Word Weavers and Spell Casters

You are What you Speak

By: Jodi Maree

Copyright © Jodi Maree 2025

All rights reserved.

The information in this manual is subject to copyright and, other than for personal use, must not be given, duplicated, copied, reproduced or transferred to any other party in whole or in part, in any form whatsoever, without written permission from the copyright holder.

No part of this publication may be stored in a retrieval system or transmitted in any form or by any means without the prior written consent of the publisher or copyright holder.

The author of this book does not dispense medical advice nor prescribe the use of any technique as a form of treatment for any physical, emotional, mental or psychological ailment or issue. The intent of the author is only to entertain and to offer information of a general nature to help you in your quest for self-development, emotional and spiritual well-being. This manual is not intended to replace advice or treatment given by an allopathic medical practitioner.

In the event that you use any of the techniques or information within this book for yourself, for others or on yourself, the author and the publisher assume no responsibility for your actions. It is advised that any technique or protocol undertaken by the reader is done so under the advice of an allopathic practitioner or physician directly or indirectly

Published by:

Pure Care Wellness, Perth, Western Australia, Australia

www.purecare.com.au

ISBN: 978-1-7640229-0-3

Dedicated to 'my people', those who never let me forget to stay on the path and follow the call.

To Mike who never stopped asking about when he could buy it.

To Steve who patiently listened to me again and again.

To Chelsi who always asked me for updates.

To Allen for all of the above and so much more!

And to my bros, the best bros a girl could have asked for, for your humour, your love, your help in so many ways and your kindness.

Contents

PART ONE 17
Chapter 1 An Exploration of Words and Power 19
    You are Here 21
    From the Inside Out 22
    New Age Nonsense 22
Chapter 2 Belief Systems and Programs 27
    We Don't Know What We Don't Know 28
    Belief Systems 29
        Limiting Belief Systems 30
    Programs 31
    Belief System or Program? 31
Chapter 3 Personal Consciousness 36
    The Conscious Mind 37
    The Subconscious and/or Unconscious Mind 38
        What's Real to Your Mind 40
        Realisations and A-ha Moments 42
        The Subconscious Mind Keeps You Safe 42
    What You Focus on Focuses on You 47
        Wonder and Ponder 49
        Unconditional Support 50
    Your Flows of Creation 53
    The Whirlpool 55
    Sovereignty 57

Chapter 4 The Time Traveler 60
  Thoughts Impact Your Environment 60
  The Incursion of Beauty 63
  You are Looking at Your Past 65
  And of course, the Power of Now 67
  Today Tomorrow and Yesterday 69
Chapter 5 Who are You? 71
  Why Do We Forget Who We Are? 72
  Avoiding Pain 73
Chapter 6 Word Magic 78
  Advertising and Marketing 83
  Abra Cadabra 85
  Speak it into Creation! 85
Chapter 7 Spells and Spell Casting 87
  Spell Casting 88
  Casting Curses? 91
Chapter 8 Word Weaving 92
  Self-Parenting 94
  Your Inner Pantheon 96
  Words and Action 99
  Monitoring Actions by Feeling 101
Chapter 9 Explorations on Words 104
  I need to 104
  I Don't Know/I Don't Understand 107
  Information vs Knowledge 108
  I Should/They Should 109

I Deserve	110
Pretending and Imagination	113
Rational	114
Nonsense	115
Want and Lack	117
Chapter 10 Word Games we Play	**119**
Truth Games	119
Protecting Truth	123
The Healing Truth	124
Judgement Games	127
Abuse Games	129
Survival of the Fittest	129
Victims and Victimisers	130
Abuse Games and Duality	132
Dealing with the Abuser	134
Abusing the Self	135
Empowerment and Success	136
Inner Bully	138
Triggering Language	139
Reverse Bullying	143
Gossip Games	144
Blame Games	145
You Own Your Feelings	148
Forgiveness	150
Chapter 11 Manifestation	**153**
Action, Change and Manifestation	157

The Clean Sweep	158
Changing Your Life with Words	162
What does this do?	163
Belief Systems and Frequency Statements	167
Mistakes are Part of the Process	170
Victory and Triumph Journaling	171
Words for Power and Creation	175
So, what are Word Weavers and Spellcasters?	179
PART TWO	181
Chapter 12 Affirmations and Frequency Statements	183
Affirmations	183
How Does the Change Come About?	185
Crafting a Frequency Statement	188
Choose and Want	190
Ownership	191
Specificity	191
Present Tense	194
Aligning with the Emotion	196
Personalising a Frequency Statements	197
Chapter 13 Practical Frequency Statements	199
Experiencing More	199
Creating Peaceful Ease	201
Realigning With Eternal Mission	205
Holistic	206
Chapter 14 Story and Stories	207
Your Personal Story	207

Tragic Back Story 211
Creation of a Hero 215
Your Hero's Journey 217
Shifting from the Story 219
Story Manifesting 223

Chapter 15 The Creation Statement and Story Technique 225
Future You and the Question 226
   The Use of The Question 228
The Story Technique 229
   Get Present, Visualise and Feel 230
   Ask For the Story 231
   Return to Presence 232
   Clear the Impediments 233
   Ask the Next Question/s 238
Story Technique Considerations 239
   Your Old Why 239
   The Minutia of the How 240
   Trust and Discernment 241
Story Questions to Consider Working With: 242

Chapter 16 Prisms 243
What are Prisms? 243
Why do Prisms? 245
The Layout of a Prism 247
Read Them Out Loud 248
How Often and For How Long? 249

Chapter 17 Specific Prisms for Healing 252

General Focus for Each Prism 253
The Audit 254
    About The Audit 254
    The Audit Prism 256
Reality Bubble Buffer 264
    About Reality Bubble Buffer 264
    Reality Bubble Buffer Prism 265
Evening Prayer 267
    About Evening Prayer 267
    Nightmares 268
    Evening Prayer Prism 269
Shining Golden One 274
    About Shining Golden One 274
    Shining Golden One Prism 275
Returning to Pristine 278
    About Returning to Pristine 278
    Returning to Pristine Prism 279
Who Am I? : Mini 284
    About Who Am I : Mini 284
    Who Am I : Mini Prism 285
Who Am I? 286
    About Who Am I 286
    Who Am I Prism 287
Morning Prayer and/ or Cleansing Prism 291
    About the Morning Prayer 291
    Morning Prayer and/or Cleansing Prism 292

Chapter 18 Closing Thoughts and Ideas 296
    Prayer Framework 302
A Final Reminder 305
About the Author 307

Terminology

Ironically, for a book about words, thought and speech, we need to begin with an explanation of terminology used within this offering. Your decisions around concepts such as God, religion, and religious doctrine, whether you are for it or against it, can very easily affect your ability to take on new ideas. It is worth recognising that the dogmas, doctrines and teachings about religion, hierarchy and terminology within which you have been raised may very well cause you to reject some of the wording or be fearful of some of the concepts offered in this book. It is important to note that any mention of God-like or deity concepts does not come from the container of a dogma, religion or church of any kind, nor does it necessarily reject any container of a dogma, religion or church of any kind.

The use of any word to refer to an overarching deity is not intended to suggest a biblical God or any deity that has been shaped into a religious concept to the exclusion of any other type of understanding about an overarching, all seeing creator of all that is.

In each usage there has been an attempt to highlight that there are many names for this concept dependent upon how you see the construct of the world we live in and the creation of life and all that it entails. The terms used within are not intended to constrain the understanding to simply western religious concepts.

Eternal Source, God, Source, Yahweh, Allah, Mother Nature, Mother Earth, the Universe, Creator of All That Is, The Almighty, Heart of Creation, Great Mystery, Sea of Consciousness, Spirit or Absolute Love are all alternative terms for the same or similar concepts of the flows and streams that create all that is and appear to have a type of sentience associated with it/them.

Please translate any terminology to your own understanding of what God might be for you. In other words, try not to get caught up in the terminology and focus on the actual message.

At your core who are you and why do you need to speak?

What do you need to speak and how do you choose to speak it?

The language you use was not yours to begin with.

You were taught to speak and given the words to say.

Is it time to choose for yourself?

Choose your own words?

We are embarking on an exploration

of something you think you know. . .

But do you?

PART ONE

The Words We Use

Chapter 1

An Exploration of Words and Power

Build the world you wish to inhabit.
Believing is seeing – regardless of what anyone else chooses.
Quiet the mind and call forth the vibration you wish to
feel, express, be, experience.
Release your old cycles and embrace the new.
Be the new.
Choose anew.
Now is the time.

Let me begin by saying, I do not profess to being an expert on words, nor on grammar, writing or orating. I do not have any formal education, letters or pieces of paper that make me anything smart or respectable by the standards of our society, or even a laudable pundit in this subject matter. I do not consider myself any sort of font of knowledge on this subject, above anyone else, or better than anyone else. I do, however, contemplate, ponder and wonder about these things a lot and they have been part of my life, my healing and my profession for a very long time.

What I do offer you here are thoughts and observations from a spiritual, experiential or philosophical vantage point based upon the many journeys of self-healing and awakenment that I have been part of during the course of my own personal growth and my professional engagements with clients over the last 20 years. You don't have to believe me or agree with me. I don't require that or insist upon that. I simply present this exploration for your open-minded contemplation as another way to understand the self and to reclaim your sovereignty. I hope to offer you a tiny starting point in contemplating who you are, how you engage with life, and what you may be aligning with through your words, thoughts and attention.

This book, this offering, is designed as an exploration of the most common and obvious way that we communicate, words, and their relationship to our happiness, our well-being and our experience of life. It is offered as an alternative way to play with and understand our communication, our connection to, and memory of, self and spirit. As well as to reignite the understanding of the power of words, thoughts and communication.

We will delve into how to understand, relate to and have compassion for your inner landscape as well as use ideas such as melodrama for your personal empowerment, a return to presence and personal healing. By the end of this book the aim is for you to have a deeper understanding of how your words and thoughts are affecting you and creating your reality and that through simple actions and explorations of self, you have the ability to change your experience of life, co-creating your reality with each utterance, thought and reframe.

This treatise on words, self-healing, manifesting and co-creating is offered as an exploration of the possibilities available when we pay attention to our presence and use our words, focus and intention consciously and constructively to create an intended outcome for ourselves. When you understand how it works, you can align and work with it to co-create your own experiences.

The human body is a magnetic and electric energy flowing and emitting biological composition. Your thoughts, experiences, emotions, feelings and actions ignite and empower some of the emissions. These can then be envisaged as engaging with the mechanisms of external reality to co-create your life experiences.

In other words, your beliefs about and engagements with your reality tend to create a certain experience that you call life – this is a manifestation experience of co-creation that occurs between you and the external. You could say it is a creation that manifests from the internal (You), the eternal (Source, God, Great Benevolence, Great Spirit, Great Mystery) and the external (3D temporal physical reality experience) as a trinity co-creating your experience of what we call life.

This exploration of words, frequencies, presence and empowered use of the electric and magnetic emission and pulsing machine that is the human, is designed to guide you into the easiest and most sovereign way to manifest your own world without impinging upon the rights and laws of others and the universe.

This is not a domination manifestation technique; it is a return to personal sovereignty and an internal embracing of absolute love that allows you to be in the flows of harmony and ease with the unfolding of your 3D reality as you choose it.

You are Here

Consider this; if all that you have done and believed, all the rules and guidance you have followed, all the dogmas, practices and worships you have adhered to, all the things you have allowed and disallowed in your life as choices of moral, ethical or any type of right/wrong calculation that you have internally chosen to honour and obey have led you to here, to this experience and state in your life, and yet here is not where you wish to be nor does it fulfil your need for feeling loved, seen, heard, understood, cared for and accounted for, then maybe it's time to reconsider at least some of what you believe and choose, some of what you understand to be right or wrong action, because whatever you have been doing hasn't been working. Perhaps it is time to reconsider and make some changes?

From the Inside Out

The aim here is the focus on happiness and health creation, the attaining and maintaining of a fulfilled, ease fueled, and joy filled experience of life for the self – and as a flow on from this, for those that are part of your life experience.

There are whole systems and protocols dedicated to the study of manifestation that are usually aimed at creating success or money, or the manipulation of someone else's choices (marketing, advertising, sales through NLP and Psychology) – these systems are usually aimed at creating or changing your world, moving from the old form to a new form, in order to achieve something, usually money, affluence, love, success or a material creation of some sort.

In this presentation, this philosophy and exploration, we are looking at this process from the inside out, rather than trying to manipulate the external and create an outer experience we are looking at understanding how you are engaged in creating your own reality by journeying within to recreate your own emanation and impact on the external world. Through such a journey, you change your external experience of life to the experience more aligned with your chosen direction.

New Age Nonsense

In the last few years, maybe the last 20-30 years there has been a vast upswell in interest in all things esoteric, energetic and mystical. It got a huge push forward with things like 'The Secret' movie but it had been slowly building prior to that since perhaps the1960s and definitely from at least the late 1980s.

Over the years there has been a sort of corruption of what is called 'new age' teachings, whereby they have become quite distorted or polluted with misinformation, ego directives and fear mongering. Some really common misinformation and fear mongering, often used for marketing, but sometimes actually believed as truth are:

"If you don't do 'this' you will fail".

Whatever 'this' is, if you don't do it, you won't 'awaken' correctly – disaster right? It's also rubbish, do your daily practice, focus on your thoughts and creations, heal the self, heal the mind and you will be fine! You don't need to do the lauded next great thing – just stay with you, heal you, love you and you'll be fine.

"The awakening is a collective thing, we all do it together, you don't have to do anything it happens automatically".

This is a fallacy told by those that don't wish to tell you; you do have to do the work, and by those who are hoping to do nothing and yet experience an 'awakening'. It's true to say that there is a natural flow awakening on Earth at this time, but that presents as more of an easing that allows for an individual to unfold with far less effort than in previous eras but you do still have to put some effort in. Nobody is doing it for you. This is especially true if you are awaiting salvation from some form of misery, it doesn't happen in a vacuum, you are part of your own salvation.

There is no cheat's way out where you can remain still and rely on others to do it for you as a collective, riding their coat tails into your own salvation. No. There is no cutting the line or cheating your way into the healing you seek *but* there are very simple and easy tools that are highly effective (like those presented here). You do however still have to do it for yourself. The more people that do it, the easier it is for the next wave of people that do it, but you still have to do it for yourself. The more truthful and open you are with the self the easier it is – but you still have to do the practices to heal the self into the upshift you are seeking.

"You must pull all your pieces and parts together or you fail".

Overall, it is very beneficial to bring all the pieces and parts of you back to you, but there are some you wouldn't want to and there are some that you actually create as separate from you for a healing benefit – we will cover these ideas in the next couple of chapters.

You don't need to own it all and integrate it all – you just need to heal the self; and sometimes that means owning and integrating parts of the self and sometimes that means dissolving and releasing parts of the self.

"The only way forward is to clear your chakras/meridians (name your energy body or practice – they've all be sold as the be all and end all)".

This has no holistic benefit; it may feel good and for some specific things be helpful but focusing on just one area is like focusing on keeping your hands in tip top shape and then wondering why your heart is failing. It's all connected.

"You must get to know your angels/guides/origin".

This is nice to do, and it can be helpful, but often it is told and sold to you as though if you can't see them and hear them, if you can't have an outright conversation with them, then there's something wrong with you and you're not doing it right (failing again! Oh no!).

These teachings often misrepresent what angels/guides etc truly are and how they actually interact with you. Let it go and expect nothing. Interaction with the unseen is happening all the time, you've just been looking for the 'wrong' thing.

Put it all to rest.

It is at best incomplete in its teaching, at worst a total corruption and lie designed to divert you and fleece you. Working on one area will not bring wholistic healing.

In addition, and without wanting to sound harsh, a lot of the teachings out there are facile and empty, simply soothing, distracting and distorting teachings about chakras, auras and angels. The teachers aren't necessarily charlatans or con people, and the teaching may help you in wonderful and amazing ways, but just remember they are only part of the picture.

Your sovereignty, self-healing and self-responsible upshift is all that you really need. Not that the energy bodies, and energy beings are not real, and not that they are not powerful but that they are so much more than you've been taught. Focusing upon them in the way that you have been taught is turning them into simplistic, childish, controlling tantrum toys – "give me what I want Angels, and give it to me now!"

So, if you feel that you 'can't afford' any of the whiz-bang teachings out there, or that you are too inept, too small or too talentless to channel or see/hear/feel angels/guides/guardians don't worry – you don't need to. You can still be deeply healed and connected just by being you, just by being self-responsible and going within.

The concepts and ideas in most teachings have been so dumbed down that you often miss the whole point and power of them. It is worth remembering that the intricacies and physics of most of these things is not necessary to know in order to achieve great things, like personal healing, awakening and peace.

What is important to understand is that when the engagement with these things is done from a reverent and respectful point of view, including the engagement with your own body, you will find that what you need to know becomes much clearer without the clutter and superficial mumbo jumbo of 'white light and clueless' teachings.

What is investigated and suggested here, in this book, is not a be-all-end-all. Presented here are ideas, philosophies and explorations for your contemplation. It may help you understand who you really are and how this really works. It may give you peace. It may give you confidence. It may help you heal and awaken. But it is not all there is to know, and it is not the only way. It is *a* way; it is *an* understanding.

Let's begin the contemplation and journey here now with an exploration of what the human is from a less corporeal viewpoint. . .

Chapter 2

Belief Systems and Programs

The human body is a biological system of magnetic and electric ebbs, flows, processes and actions – it creates itself, recreates itself, cleans itself and repairs itself constantly and continuously. It is a well-documented idea that each cell in the human body self-replicates and dies off such that at any given time the oldest cell in your body is only about 7-10 years old. So, if this is the case and the body is constantly replicating itself, why doesn't it wipe the slate clean and replicate itself as a newer, better, healthier, stronger and fitter version? Why doesn't it return to perfection each time?

Many reasons have been postulated, but the basic root of the issue appears to be because the DNA or the cellular replicating mechanisms of the body are operating from old information, perhaps tainted templates, or not being given enough time and fresh input to replicate itself in pristine perfection once more.

The idea behind this book, this exploration of words, focus and the stories we tell ourselves is that your attention has a magic to it that creates response from what is attended to. Your focus or attention continuously placed in an area of your life repeats the creation of that area of your life, and this includes the recreation of your physicality in each replication as a mirror of the current version of impediments that you are dealing with physically, emotionally, mentally or psychologically.

Simply put what this means is that if you could somehow change your attention and focus, if you could change the story you tell yourself and if you could change the repetitive thought loops of self-story and self-validation that you endlessly tell the self, then you change the cellular creation of your own emanation. This has the potential of changing your physicality and your experience of life, you may literally be able to change what occurs in your life.

This is all done via self-responsibility, repetition and personal healing, there is no manipulation or dominance over self or anybody else. This is done through understanding the flows of self, the engagements with life and going within to ignite, magnify and emanate flows of peace, love, forgiveness, self-responsibility, truth, integrity and joy. The aim is to enhance and increase those flows, magnifying them into your life in known and unknown ways and ultimately change your personal experience of life.

We Don't Know What We Don't Know

The concept is simple; the engagement of it and enaction of it can be slightly trickier. Fundamentally you don't know what you don't know and in addition to this, you usually think you know what you know and never dispute it with the self!

This convolution we do whereby we have certain fundamental truths that we never investigate and yet we don't know what we don't know, means that it is very common for us to be believing something that is not true and yet never questioning that belief, whilst at the same time not believing something that is true, and being quite convinced in our superiority over those who believe this thing we call 'nonsense' because it is, in our belief system, 'not true'.

We then continuously validate our lack of questioning or investigating around the belief. Said questioning or investigating might prompt the discovery that what we believe is, in fact, not as true or false as we have firmly decided. If something we believe is not true is in fact true, then the internal self-perpetuating belief system will, in one way or another, deter us from hearing, investigating or taking on board any evidence to the contrary of the currently held belief. The opposite is also true, if we believe something is true, we may spend our time being blinded to all evidence that it is in fact not true.

We are complicated creatures, with many blind spots, and an overall compulsion to 'not look foolish' and 'to be correct' – mostly these compulsions come from a fundamental desire for or orientation towards feeling safe in one way or another. We decide what is true for us based upon the type of evidence we require to prove to ourselves that it is true. We find that to be a relaxing, reliable and safe position to be in, which is why, from that point forward, we don't tend to re-investigate it for ourselves.

What we tend to do, once we've made a decision, is to never investigate whether our belief systems or foundational decisions about life are still true or not true. We simply dismiss as fallacy or nonsense anything that doesn't align with our currently held beliefs and get on with engaging with life from the point of view of that which we believe (have decided) to be true. There are two main mechanisms within that dictate our view of life and our engagement with or reaction to life. These two mechanisms could be referred to as belief systems and programs.

Belief Systems

Belief systems are those mechanisms that dictate what we believe to be true or not true. They dictate our engagements with life and what we can see or focus upon and what we cannot. Think of it as akin to the experience of buying a car, before you researched and decided upon the type of car you liked, you rarely noticed them on the road, but then you decide you want a certain type of car and suddenly you see them everywhere. Those cars were always there, you just weren't focusing on them before and so they operated in your peripheral awareness, not your specific focus. Belief systems are like this, whereby they operate in silence in your system, dictating how you view or engage with life.

Our reality is created by our perceptions, and our perceptions can be limited by our belief systems. Belief systems are held within and continuously pulse us information about our reality, telling us what we think is good or bad, what we think is moral or not, what we think is possible or not, but until you notice them, they operate subversively keeping you in alignment with them.

We can be very unaware of how our belief systems cloud our perceptions and make our perceptions seem real when in fact they are self-created based on perhaps erroneous or at least unhelpful belief systems that can be recognised and changed.

Not all belief systems are bad, and not all are good – they just are, they are part of the make-up of self and may be helping or hindering you at any given time.

The ones that give people the most issues are those that could be termed 'limiting belief systems'. These are the belief systems that limit your experience of life in certain areas, they tend to disallow investigation of new information that might change your viewpoint, or affect your tolerance levels for certain behaviours, actions, experiences or life circumstances.

Limiting Belief Systems

Belief systems are most often formed by experiences and childhood. Some of them can be really wonderful and life enhancing! If you were raised in a circumstance where you were very happy and experienced your parents and community being kind, caring and sharing with other, then you may have formed the belief system that kindness is empowering – and this belief system may have served you well through life.

However, if you were raised in a family where kindness was ridiculed and humiliated, because the family belief system negated kindness as weakness. Perhaps you were taught that if you have something you defend it and try to get more of it, that's what winners and survivors do! Then you may find that during your engagements through work or society, your attitudes and actions tend to repel people.

Belief systems such as these do not help you make friends or connections that may help you get ahead in life. This would be an example of an unhelpful, perhaps damaging, belief system that limits your ability to find happiness and peace. This is often referred to as a 'limiting belief system'.

Programs

Programs, as compared to belief systems, are often more deeply ingrained and can be practically invisible to you as a program. A program is often what you think of as 'just the way life is'. They are often things that are completely unquestioned, they seem to make sense logically and are often backed by your schooling and those around you.

In a similar way to belief systems, not all programs are bad nor incorrect! In fact, some of them seem so logical and backed by science that there is no evidence at all that they are 'wrong' or 'untrue', but they are still ideas, decisions, and foundations of or about life that we think of as true and hence they are programs.

Programs usually come from family and schooling, not necessarily experiences. For example, if you have been raised Catholic then it is likely that one of your programs will be strongly oriented towards sin and the badness of self for sinning If you weren't raised Catholic you may actually view 'sin' as just a 'good time' since the concept of damnation via 'sin' is not something that you operate from as a base program of self, so, it is less likely that you feel guilt over the things you do for fun.

Belief System or Program?

Generally, programs and belief systems dictate the way you view life and engage with life. Their precise definition can be a bit fluid whereby to one person it is a program but to another it is a belief system, but both belief systems and programs, in tandem, tend to form your limitation in possibilities. They tend to dictate what you believe life is and isn't, as well as your ability to engage with and change that.

Ultimately the first area to address when you wish to change your life are the belief systems and/or programs that you hold that do not allow you to experience the life you desire. You don't need to specifically discover them and name them necessarily, just recognise that they exist and may be holding you back – if you discover exactly what they are and name them, that's ok too!

What does this mean? It means that *you* are your first limitation. Your ability to, willingness to and dedication to changing the belief systems and programs that prevent you being in mastery of your own thoughts, actions, and words, your own life, will dictate the degree to which you can claim your personal sovereignty and co-create your life into an upshifting experience of success, joy, peace and fulfilment.

Only you can really figure out what your belief systems, limiting belief systems and programs are, because they are often deeply personal and related to your family lineage, childhood experiences and the various education, political and religious systems you were exposed to, indoctrinated into and/or raised within. There are, however, some very common overarching belief systems and programs that a lot of people hold variations upon:

- Belief systems and/or programs aligning with or resulting in poverty, destitution, break-even living or struggle.

- Belief systems and/or programs around your own superiority or inferiority.

- Belief systems and/or programs around love such as your ability to be loved or find love, faithfulness, commitment, what love really is or what is acceptable or expected from love.

- Belief systems and/or programs that limit your ability to succeed or even commit to succeeding.

During my time working as a mentor and spiritual counsellor I have come across many different belief systems or hindrances that emerge throughout a self-healing journey. The story of one client's experience can be used to illustrate this concept.

This client (let's call him Dave) has a long history of believing that he is stupid, gets things wrong all the time and lets people down. He also struggles with depression and crippling self-doubt and self-worth issues. I have worked with Dave for some time and can objectively say that he is intelligent, thoughtful and has very heartfelt insights. He is far more than he considers himself.

Dave's belief stems from childhood experiences whereby he was treated as a burden, as an inconvenience, as annoying or unacceptable in some way. For instance, whenever his father was telling him something, maybe something as simple as a story, if Dave lost the thread of what was being told to him, his father would instantly lose interest in telling him any more of the story. Dave became suddenly an inconvenience or annoyance to his father at that point because his father deemed him too stupid to follow the story – never taking into account that the father himself may not have been a good linear narrator of detail, perhaps the father told garbled stories that didn't make sense, which is common amongst those that do not know how to communicate strongly. Dave however, being a child, became convinced that it was he that was the problem – he was too stupid to follow even a simple story, and because he was too stupid to follow the story, the first guardian of his innocence (his father) who was supposed to love him, turned away and withdrew from him.

This action of the father was hurtful and upsetting to Dave as a child and was taken on board as a type of 'withdrawal of love' by the father. This has resulted in a series of belief systems and programs along the lines of 'I am stupid', 'I cannot get things right', 'I am not loveable because I am stupid', 'all of my efforts must be towards the other person, or they will stop loving me'. Which means that he now operates from the program 'no matter what is showing up in my life, I am stupid, I don't deserve good things, I don't deserve love, so if good things are happening something bad will take it away or happen very soon'.

The above is a very simplified story of how we can take a childhood experience and create for ourselves a lifelong debilitation by forming inner understandings or decisions about what is true and what must be done to fix the self, based upon the decision about what is true. In this instance, what is 'true' is that Dave must be stupid because he lost the thread of the story and his father withdrew his attention. As a child Dave needed his father's attention as a type of validation that he is loveable and acceptable. Dave's solution, derived from his child's mind in childhood, was to prioritize others' needs and wants over his own in order to maintain the attention and love of that person and avoid the criticism or withdrawal of love from them. As long as the attention can be maintained, as long as the withdrawal of love does not occur, then by 'logical conclusion' he remains loveable and acceptable. Except the conclusion isn't logical.

The conclusions that are formed are the conclusions of the wounded child that has decided what must be true and how to fix it. They are not the conclusions of the adult who understands that their parent is perhaps a wounded and deficient person themselves. It is the conclusion of the child who thought their parent was perfect. The parent's role is to teach the child how to be human, hence the child considers the parent to be the font of all wisdom with regard to how to be a better human, and a more likable and acceptable being.

These types of hurts, and conclusions, are taken deep within and form the makeup and expression of self throughout our lives. They condense themselves into our foundation and become that which shapes our personalities, our decisions and our beliefs about what's ok, what's not ok and what's right and wrong about life, us, experiences, actions, and others.

BELIEF SYSTEMS AND PROGRAMS

I hope you are getting at least glimmers of what a belief system is, what a program is, and how they may be a convoluted tangle within you that are preventing you from co-creating the life you desire – or perhaps preventing you from even seeing that they exist within you at all!

As mentioned previously, we are complex and convoluted creatures. We create conclusions about ourselves, and our lives, based upon our experiences and then operate from these conclusions as if they were real and indisputable! We do this to create a form of safety and stability; a foundation we can rely on.

Ostensibly we are doing this to keep ourselves safe, functional and together (emotionally and psychologically) but ultimately these conclusions can block, limit and/or hurt us by restricting what we allow ourselves to experience in one form or another.

Chapter 3

Personal Consciousness

You could consider yourself as made up of at least three minds; the conscious, the subconscious and the unconscious minds. I'm sure you've heard about all of these minds; they have been discussed ad nauseum since the days of Freud and Jung and more recently given great pop culture credence via the new age circles over the last 20 odd years. So, what we are doing here is simplifying the idea and offering an understanding of it that allows you to see the various levels of self you are always working with.

It is commonly accepted that the conscious mind does the thinking and is the present, obvious and interactive-with-the-world-around-you level of mind, but the subconscious and unconscious minds can also have some conscious and interactive domains of activity in the human.

In many ways it depends on your school of thought and which doctrine of education and definition you adhere to as to which of these minds (the subconscious or the unconscious) does what. Ultimately, unless you want to delve into the deep dark recesses of the psyche and publish academic papers and pontifications on the specific level of mind you are investigating or expounding upon, it just doesn't matter whether it is the subconscious or the unconscious that is the culprit apropos your personal situation and/or concerns on a day-to-day basis.

There are levels of mind that are more spiritual or holistic in nature. These aspects of consciousness are often inaccessible to the everyday awareness, as the experience of touching them is rarely remembered clearly. They are known by various names—such as the superconscious mind, the dream-conscious mind, or the over-conscious mind—and are typically accessed through altered states. Though they are integral parts of you, they tend to be elusive and ephemeral to the conscious mind, with connections to them occurring at depths beyond the reach of ordinary memory. However, when it comes to presence, wounding and co-creation of a peaceful happy or fulfilling life in the 3D the conscious, the subconscious and the unconscious minds are the minds to look at.

The Conscious Mind

Personal consciousness is the energy that runs through you, mostly you feel it or recognise it as your emotions, thoughts and feelings. It is the ephemeral flows of energies that form you, that are you and that feel like your thoughts, emotions and feelings. It is the you that is thinking, and the you that is aware of the thought that is being thought.

You are formed by your personal consciousness, literally and metaphysically. What you think and speak is part of your personal consciousness. When you think and speak happy thoughts, you flow happy consciousness, when you think and speak victim thoughts, paranoid thoughts, angry thoughts you flow victim, paranoia and anger consciousness. That's a simplified understanding of it, but at the root of it all, your thoughts and words, written and spoken, are all creating your next moment of experience. So, think and speak as you wish to create.

What type of life do you wish to have?

Focus your attention, your words and your emotions on the feeling of that life and think and speak as you wish you were experiencing in 3D reality – think happy to be happy, speak kind to experience kindness, focus on peace to live a life of peace.

It sounds trite, it's probably something you've heard many times before, but before you dismiss it out of hand as more of the same information please read on and experience the depths of understanding of what these simple ideas really mean.

The Subconscious and/or Unconscious Mind

The subconscious mind (or unconscious mind) is the aspect of you that is not present and conscious. It contains, stores or manifests the memories, emotions and automatic reactions (including programs and belief systems) of you. It also runs many of the body processes and actions that keep you alive – you don't have to think in order to make your heartbeat, because the sub (or un) conscious mind does this for you.

It has been suggested that the sub (or un) conscious mind runs about 90% or more of your thoughts, your reactions, your instincts and actions. So, the truth about the human is that whatever you think in the conscious mind is tiny in comparison to the hold over you that the subconscious or unconscious mind has!

It will depend on the school of thought as to whether you think it's the subconscious or the unconscious that operates on this level, but for ease of expression we will mostly use the term subconscious because it doesn't really matter which one you decide does this, we're just saying that it's not the conscious brain mind that does this. Which means that you usually cannot consciously decide to operate in a way that is the antithesis of the programming and focus of the subconscious mind and be able to sustain that action because the conscious mind generally has very little impact.

Aside from the operating of the body, the subconscious and the unconscious also connect with the emotional body and a few other aspects of self, and simply put, they hold the traumas that you've been through in this life (and potentially other lives). They seem to compartmentalise your memory, holding the trauma or traumatic incidents separate, so that you are safe from its constant reverberation in your system. It is quite common that you don't even remember much about the traumas in your own life or your childhood because of this compartmentalisation action of the subconscious mind. This seems to be a safety mechanism of the body to take assaulting or confronting, potentially traumatising, memories and experiences and separate them from the conscious mind to enable the human to process them at a later date. This might even be why we don't remember things such as past lives (if that is your belief system).

If the minds did not do this for us, we would be in a constant state of shock and over reactivity to the dramas and traumas that occur to us every day in our lives – the big and the small ones – unless we resolve them as and when they occur.

The idea is that the minds do us the kindness of compartmentalising these experiences and emotions, these wounds and hurts, that shape us and form us, and at some point, in our journey of being a human, we go back and sort through these compartmentalised aspects of self and neutralise them in some way.

This neutralisation is also called healing and can be done in so many different ways that it's really just a matter of finding the right action, technique, therapy or personal experience which helps you do this.

The subconscious holds these compartmentalised traumas and wounds or distils these experiences into a conclusion of some sort (which we call a belief system or program), but it does not resolve them or neutralise them. It holds them separate so that the human can function in day-to-day life, but you still have to neutralise or resolve them for the self at some point in time. The subconscious whilst holding the impacts and feelings of these traumas is also, in silence and invisibility beyond or beneath your conscious knowing, pulsing a perhaps diminished form of the stress from these incidences into your system such that you are continuously emanating the feeling, the hurt and the frequency created by the wounding or the trauma held – whether you know it or not – until you heal the effects of that trauma.

You are continuously experiencing a subliminal form of the stress from these woundings, and you are continuously honouring the programs and belief systems formed from the woundings. Each experience that resonates with any sense of similarity to the original compartmentalised trauma/wounding (which resulted in the formation of the belief system or program) triggers the validation of or reaction imprinted by the belief system or program.

This pulsing of the stress creates what could be thought of as a schism in your system. It affects the hormone flow, it affects the neurotransmitters, it affects your personal triggers, like your emotional trigger points, and it also affects your muscles, your nervous system, your ligaments, your tendons, your fascia, in fact your whole physical, emotional and mental well-being.

Releasing the charge of these internal continuous pulses occurs via self-healing. This self-healing can happen on many levels, it may be via talk therapy (mental level), it may be via prayer or meditation (spiritual level), it may be via movement, massage or stretching (physical level). However you do it, it aids your entire system by releasing the continuous emanation and pulsing of the traumas, wounds and ancient hurts you hold within. These are mostly held in your unawareness but sometimes you may be quite aware of the difficult times you have had in the past that you are holding onto within. Except it's not past.

It may be the past in your timeline. It may be a distant memory in your timeline, perhaps a past guilt or terrifying memory, but to your body, to your minds, it is current and occurring again and again. It will continue to do so until it is neutralised. It is not occurring to you as a 3D physical in the now experience or conscious concern in your present, but it is pulsing in your system presently and continuously.

What's Real to Your Mind

In your subconscious and unconscious there will be housed your personal traumas, wounds, dramas, there will also be housed your belief systems, your programs and your fight flight triggers. These will be things that you have been through in this life, experienced in this life and/or that you've experienced in any other lifetime (if that is your belief system). But what you may not have considered is that within you there are also those things that have been imprinted through what you've seen on TV, what you've seen in the movies, the conversations you've had, the things you've watched on YouTube, books you've read, articles you've read, things you've researched. All of it.

Which means you may actually hold a traumatic imprint within from something you personally did not experience, from a movie that you've seen for instance. You didn't experience it physically, but your system experienced it via the movie. And that sort of non-personal experience houses itself in your subconscious and/or unconscious self. It just keeps flashing into your system, into your flows, into the streams of data that makeup the energy plasma self which feeds into the makeup of the physical self.

This is simply the surface level of what you have watched and experienced at arm's length such as movies and TV shows – we are not talking here about subliminal messaging via movies and TV shows. Consider the depths of what is taken in by your minds when you add in the ideas of subliminal messaging on top of all of this.

The minds do not know the difference between what is 'real' and what is a movie or imagination – if it has an emotional impact, it is a real experience to the mind.

How many times have you been watching a movie or reading a story and noticed your whole body being tense and your breath changing in line with the tension in the story being told? How many times have you experienced the release of that tension via the relief or happiness at the victory on the screen or in the book? Your mind is experiencing all of that as real!

So, the imprints and impediments in the subconscious and/or unconscious minds can be many and varied and some of them are not even your own experiences, they can be from ancestors, the news, stories you've heard or even books you've read or movies you've seen.

Epigenetics is now showing us that we can hold the effects of emotional traumas that occurred to our ancestors within our own systems, affecting us as though they happened to us personally. It is extremely complicated and convoluted! It's worth recognising that what you may be emanating and pulsing, what you may be thinking and reacting to, may not be specifically yours, and yet it's creating your experience of life.

Realisations and A-ha Moments

When you have an aha moment, when you have a pulse of realization, a conscious present epiphanous moment, this has a subconscious/unconscious, perhaps super conscious and over conscious, impact sending a neutralising wave through your system. That can happen from a conversation or a teaching for instance, which gives you a realization and a-ha. It can happen through meditations, activations, divine realizations, connection to the heart of creation or running the flows of absolute love. It can happen in many ways, sometimes spontaneously, sometimes directly sought out and sometimes unexpectedly.

The realisation, the epiphany and/or crystallisation of understanding along with the energetic neutralising potential it holds to diminish, resolve or dissolve your subconscious and/or unconscious emanations of trauma also gives your conscious mind the idea that the issue is resolved – which again sends a pulse through your system of neutralisation.

Realisation, epiphany and understanding of self and belief systems can be a very healing experience. It can deliver what seems to be instantaneous healing, but it can also open the door to deeper understanding and exploration of self to truly profoundly remove the deviation influence of the inner wounding that disallows your life becoming and continuing as the experience you would prefer.

The Subconscious Mind Keeps You Safe

The subconscious mind is usually quite literal and responds in ways that sometimes make no sense to the conscious mind. You may consciously believe something to be true, consciously decide to pursue something and yet the subconscious mind, which is a collection of your memories, experiences and emotional reactions to the experiences, may be working against you. Your subconscious mind may hold the belief that what you consciously believe to be true and beneficial is in fact harmful to you in some way.

This is a convoluted system of feedback, action and reaction in the human, and the idea that the subconscious mind is literal, reactive and can have distorted ideas about what is helpful for you is very relevant.

You will know that your subconscious mind could be harbouring ideas, emotions, conclusions and decisions that may not allow you to be your best self and heal yourself into the life that you desire by looking at what it is that you desire. Look at what you dream of and what you believe is consciously true then observe whether you in fact have that in your life.

Do you dream of great wealth? Do you know that you have the skillset, the talent and the idea that will get you great fulfilling successful wealth and happiness? And yet you are not living that dream in reality? Then it is a safe bet that you are harbouring a belief system, program, idea, automatic reaction, understanding, self-worth and/or esteem issue that is contrary to your conscious thought.

These are likely held in the subconscious mind and are likely that which convinces you that there isn't enough time in the day, you don't have the necessary qualifications or that nobody will take you seriously and so on – all of the ways you self-sabotage your own success often stem from the subconscious mind and its literal response to your life, along with its aim to keep you safe. Note that it is always trying to keep you safe, but it is often distorted in its action and that action does not serve you or help you find your happiness, find your joy or change your life.

The subconscious mind appears to be both literal and listening, which means that when you use your words specifically and aligned with feeling, the subconscious mind will attempt to literally manifest that choice into being. Your subconscious mind is waiting for the picture, the word, the agreement and the image of what your miracle life is and will bring it about in ways you know not of and are beyond you finding out.

How do we know this? All you need to do is look at the root thoughts that you have about life, the automatic responses you have to suggestions of something new to you, and the regular jokes, expressions and replies you use every day. These will illustrate your base emanation and as such you will find evidence of agreement with these in some form in your external manifest life.

Do you think life is all about the hustle? And so, you hustle.

Do you think love is all about the look? And so, you spend much money and time on how you look.

Do you think that nobody understands you and how hard it is for you? And so, you spend your time feeling misunderstood, separate, unseen and alone.

Are you experiencing it and so believing it? Or could it be that you are believing it and so experiencing it? Your subconscious is emanating who you are and what you believe every day. It is then helping you create emotions and have feelings that are aligned with the choices/conclusions of the subconscious mind this in turn keeps you in alignment with the ideas, beliefs and understandings you have about life.

Now you may say to me, well I don't get that, how can it keep me safe by preventing me from achieving my dream? Why would it work in such a manner? Ultimately the machinations and manoeuvrings of the various minds (conscious, subconscious, unconscious) of the human and the psychology of the human are a bit of a mystery, there are many theories and many operating models to understand the decisions and formations of the minds and the ultimate effects of the construction of the personality and actions and resistances of the human therefrom.

One way of attempting to understand this is to consider that the subconscious mind's goal is to keep you safe. It does this by making conclusions, or deductions based upon upsetting or traumatic experiences that have occurred to you. When you experience something, its emotional impact is felt within and the consequences of this are stored within.

The subconscious mind takes this information and forms a conclusion that is then formatted in such a way that it will prevent certain things from occurring to you and encourage other things to occur all in an effort to avoid experiencing the impact and/or repetition of that trauma again. It effectively changes your emanation and frequency match disallowing certain things in your life that are believed to trigger the same traumatic effect and hence have been designated as harmful to you in one way or another.

As a very simple example, your subconscious mind may make a conclusion that money is bad, or that rich people are mean, based upon some parental teachings you experienced, or some childhood experience/s that you had.

What sort of childhood experiences could create this type of subconscious mind conclusion? Perhaps money was a cause of many arguments when you were a child leading to a traumatic imprint in response to money? Perhaps money was what caused the biggest scariest fights? Perhaps it was always over money that your parents had emotional disparity or friction that you as a child experienced as a type of verbal violence and breakdown of the love in the family? Perhaps, to an adult, the disagreements were mild but to the child that you were they felt significant? Perhaps the child in you simply decided that any cause to disagree was not the love you came to experience hence money is 'bad'?

Remember this is a child's experience and hence a child's conclusion – it may not make sense to your adult mind and adult reasoning. The anger or disagreement is experienced as a physical experience that the child often takes on board as their fault in some way. This is the original 'trauma' that caused a belief system/program around money to form, and the subconscious mind now enacts and pulses this constantly throughout your system.

Your conscious mind is perhaps focused upon 'making money' or 'being rich' and yet your subconscious mind believes that to keep you safe, you cannot be rich.

Why might it believe this? Because in your experience, maybe not your conscious memory experience but it is in your system, money causes friction, money takes away the love and money causes arguments! Your system, which is a life preserving system, designed to keep you living (physically, mentally and emotionally) will keep you whole and safe by denying you money. Thus, you may find that you struggle to make and/or keep money.

How is this decision keeping you safe when it obviously keeps you from being in a financially thriving state? The subconscious mind isn't thinking in terms of money providing the life you desire; it is thinking in terms of money leading to conflict, friction, violence or sadness. It attempts to keep you from becoming sad, angry, torn apart or being associated with that "bad" money by creating belief systems, actions and behaviours that minimise your effectiveness at creating the wealth you are consciously focusing upon.

The conclusion is unhelpful and actually works against you, and yet the subconscious mind is really attempting to keep you safe.

This is a very trivial and uncomplicated example to illustrate the point, in reality humans are deeply complex and create convolutions within the self that prevent them from experiencing and living the happiness, wealth and health they desire based upon many factors – some truly trivial yet powerful and some truly powerful and overarching.

What does this mean? In brief it means that you already are the product of all that you have thought and experienced in the past and all the decisions and understandings you have come to about those thoughts and experiences. Thusly, going forward, you are emoting, feeling and acting (or not acting) from the space of belief about life that you have already created. Is this creation real? Is it based upon what is objectively true? Or is it based upon what your subconscious mind, your inner child, your inner wounded one, your hurt and your psyche have all decided is the only thing that can be true for you in order to keep you safe and protected from experiencing that wound, that hurt, that humiliation, that devastation again (whatever the original wound, hurt, humiliation or devastation was that created the decision in the subconscious mind that still rings out today).

What You Focus on Focuses on You

It has been paraphrased and quoted oft by many and perhaps it was Nietzsche who originally said it as it is so often attributed to him:

"When you gaze long into the abyss. The abyss gazes also into you"

Which is another way of saying, what you focus upon, focuses upon you! The original statement seems more attuned with negative thoughts or depressive thoughts, the idea perhaps being that when you focus on the darkness/negativity (gaze into the abyss) the darkness 'looks' back and magnifies in you (the abyss gazes into you). You cannot escape that which you gaze upon (focus upon). This understanding also, however, holds true across the board, not just for the negative foci.

If we put this into the context of co-creation, manifestation or even just on how we are feeling, then we can interpolate this into the understanding of 'what you spend your time focusing upon, focuses back upon you'. Another way of saying this is what you put your attention upon, what you regularly think and feel, is what you generate in your external circumstances and is returned unto you as the contemplation's outcome.

So, your personal consciousness, your flows of thought and feeling, create your reality by being the emanation that is reflected back to you by the external – or perhaps more correctly, it is that which is attracted to the emanation (frequency matching) that exudes from you as a consequence of the flows that imbue you from your thoughts, feelings and foci.

There is nuance to this whereby what you think and feel can either be your actual thoughts or those imprinted upon you by others; by their opinions, deductions, teachings. If you take your thoughts and feelings at face value and do not contemplate their origin, repeatedly looping them through your mind by revisiting the same concepts, the same ideas, the same feelings and strategies then you will find that the external reflects this back to you through its presentations of experience for you. Simply put, your thoughts create your realty.

You may have experienced this as the external validating what you are thinking, and you have believed that what you are seeing is *why* you believe what you believe – but maybe what you are seeing is *because* you believe what you believe! It's a chicken and egg idea – what came first? The belief that is validated by the external? Or the external creating the belief?

From the point of view of focus and magnification, what you spend your time focusing on, focuses back on you and hence becomes a part of your reality, it becomes what you see, it becomes present in your life. So, did you draw it in by your focus, or did it exist and hence created your focus?

Ultimately, we may never really know the answer to this, but what I can tell you through experience and through witnessing and hearing much anecdotal feedback, and client experiences is this: when you change your focus, when you change the repetitive thoughts and responses that you currently operate from, things change in your external. This leads me to align with the idea that the external is responding to your internal.

Thus, change your thoughts, change your feelings and responses and you change your external. This internal change in thoughts is reflected back to you with a change in the external that is in alignment with the new thoughts, beliefs, feelings and foci.

The question becomes are they really your thoughts? Are they your pure and pristine original thoughts about yourself, life and everything in it? Or are they the melange, the imprint, the entrainment of everything you have been through, and everything you have taken on board as true, and everything that you have internalised and used to recreate the self in an image that the world would, could or should find acceptable?

Wonder and Ponder

So, what you focus on you get more of, yes in a trite "The Secret" nonsense way but also in terms of self-validation and perpetuation of belief. You believe life is difficult and so you notice all the difficulties in your life, and you keep focusing on them and become further convinced life is difficult. Yet you have forgotten that your myopic focus is blinding you to the other things that exist. They are all around you, you are just not focused upon then, maybe you are multiplying the difficulties because that's where your focus is. Your focus creates more of it.

Start to notice other things, wonder and ponder about the number of miraculous things in your life from the simple to the magnificent – water, tea, food, shelter, a warm bed at night, a hot shower, happiness, love, peace, opportunity.

Consider, for instance, a humble cup of tea. It is on the surface a simple convenience that is readily available. Yet, think of the journey that tea has gone through in order to now be available in your home cupboard. Ponder what it brings to you, all the experiences it has been through to now be in your cup – that's miraculous!

That beverage arrives in your cup, ready for you to drink, with a multitude of experiences. How far has that tea travelled from where it was grown, harvested, dried, packaged, transported and stocked for you to buy. That tea may have travelled more than you have! Focus on the journey it has gone through, everything it have gone through to get to you, the miracle of it being there in your cup and you change your focus from the difficulties in your life to the miracles in your life.

Lift your mood and enthusiasm by noticing all the good things, wondering and pondering on all the miracles and celebrating all the victories in your life, even the tiniest of tiny ones! The wondering and pondering are the gateways to igniting the optimism and hopefulness in your heart – wondering and pondering, looking for the amazing in the ordinary, are the avenues to increasing the love, pleasure and happiness that you emanate. This change in focus eventually leads to a change in your external in response to your change in focus and change in emanation.

Unconditional Support

What you focus on magnifies in your life – or so it appears, but is it magnifying or is it the only thing you are acknowledging? Your inner self, higher self, guides, guardians, God however you wish to consider this, responds to your focus by 'sending you more of that', the idea being that by placing your focus upon something you are dictating to the 'beyond 3D' aspects of self, the beyond mind aspects of self, that this is what you believe life to be made up of and hence you get more of it.

The universe, the flows of life and streams of reality are non-judgmental and will 100% unconditionally support you in creating what you believe to be true. It is a 100% unconditional support system.

Now, consider what unconditional actually means – it does not mean that you will be corrected onto a more benevolent pathway or one more aligned with who you are at your core, or where you wish to be in life, it means that you are supported exactly *where you are at*.

No matter what your focus, no matter what your beliefs, no matter how you engage with life, nor how you disengage with life – you are unconditionally supported exactly where you are at. Unconditional is unconditional – there are no conditions. You are not corrected; you are met where you are and supported all the way.

This means that you are supported in your downward dive into the spiral of chaos and path of sorrow AND you are supported in your upward explorations and exertions in alpinism and climbing beyond your spiral of chaos. You are unconditionally supported no matter which direction you choose. So, what you focus upon becomes your message to the universe about what you believe is true about you and your life. It becomes the message to the universe about what you want more of and it becomes the message to the universe about what you cannot have or experience.

Now, the good news here is that it is not just what you focus upon but how you focus upon it, because the emotional state is the big broadcaster of who you are and what you want more of.

If you are in the midst of something you do not prefer, then focusing on it with anger, outrage, sadness and helplessness broadcasts your message to the unconditionally supportive universe, flows and streams of life and eternal source that this is what you want more of.

All your focus is here – and all that focus is very loud with powerful negative emotion! That is all you see and experience – your emotions and beliefs all align to 'this is what is here and what I am experiencing'.

On the other hand, if you look at where you are at, understand that it is a personal creation stemming from your internal self and eternal relationship with the streams of life (God if you will) then you can look at it objectively (not subjectively and emotionally) and realise it is an expression of something from within you. It is an out-picturing of who you are and what you believe – it is your creation.

This means that what you are experiencing now, should it be unpreferred and not in alignment with what you would prefer to be experiencing, is currently giving you information about how to refine your focus, about how to change your emotions and self-correct your reactions.

Additionally, it is giving you information about what traumas, wounds, dramas or hurts you are holding within, that may have evolved into programs and belief systems you have become blind to. These programs and belief systems are currently dictating your reactions, your responses, your emanation and your personal frequency. Through this you are, on some unconscious level, informing the universe, the flows of life, the higher self, your god, and whomever or whatever you believe guides you and your flows of life, that this is what you want more of.

When you embrace self-responsibility and, during unpreferred experiences, begin noting that what you are experiencing you do not prefer to experience, then take a moment to be peaceful about the current circumstance. Release raging against it or capitulating to it and simply take that moment and consider 'ok, this exists, I do not prefer this, what else is there?'.

At this point you switch your focus to something pleasant and preferable (no matter how small) and begin to focus upon that.

Feel the joy, peace, and love in that moment about the 'something preferable' and you will move through the current difficulty much more swiftly and through a sort of osmotic release and magnetic collective process, over time your out-picturing moves into that which you would prefer. The more time you spend in genuine peace and preference the more peaceful and preferable your out-picturing becomes.

Each human has a very convoluted expression of self, there is much hidden to self, much masked and shunted to the side to pretend that it does not exist, it does not hurt, it is not you, yet your life will show you precisely who you are, nonetheless. It is a frequency action; it is an out-picturing of your true understanding of self and what you can and cannot have.

Thus, what you focus upon you get more of, yes, but it's not just about focus, it is how you focus upon it. Do you focus upon it with the tantrum energy of a child or the limpness of a victim? Continuously expressing your anger or sadness at what is? Then you will likely get more of what you do not prefer or enjoy. Do you recognise that it is not preferred and choose to use the current circumstance to define what you would prefer and feel into the hope of a new creation and better times? Then you will likely move through your difficulties quickly, experience solutions and new options regularly and easily and change your outcomes more rapidly.

Your Flows of Creation

Your personal consciousness, the thoughts feelings and conclusions that you flow daily in your contemplations, in your actions, in your reactions, these create your reality.

If your reality is not as you would wish it, if you are not feeling the depths of peace and tranquillity you would desire, if you are not having the relationships you desire, if you are not feeling safe, loved, supplied and contented, then what is it about your flows of personal consciousness that is emanating a deviation from these states of being that you are seeking?

Streaming your dream occurs by regularly checking in with yourself. What is it you would like to see out-pictured as your life? Who are you at your core and what life would you like to live? Are you emanating that?

Are you regularly monitoring your thoughts, and mastering your emanation to reflect that, to co-create, to resonate with that which you would prefer to be experiencing in your life?

You flow it, you stream it, you choose it from within first.

You create your reality. This is mostly done via the various flows of personal consciousness. Your flows express in the world through your thoughts, emotions, feelings and words, your engagements and interactions. Understand that what we are flowing from is light and sound, words that are light and sound making up our thoughts and assessments of our feelings and emotions. Generally, what the words are creating is not what we are looking for, not the life we desire and yearn for.

As an electric and magnetic flow system, the human being streams consciousness as an emanation of the self. What you spend your time thinking, feeling and emoting is the fuel for the creation of your reality.

When you change the flows of attention and intention through your personal consciousness flows, you change the out-picturing of your reality. You then experience this as the manifestation of the life you desire, or at least the evolution of your life into something more desirable.

When we engage with life, we are making a choice. Whether we make a conscious choice to take action or we commit to inaction, it is still a choice. That choice is made by the personal consciousness that we stream through our being. Who we are goes into that choice. This choice streams from us as a pulse, a wave engaging with the external reality imprinting and informing it as to who we are, what we believe and what we choose.

You may think that what you choose does not come to pass – but I choose prosperity and yet I am not prosperous! And I say unto you, you may have chosen prosperity, but did you flow it? Was it imbued into you as part of who you truly are? Or was it the conscious mind choice that you wished for, hoped for, tried to align with and yet you flow the personal consciousness of 'this will never work, I don't earn enough, I don't have the education needed to make the big dollars, I am not smart enough, I am not worthy enough, there are not enough opportunities for my skill set, it'll never happen to me, I can't do this right' and so it goes on?

We flow all sorts of doubts, worries, fears and limitations with our personal consciousness, and sometimes we are not even aware that we are doing it! This manuscript is designed to help you gracefully face your limiting flows and help you upshift and uplift those flows so that you can create again, allowing you to out-picture the life you yearn for.

Whether you realise it, acknowledge it or not, you have within you all that you need to radically transform your life. It is all within you. You are the master of your life by recognising that you are the chooser of the emanation of your own energies and flows. You are the chooser of your emotions, actions and reactions. When you own that, when you take personal presence and mastery of that in repetition, repetition and repetition – when you truly remember and own the personal mastery of your presence on this planet, then *you make it happen*.

It all comes from you in Mastery of you.

Your life becomes your creation, and your outcomes become what you desire rather than those confronting, unexpected, demoralising or upsetting outcomes that you are experiencing. Your outcomes become joyfully glorious, happy occurrences of resolution of difficulties and peaceful moments.

You cannot control anything. You cannot predict everything. But you can be in the flow of your own peaceful thoughts and actions and watch as those mountains you dread turn into molehills and become so petty that the life you lead gets easier and easier, more peaceful and calm, more bliss filled and loving, with so called miraculous events occurring regularly.

Give up the expectation that someone will 'do it for you' and grasp the reigns of self-actualised self-responsibility, becoming the master of your own self, your own happiness, and stream the flows of your personal consciousness aligned with love, with peace, with prosperity of self and with the grace filled light and love of self-healing. And get ready for your life to transform into a thing of beauty!

The Whirlpool

You are directing the path, controlling the path with your conscious mind, really it is an intuitive dynamic choice of direction. Co-creation is very much an in the moment occurrence.

That doesn't mean that you can't plan anything. What it means is learning to become responsive to your environment, as opposed to just throwing your hands in the air and becoming a leaf on the breeze and allowing the environment to push you around.

Co-creation is going within and really feeling 'OK what's thrilling me today' and putting your energy into that.

There are lots of different levels of matter and self that create the human setup – not just the physical body, the mind, the emotions and the spirit. It's so much more complex than we consider ourselves, and there is no need to decipher it all, there is just a helpfulness in recognising that we are far more physically, emotionally, mentally, spiritually and etherically complex and vast than we give ourselves credit for.

Trying to understand it all may be of interest to you, but it is not necessary in order to heal the self and co-create the life you desire. For now, let's just work from the understanding that the human setup is a lot of different layers or stations of identity, layers of emission, pulse frequencies, different dimensions, colours, sounds, connections and so on.

The energy of your internally held and operated from dramas, traumas and wounds makes up part of, or at least heavily impacts, the flow of your system. Your flow can be completely unimpeded or completely impeded or anywhere in between. Most people are partly impeded partly unimpeded, and the ratio or the percentage of flow or impediment is determined by how much trauma (as an example) they are operating from, and how much of that trauma they've healed truthfully or compensated through.

What that means is the human system has flowing circuitry, and it has flows of Eternal Source, Eternal You and the dramas, the traumas and the wounds, as well as memories, personality, ego etc that are streaming throughout you.

When you have a certain experience in society that is aligned with something within you that is less than desirable, an experience that in some way awakens, or resonates with, a previous drama, trauma or wound you have experienced, it works incredibly rapidly to amplify in your system. It creates a type of whirlpool effect that draws you straight back down into the original emotional aspect of the drama, the trauma, the wound that it is resonating with. It works very very quickly to draw you off centre and off trajectory.

It is an energetic action that you then experience as an emotional response as it plays out in your reality – you may feel it as depression, anger, irritation etc. Energetically, what's happened is you've been caught in a maelstrom, a whirlpool of powerful currents and it's ripped you down to the original emotional aspect of the drama, the trauma, the wound and knocked you askew. So, it has a lot of power.

The negative always feels more powerful, it easily draws you back and pulls you down. It is, however, not more powerful. It is just more known, more recognisable. The older paths are more well-trodden.

You are used to thinking negatively, powerlessly or dominatingly, so when the negative experience or thought appears, it is familiar, and it seems to have more power than the new and preferred way of thinking. It seems to have the power to knock you askew very quickly, but this is mostly because you are used to the well-worn and trodden paths – it takes effort to break new ground. Give it a little bit of effort to correct your focus, to try again with the upshifted thoughts and emotions, and soon enough you will have created a well-worn and well-trodden path in the peaceful and powerful realms of self.

Sovereignty

The peaceful and powerful realms of self are aligned with sovereignty of self. The concept of self-sovereignty has been talked about and explored a lot in new age circles as well as various conspiracy theory type ideologies. It can be a very misunderstood concept and is often spoken of as some type of extraction from the domination of the societal systems and overbearance we live amongst.

Claiming or reclaiming sovereignty is not about retribution against those who took it. It is not about fighting the king, or the government, the church or the cult who took it. It's not about rejecting God or standing alone in the universe as some type of solo one person army. It's actually not even about fighting at all!

It is about your state of consciousness, the personal consciousness that flows through you as an energetic stream and forms you as the person that you are. It is about the reclamation of your free thinking, your personal discernment and analysis of what is being presented to you and then making your own conclusions, not just towing the line or believing the narrative of the environment you are in.

Claiming or returning to sovereignty involves recognising your entrainment, the training, and imprints that your upbringing, your society and your environment have all contributed. These entrainments have formed the way you think, contained the way you think and instructed you how to think, and often thusly created a limitation in your expectations of life and of self.

This is a type of compartmentalization of the way you analyze, process and recognise that which is outside of your experience or entrainment, and whether or not you dismiss it, fight it, investigate it, or allow it to be observed in neutrality.

Sovereignty is like seeing it all as an à la carte menu – taking what is true for you and allowing the rest to just be a part of that which exists but does not form your set of ethics, morality, belief systems, programs or the complex make-up of ideologies that you hold. Allow all of your ideologies, theologies and other ologies to be fluid. That which you believe and operate from, that which you engage with life from, should be investigated regularly along with any new information you are attempting to assimilate into the creation of self.

Expose your old beliefs and programs to the self and investigate whether they still hold true for you. Bring them to the surface and prune them, tend to them, discarding that which is old information, that which was formed as a conclusion from the younger mind, from the earlier feelings, from when you didn't know what you know now. Refine them to reflect who you are now. Perhaps even look at what you had previously discarded and reassess it for any current relevance it may have for you – was it erroneously discarded? Could it be that it is true and helpful for you now?

Look at what is good about your current belief systems, are you honoring the good about them? Have you forgotten the joy that they brought to you? Nourish those parts, bring them to the forefront and explore them from many angles, in a multitude of ways. This allows you to form a flourishing creation of nourishing ideals with multiple foci of the self, of your consciousness and a true sovereignty of thinking that encourages the embodiment of the happy, free and sovereign human.

A state of personal autonomy and sovereign being is a consciousness that allows the flowing of self, in peace, in calm, in presence, and in happiness without the rage and anger, the outrage and violence of fighting the system, of sharing your vitriol or naming and shaming. It allows you to see all that is occurring around you and in your environment whilst staying neutral to it, bringing the Self back to the self, and flowing with the streams of peace, calm, happiness and joy. Yes, 'it' exists, whatever 'it' is that you are focused upon, but so does everything else, so what is your attention on?

Your attention is a magnifier, so what are you magnifying? Bring your attention to the state of sovereign consciousness and stream the flows of peace, calm, love and presence whilst monitoring how you speak and engage. Monitor your engagements with others and diligently disallowing all forms of abuse, including the self-abuse of focusing on the 'horror out there'. This is how you change your mind, your flows and emanation. This is how you change the world.

Chapter 4

The Time Traveler

The human exists in the past, present and future at once. Yes, as a truth for the actual soul and embodiment but also as a truth for the brain and the thinking spectrum. Each day you spend time in the moment, not much for most of us, it is true, but we do spend some time there. We also spend time thinking or reflecting upon the past, we remember things and we explore regrets and beautiful moments we have had, and we think upon the future, we worry about tomorrow and all our tomorrows and we wonder if it will be ok if things will turn out. We spend a lot of time in both the future and the past. Even though the present is the place of power.

The present is where you neutralise the past and create the future. The present is where it all ends and begins, because in most cases the present is where none of the worries are actually happening, it is the place of ground zero with the option of recreating the way you are thinking about and experiencing both the past and the future.

Thoughts Impact Your Environment

This time travel nature of the human, of the mind, of the consciousness has an emission aspect, a frequency aspect, where the thoughts can be seen as creating an electrical impulse in the brain.

It has also been shown that the feeling of emotions has a measurable effect on the emissions of the body, the electrical or magnetic fields from various organs and parts of the body – the most notable and well-studied in comparison to other areas of the body is the heart.

The fields of energy around the body have begun to be noted and explored by the mainstream sciences, although these have been well established in history and alternative areas of spiritual worship and medicine on our planet for many thousands of years – things such as chakras, nadis, meridians have all been part of various religious and "alternative" healing modalities for a long time.

Along with the ancient ideas of energy flows of the human body and the more recent studies of the heart field and its response to the emotions felt or encountered by the human, there is also the science backed observation of the human brain in the midst of various emotions/situations and its measurable responses that show as electric and/or magnetic processing in the brain. These emanations and ignitions can all be measured in response to words thought or spoken, or feelings experienced from various stimuli.

Thinking or speaking with violence has been measured as having a very different and disruptive effect on the emanations of the body than thinking and speaking with love. You may even have experienced being in the presence of someone in a rage and noted how different it feels to being in the presence of someone experiencing peace and love. Or perhaps you have walked into a room where an argument has just taken place, or where someone is currently seething with anger, and you may have noticed that you can palpably feel the energy of that.

These are simple examples of the emanations that come off the organs/body based upon an emotional state and occurrence – elicited by words or thoughts.

You cannot sit in anger, seething resentment or outrage and have no thoughts running through your head that are fueling that anger. If you sat in internal silence, there is nothing to perpetuate the anger state – or any emotional state in reality.

Inner contemplation of nothing brings about a neutral state. The neutral is not 'the nothing', it is the uncharged state of being. This is not a bad thing to pursue. It is different to the numb state or the perpetually seeking happiness state and can be the first step towards the peace and joy state that is often sought as part of the pursuit for enlightenment.

The idea that your words or thoughts may affect your outer reality can also be evidenced by research such as the plant and water experiments that have been going on in science for quite a few years now. You've probably come across the work of Masaru Emoto, the Japanese author who did many experiments that seemed to show that water recreates itself into different crystalline structures in response to the words or sounds directed to it or spoken to it.

Plants have similar responses to words, sounds or music directed towards them. The more negative or unpleasant the words, sounds or music the less thriving and beautiful the response from the plant or water.

It's possible this all comes down to water – plants contain water, so do humans. We are in fact anywhere between 50 and 80% water, so these experiments with water and its response to violence, anger and fear or love, peace, and gratitude, could be very important for us as humans to consider.

You don't need to take my word on these things, in fact please don't! It is very easy to find experiments and outcomes, theories and conclusions about these things – simply go online and do some research. You will be presented with a plethora of theories and conclusions based on many experiments, some following the scientific methods that we so highly prize for delivering the truth, that may lead you to at least be open to the ideas being presented here.

Let's put this together, we have the measurable impact of thoughts on the neurology and activity of your brain, we also have the measured emanations from the body and the personal experiences of the emanations of other's (their anger is usually the easiest to personally register within your own body, you will feel the discomfort of it within you), then there is the measurable responses of the other (in this reference we are meaning plants and water) to the external input of words or sounds leading to alterations in the integrity and/or thriving of the water or plant that is exposed to these words or emotions. Perhaps this is enough to start you considering that there may be a response both internally and externally from thoughts and emotions felt, projected or experienced? Or at least, that it is a possibility that playing with changing your thoughts or emotional focus may have some type of effect on your emanation, on your happiness, contentment or even your experience of exterior reality.

Now consider from the above that you are made up of water, you are a flow system of circuitry directed by the mind and heart, and you are measurably emanating a frequency into your environment. This frequency automatically interacts with and impacts all that surrounds you. So, your thoughts and emotions, your words and sound, will impact not only your internal landscape but also your external landscape.

The emission of the thought bathes the cells, the heart and the external with the same frequency and vibration of the thought. From this you may be able to deduce that your negative thoughts will bathe your cells, heart and external with a negative vibration. This will affect the ability to thrive and the growth of your cells, it will affect the health and orientation of your emotions, and it will affect the love and joy you feel in your heart. Flip this around and you get the idea that if you think peace, you experience peace, think joy, and you experience joy, think love, and you will experience love.

The Incursion of Beauty

How do you 'think peace' when you are in turmoil? The simple answer is practice. The more complex answer involves resilience!

You first remember that turmoil is not all that there is, it is just all that you are focusing on and experiencing right now. If a plant can grow through the pavement, if a plant can sprout in a prison yard, then that is your evidence that life and beauty can return to the most barren and hard, the most violent and bereft circumstance.

There is always at least a tiny option for an incursion of beauty wherever you are, in whatever your situation. In some situations, this incursion of beauty is more difficult to find and perhaps more difficult to trust in and rely upon, but it is always there!

Find that incursion of beauty and make it your focus, give it most, if not all, of your attention and find the magic in its existence, find the joy in its presence and believe in the wonder that it should even be able to be there at all!! This is your starting point for returning the flows of peace, joy, love and ease into your life – through the power of wonder!

This takes practice and repetition. This takes focus and attention. You have long and far been drawn from the path of peace, joy and love, you have been many times told that it is not powerful, it is not sustainable and it is not viable for the world you live in. Yet, all the other ways have led you to this feeling, this place of negative distrustful damaging and hurtful thoughts that leave you feeling angry, bereft, unloved, unseen, unheard and frustrated, without a connection to who you truly are, without the peace of quietude and presence, without the calm of faith and love and without the reliance of being supported by life, by those around you and by yourself, just for being you.

What you are engaging with and what you are experiencing and expressing has brought you here. It has created you thus far. Your life is an expression of who you are and what you are thinking, believing and expressing into the world.

Is it what you enjoy? Are you deeply feeling and living the love and happiness you want? Then think again. Speak again. Feel again.

If what you have been doing has led you to this now, if what you have been thinking and speaking has led you to this now, and this now is not what you want or what you hoped for, then change the way you think and speak. Change the way you weave your words and spell something new into existence.

You are Looking at Your Past

What you see as your world, your reality, is the out-picturing of your thoughts, beliefs, programs and decisions about life and how life works and what it can be for you. The out-picturing of your life is the past.

You are looking at the past. The past that you thought into reality. You are looking at, living in, tending to and experiencing the out-picturing of the past thoughts, occurrences, conclusions and actions that you have had or taken.

Your own reality reflects what HAS been. Reacting and responding to it perpetuates it or changes it because your reactions in the now create your future.

The outer reality or out-picturing of your moments, hours and days is created in the present and out-pictured as your future present moment.

Each moment is an image, a creation, a presentation of what you have already set in motion, set in place. Changing your in-the-moment day-to-day focus, reactions, thoughts and feelings creates a new out-picturing in your next moment, in your future.

How long will you keep reacting in violence, anger, fear and/or outrage in the moment before you realise it is this reaction that created the out-picturing of what you are currently experiencing and reacting to?

Continuing to react in these ways, continuing to worry, continuing to fret, continuing to believe in life as, or see life from a point of, fear, anger, opposition and separation is what is creating the future of fear, anger, opposition and separation.

What you do now, what you think now, what you believe now, how you react now, is what creates your future. Nothing exists in your life without your focus, without your attention. What are you focusing on and how are you focusing upon it? This is what you are perpetuating in your life. This is the future out-picture you are creating.

Whatever you are focusing on may exist, it may, or it may be something you are creating, it may be, but whatever it is, whether it is 'real' or 'not' it is still holding your focus and thusly will become real to you.

If it exists it may hold your attention strongly, but remember it is not the only thing that exists! It is simply the thing that is holding the most of your attention in the strongest way right now.

Shift your attention, what else exists?

What is there that is joyful in your life?

What is it that is beautiful in your life?

What is there that has less negative charge, that ignites you into less anger, fear, doubt, worry, confusion in your life?

Focus on that, give that your attention.

Place your focus on that which lifts your joy and your frequency thusly creating this feeling and experience as your future out-picturing.

Your focus provides energy and magnifies that which you focus upon – what are you focusing on? Consider the uses of your attention by others. Perhaps it is worth wondering upon concepts such as why the media and other sources of information bang the drum of fear, doubt and worry? What is the media drawing your attention to?

Your attention, your outrage, your shock, your fear, your frustration and impotence in the face of seeing the disintegration continuously in your environment and world fuels that which they are showing you. Yet your focus on it now, your outrage about it now, your myopic attention to this and only this, creates it as part of the out-picturing of your future. So, is the media reporting on what is so, or are they fueling your creation of it continuing to be so in your environment?

Your mantra may become, 'yes, this exists, this is here, but what else is there, I hold hope for better things to come' and then choose your focus and switch it to something joyful that ignites your feelings of hope, your feelings of wonder and your feelings of optimism for a bright future knowing that the whole time you are fueling the creation of that bright future in your now.

There may be action you need to take in the face of the 'thing that exists now' but holding to the joyful focus creates the cessation of the despair that comes from focusing only upon the negativity and that which currently fuels your outrage and less than desirable circumstances.

And of course, the Power of Now

It is quite possibly true to say that time, as the human experiences it, is not how time works at all. The human experiences time as linear and yet we spend each day focusing upon and obsessing over the past and the future so, in a very real way, it is all happening now.

I'm sure you've heard about the power of now, it's been talked about a lot over the last 20 years or so, and many have spent much in the way of time and money on understanding the concept and integrating it into their lives for transformation.

Ultimately understanding 'now' is very simple.

Now is the place where all choice is made. It is thusly the place where the next moment is chosen and co-created by you as the consequence of your current 'now moment' experiences, expressions, emotions and emanations.

Pulsing your now moment as an expression of peace, of love, of gratitude and of joyfulness, creates the next moment as an evolution or consequence of that pulsing from the now moment. You are always in the now, and yet each now is creating the next now. Your pulsing, your choosing to hold a state of an explicit something creates the next moment from that explicit something. Each now moment neutralises all past memories and creates all future moments, but in each now moment we spend time remembering (re-creating) the past and fearing (creating) the future.

Choosing to return to You, in presence, and pulsing the peace of now, creates a future that is aligned with that peace. It creates the next moment that is aligned with that peace, and eventually you are creating all your moments aligned with that peace. Your present is the place of power. Your present is the place of manifestation and co-creation, the place where you create all your future moments from that moment of now. Holding your focus, your feeling and your emanation in the now as the place of peace, the place of joyful choice of love, you emanate that into your future space to create the next moment as a reflection of that emanation.

Returning to self often and re-choosing to hold the emanation of the preferred outcome, of the preferred state of being and experience of life, is the way we create the future into the image of our choice. If what you see out there does not match your choice, then go within again and choose again, to feel the peace, to feel the joy, to feel the love that you wish to experience 'out there', emanate it from within and it creates the future moment as an emulation of your emanation.

Externally, all that you look at is a reflection of your past moments' emanations, your past moments' choices. You are literally looking at the past.

Some of those choices were made by the collective, and some of them made by you, but your ability to master your own emanation is what co-creates the life you desire, the life you enjoy, the life you are looking for even in the midst of collective choices that bewilder you or perplex you.

Go back within, soothe the self and release the triggering.

Go back within and calm the self and release the outrage.

Go back within. Breathe peace, breathe love. Remember the eternal being that you are and release the frustration, the anger and the bewilderment at the choices of the collective. Return yourself to peace. Breathe and love. Tend to you. Tend to your life and stay focused on emanating it from within to co-create in the external for the self as the outcome that is desired. You cannot control anyone else, but your emanation in peaceful flows of joy is completely enough to transform your life experience into that which you seek!

Today Tomorrow and Yesterday

Today creates your tomorrow, in a very real way tomorrow does not exist until you create it. We create tomorrow in every moment with our expectations of tomorrow. Our expectations of tomorrow are based upon our remembering, repeating and regenerating yesterday. Our past (yesterday) is out-pictured as our today and our thoughts on this, our feelings about this, our expectations generated from this, create our tomorrow.

Consider thinking again, expecting differently and allowing for something new to show up in your tomorrow. There will be successes and failures as you learn to do this with consistency. As you begin to understand the moment of now as the void point, the creation point, the choice point and the experience of today as the end result, the out-picturing, the manifestation result from all your yesterdays, then you will begin to have more success, more impact and more of your chosen results in your tomorrows - by not repeating today what you did yesterday.

Choose again in this moment of now, today, and create a new tomorrow.

All of your tomorrows are created today. It is your choice to begin again or to dismiss this as not possible or too hard as you continue to generate your tomorrow based upon today's thoughts from your yesterday.

You are the one creating it, in partnership with the Eternal Source, hence it is a co-creation from your direction. You give the direction.

Eternal Source fuels you, supports you and guides you. You choose the focus and intention thus co-creating your outcome from your attention and intention through the fuel and support of Eternal source. This is not about religion; this is about the spark of life that animates you and encourages your existence. All doubts to the contrary, all deviations and distractions from this are not from Eternal Source. They are your beliefs and understandings of the power of something else, something stronger or more powerful than you and your choices, that lead you into the path of sorrow, the path of incompletion of your dreams and the path of doubt, fear, anxiety and stress. That's ok, that happens. Choose to remember again that the detour was temporary, and you are eternal! Breathe, be present and begin again.

You can begin again as many times as you wish, just stay focused on now and today, as the creator of all your tomorrows, disallowing all your yesterdays in having a say in neither your today nor your creation of your tomorrow.

Chapter 5

Who are You?

The fundamental question most people ask themselves is 'Who am I?' and yet when asking this question most people will answer it from an internal data point of view, from their subconscious programming;

"I am a mother"

"I am a son"

"I am an accountant"

"I am a teacher"

These are usually simply roles you play, and you are so much more than this!

You are an infinite expression of sound light energy that aligns with, connects with, engages with DNA technology, seed and egg technology, donated quanta and DNA from a male and female. You then go through a womb and birthing experience where you take on a form of forgetting associated with freewill and incarnation on earth.

From here you mostly forget your light experience, your infinite nature, and become the finite being, within a dictated timeline held within a DNA informed physical being.

You are here on purpose, as a remembering of self-mastery, the power to co-create from within.

You are here on purpose to remember who you are and reconnect with the flows of eternal life, the flows of divinity, within you.

You have an inner being that's always been, that joined the body here to be here, to co-create here. You are a carbon-based bio form that is a 'person of the earth'. You are one of the 'people of the earth' and as such you reflect and mirror the changes she goes through. Everything that happens to her on a macro scale happens to you on a micro scale. Even your chakras reflect the aligning of the planets, and your cells reflect the stars. You are a gathering of the cosmos and a reflection of the cosmos

Most people go from day to day without so much as a casual thought about their energy system, their cells, their body or its condition – about their own inner cosmos, connection and magnificence. Your energy frequency body is a system which can function automatically, without any overt or explicit direction or attention from you, but it is designed to respond to your intentional input. It only operates at peak efficiency when such is the case. Without intentional input and regular attention from you, your aura, chakras, meridians and other energy bodies and aspects operate in a kind of default mode whereby they pick up information from outside sources, from the collective and from expectations.

You incarnate as a co-creating photonic light-being with a 'clean slate'. It has been said that planet earth is a place of 100% freewill, in a galaxy of 100% freewill. You arrive as this incarnation through the birth canal which wipes your memory (sometimes called 'the great forgetting', 'the mind wipe' or 'the veil') – why would this happen?

Why Do We Forget Who We Are?

Why would the human be created and birthed on this planet with amnesia of who they really are and what they really can do? If the human is so powerful, why don't we remember this after our birth? Ask a small child about healing and love, they remember! They have what we call innocent ideas and fanciful ideas about friendship, love, affluence, availability, peace and healing that we simply cannot understand or believe in as adults.

We consider ourselves more learned than the child and thus we teach the child that what they believe is not so. And yet, all children come through with these beliefs and are often bewildered by the way the world actually is. We forget who we are, where we have come from, and our original ideas, hopes and dreams about life as we get older – some of it is wiped during the birthing process, and the rest fades away like a forgotten dream as we engage with life and those around us.

If we have forgotten who we are, why we are here and how powerful we are/can be, doesn't this put us at a disadvantage? Doesn't this then allow us to be very easily manipulated, misled and deceived? Yes, it does!

Remember though, that this is a freewill situation and choice, the choice is made prior to birth to honour the circumstances of a human life and life on Earth and this memory wipe or amnesia is part of the 100% freewill of the planet earth and her bio forms.

Perhaps it is the case that in order to have 100% freewill one needs to not be sidetracked, overloaded or operating from the memory of past karma or past timelines. You need to be able to come in essentially 'clean' and 'start again' in order to grow and learn beyond where you have been stuck.

You may repeat some past situations, meet with others you have been with before, or enact situations and emotions from previous circumstances, but you do this without the memory of the history of those circumstances allowing you to experience them fresh and without judgment thus giving you the opportunity to swiftly resolve them and move through them thereby dissolving the karmic imprints of them.

Avoiding Pain

We as humans tend to not resolve our pain swiftly. We tend to avoid our pain or ignore it until it cannot possibly be shunted away anymore, until it overwhelms us, and even then we sometimes just collapse beneath it wailing and chest beating that it is too hard and we just can't do it. The human usually avoids any type of healing of the pain until the pain itself is far more painful than the work involved in healing or releasing the pain.

It's a little counterintuitive, but it is what we do – it's like spending your life walking with sand in your shoe that is uncomfortable and causes friction and chafing but 'at least it's not a pebble'. If it was a pebble, you'd actually stop and remove it because walking would be too difficult with the pebble still in place.

This avoidance of resolving our pain often means that we tend to repeat circumstances that trigger the same type of pain in our lives over and over again. Each time it occurs you almost certainly have some type of eye roll experience about it 'Oh no, not this again!' and eventually you create an inner knowledge bank that feeds you the idea that this is just a truth about life – all jobs are onerous, all bosses don't understand, all men/women are unfaithful, you can't trust anybody etc.

These types of decisions about life tend to form hard and fast ways we engage with people, places, things, experiences and occurrences. And yet, it is truly the case that 'wherever you go, there you are' – you are bringing your experiences, your expectations and your engagement to every situation and circumstance that you are part of. So, does it happen because it happens, and this is true about people and life? Or does it happen because you expect it to happen, and you are just that powerful? Perhaps you created it and thus it happened thereby fulfilling your expectations?

Here's a simple example of how this might play out:

You walk down the street feeling like a freak in some way (not dressed right, too tall, too small, too fat, too thin etc), and everyone looks at you. Are they looking at you because you actually are a freak? Are they looking at you because you expect them to? Are you looking at them hoping they don't look at you, just checking that they are not looking at you, and yet by the very act of looking at everyone you are encouraging them to look back?

WHO ARE YOU?

Are you, in your fear of attention and judgement, putting out an energy in subtle and overt ways that will cause those around you to react to you as though you are the freak you think you are? Or are you acting defensively, aggressively or antagonistically in the expectation that those 'out there' are going to act toward you like you are a freak?

You don't want to feel vulnerable or get attacked by their opinion that you are a freak, or their actions about you being a freak, and so you 'go on the offensive' and behave in such a way as to put them off, or push them away, just in case they treat you like a freak and/or hurt you.

It's entirely possible they were looking at you because you are beautiful, unique or interesting, and yet your behaviour and expectation is causing the perceived reaction of others toward you or causing you to perceive them as judging you in a negative and hostile way.

Now it is fair to say that there are those in the world who are so shut down, so oppressed and depressed within that they have made decisions about folks of certain colour or ethnicities, or about certain genders or other, or about certain education levels or other, and of course these folks can definitely consider another as the enemy or 'less-than' based upon their own prejudices against the other's skin colour, education level, gender, dress code or height or weight etc. And yes, these people are often quite demoralising to come across, but recognising that in reality it is usually your sense of what you think is going to happen when you encounter folk 'out there' that dictates their response to you, will go a huge way to help you notice that most often you are creating the experience you expect to occur.

What does this mean? It means that your thoughts about yourself, your thoughts and expectations about any engagement, occurrence or experience in your life will usually be correct. You will get what you think you will get.

A very simple way of illustrating this to yourself is for you to go out into the world and do something that you wouldn't normally do or do something you would normally do but do it in a different frame of mind and with different expectations.

For instance, if you would normally engage from a fearful perspective just waiting for someone to put you down, or for someone to frown at the way you are dressed, or the way you speak, or the colour of your skin, why not try engaging in the outer world with a smile, or with pleasantness in your heart, with the expectation and continuous self-parenting internally of seeing and being the good things in life.

Try it at the supermarket. You don't have to talk to anybody if you don't want to, just hold a smile in your heart, hold the optimism of a good experience, and put a small smile on your face, especially when someone looks your way. You may be deeply surprised by the answering smile, the answering nod or even someone actually saying hello to you. Maybe they were never looking at you for all the faults you think you have, maybe they were just lonely people in a sea of strangers and looking for those around them that are also experiencing the same loneliness.

Everyone is experiencing some form of disparateness from the 'norm' for one reason or another. Pretty much everyone considers themselves to be less than what is expected by 'those out there' or society in general. They're not kind enough, smart enough, successful enough. They're not tall enough, slim enough, strong enough. Everyone has something inside them that tells them they are imperfect, or unsatisfactory in some way and hence every situation they are in they are expecting to be judged for this.

Perhaps it is the case that you are creating the situation that validates your inner decision about the self? Perhaps it is the case that you can uncreate it by expecting something different? When you go out in the world with an expectation of kindness and peace, you are not fighting the world for your place in it. When you are not aggressive and defensive in the expectation of having to fight your way through circumstance or defend yourself against the prejudices you expect to experience from others your engagement with the world changes.

When you present in the world calmly and kindly, you don't provoke the self defense mechanism of others because you are not a threat, and hence you get less of the judgment or prejudice you are expecting to receive. You get more of the kindness and acceptance you actually want!

It is not weakness to be calm and kind, it is simply recognising that fight begets fight. Maintaining the expectation that you will experience judgment and difficulty is the same as creating it for the self. Maintaining the expectation that life is easy, and people are kind, is the same as encouraging that experience in your life. There will be anomalies, there will be unexpected confronting experiences, but it is highly likely that your overall experience will shift to one of more happiness, and self-validation.

Chapter 6

Word Magic

And so, we come to the titular subject, words. Let us first consider that our language is a sound-based expression of a light-based aspect of life. You were given/taught language in childhood as a way of communicating and expressing externally – which means that in a very real way, your feelings and emotions have been condensed down to fit the language that you are capable of using to describe them.

Verbal language is the sound expression of thought, it has a vibration, it comes out of the mouth via a vibration from within to without. Language has a sound component; it must have this, or we wouldn't be able to hear it. Putting aside sign-language and body language, here we are talking about verbal language. Sign and body language are more physical languages, and less light based – they are important for communication and understanding but they are not as vibration and light based as verbal language and thought in this context.

Verbal language is an expression of that which we think, often filtered to only audibly express that which we believe is socially acceptable (or perhaps socially disruptive!) to the situation, the listener or the society, but still, it is an expression of thought. It is the verbal expression of that which is within, the various thoughts, ponderings, wonderings, or self-screenings that we filter through internally to then express externally. As such it is a sound expression that is built from our conditioning and forming throughout life. Our verbal expression is created from our society, community, parents, schooling, and the various machinations and moldings we go through or put ourselves through to become what we perceive to be acceptable, successful and perhaps even dominant in our situation.

Words are a form of communication, they are a way of thinking, a way of expressing, feeling, emoting and a way of connecting and creating. We use words to create bonds with other humans, to express our needs, our feelings, our thoughts and desires, to other humans. We use words to create camaraderie and friendship, or to seduce, convince or romance. We use words to deceive and manipulate and to lie and mislead.

Words, whether spoken, thought or written, are the human's stock in trade and go-to method for expressing to, connecting with, informing or convincing other humans. We use words to, individually or collectively, help other humans come to an understanding of who we are, to believe what we say or to join us in our quest to be who we think we are (or think we should be or should be perceived to be).

Thoughts are words that are unexpressed to the world, they often come with images and feelings personal to the thinker and so could be considered words expressed internally with light. Spoken words are words expressed externally with sound; however, they too may come with ideas, images and feelings and hence could be considered expressed with sound *and* light.

We may consider words as our expression of who we are to others and yet mostly it is actually an expression of who we *think* we are and/or who we would like others to think we are. Our thoughts may be the polar opposite of our words spoken. We may think we are worthless and yet speak with a sense of authority. We may think the request from another is futile, imposing or incorrect and yet we politely agree. Both thoughts and speech are words, and both affect your emotions, feelings and being – even when they are in conflict with each other.

The human is an emanating machine; the biology itself pulses and flows with magnetic and electric movements and circuitry. Our thoughts and processes 'light' up the brain as evidence of activity, of life and of consciousness, often interpolated as individual identity and sentience.

We use words to express, to convince and to explore ideas. Weaving words into a narrative that makes sense of our world or creates the persona that we wish the world to believe of us. We use words to make money and gain popularity, to get likes, to get laughs and to receive the accolades we desire. But what are we really doing?

We are sharing an emission of self with the external and an emission of self through the internal. We are speaking our words out there and thinking our thoughts in here. Both are emissions. Both are electrical or magnetic (or both) frequencies of self, shared externally or internally, and both are involved in the creation of self and life.

We are weaving our narrative. Weaving our world through narrative via both internal and external mechanisms of flow, programs and belief systems. We are creating an emanation of self, a frequency emission that is sometimes in flow, sometimes distorted and yet always emitting to the world at large, to those that are paying attention, who you really are.

Your thoughts and words become the world you live in.

They create it.

Your words are first given to you by your parents, you usually learn to speak at home through engagement with family. You learn to define your world through the words and understandings delivered to you by your parents. Then you go to school and learn different ways of speaking from your teachers, your friends and the other beings external to family that you become exposed to. This offers you new definitions and usages of words, and new words for new situations and learnings.

This is followed by your own investigations, your own attempts at personal growth perhaps, or your career decisions and the channels and funnels of life's trajectory for you, that lead you to learn new ways of expressing the self, of hiding the self and euphemistically referring to feelings or glossing over situations.

Your way of viewing the world and expressing about the world is created by all of these channels in life and all the decisions you make that take you further into various channels and funnels of life.

For instance, you may work in an area that is very much preoccupied with describing things without emotion and without specificity, using euphemism and jargon, as in many boardroom and business circumstances. On the surface this seems optimal, by not blaming and shaming we are being kind, perhaps fair, we are dealing with the issue and not the individual, right?

On the surface, this may be true. There is a strong argument against blaming and shaming, it is unnecessary and is in fact a form of abuse in and of itself – where does identifying perpetrators and learning from actions and outcomes stop and salacious abuse of character and sharing gory details begin? An interesting question about boundaries and parameters.

Having said that, as we veer into the habit of not speaking the truth and using euphemisms and circumlocution to express our thoughts, we run the risk of a disconnection or detachment from feeling and reality, a type of glossing over of the true horror of what has actually occurred. Consider, does the euphemism 'minor attracted person' minimize the feelings towards the behaviour of a pedophile to some degree? Simply by using a less inflammatory word we create a circumstance where the true damage of the behaviour becomes glossed over.

This habit of using euphemisms, corporate speak and politically correct language for even the most abominable actions may create a detachment within self, affecting the ability to connect to your own loving and expressing nature. It may create an engagement with others that is disconnected from any of your true opinions and feelings but is appropriately expressed through euphemism and politically correct language so as not to cause any ripples or reactions in those you engage with. Or it may be entirely appropriate and helpful for you. The questions to ask the self are:

Does this way of speaking express who you truly are? What happens within you when you speak this way? Does your mind churn and rebel against the thwarting of its desire to express your actual feelings and true emotions? Are you becoming so switched off and disconnected from your feelings that you cannot even identify what they are? Is this way of speaking creating the world you wish to live in?

Of course, as a community we need to speak and engage in a productive, uninflammatory and yet expressive way, we should be focusing upon non-castigatory and helpful forms of expression, doing so without using abuse or abuse language.

At the same time, we do still need to have a connection to, understanding of, and an ability to express, our true and real thoughts without hiding behind lingo and politically correct or virtue signaling speak. Bringing the darker elements of our environment to the surface for recognition and healing is important to do without glossing over them and without adding to the darkness by gossip and salacious personal attack.

Your emotions and feelings, your thoughts and ponderings, are all connected to the expression of who you are. Your consciousness and sentience are both associated with and connected to the expression of self. Understanding this can help you recreate your life, reconnect to your happiness, by the exploration of where the suppression of self is occurring.

What are you protecting the self from, and why?

Where have you reformed the self to be something that is covering your true essence and how can you safely, easily and gently dissolve the overlays, the suppressions?

Encourage the true beauty of the self, the butterfly within, to emerge in its own personal glory for the success of you and your life in this incarnation. Reclaim the expression of you and you reclaim yourself and your true trajectory in life.

Advertising and Marketing

We live in a world of advertising, and the role of advertising is to convince you to buy something. In order to do this, they convince you that you need the item. How do they do that? They generally don't give you scientifically validated statistics and actual hard facts, they sell you a lifestyle, they sell you happy families, beautiful successful partners, joyful fun, fit bodies, success and adventure.

We know that the item being advertised won't really give us the happy family and successful life, however we are constantly bombarded by this type of advertising and what it does do is leave us with a 'something is missing' feeling within. It leaves us yearning for something, trying to fill a hole within that has been created by the vision sold to us by the advertising and/or marketing campaign– and often we don't even really know what we are yearning for, we think it is the product we yearn for, but it is actually the satiation of the emptiness that has been created.

The assault of advertising leaves us with an empty state, an emptiness that is artificially generated by advertising and unsatisfiable because it is not real – so we want more, and more, we want the newest and the latest, but none of this satiates the emptiness that has been created. The only way out of this state is within, with presence and self-love to reassure the self that nothing is missing.

So, if words have this much power and impact, what does this tell you about the advertising and marketing industry? How much of what you think are your thoughts and conclusions, your true desires and wants, are actually imprinted upon you by advertising and constant exposure?

The human is quite easily entrained into certain behaviours, thoughts, wants and needs via constant exposure and the repetitive subversive persuasion techniques used prevalently in the advertising and marketing industries – but also in other areas of our lives.

This book is not about the guerilla tactics of the advertising and marketing industries and how strongly they impact the human mind, the freewill choices of the human and the delivery of your dollars to those that do not have your highest interests at heart. All of this is mentioned here as a side note for your contemplation.

How much of what you are aiming for is really what you want? How much of what you term 'success and happiness' is truly that which would make you happy? And how much is an induced concept delivered to you by the steady stream of words and light shows presented by the advertising and marketing campaigns that plague our reality leading to constant exposure to the messages and ideas of others' definitions of success, happiness and enlightenment?

This advertising and marketing campaigning works on every human and envelops them in an ignition of thought and a lure of focus that is a disruption to their true presence and peace. This happens to all who are immersed in it (as we are just by living in our society and engaging with technology). It is only the very wary and present-minded that can catch themselves and draw back from the overpowering internal compulsion born from the deception and manipulation used to capture your attention and your money. Can you imagine how easily the distracted non-present yet perhaps seeking human is entrained into the wants and the pursuits of desires that are not their own?

On the more optimistic side, consider why the advertising and marketing industries work the way they work – with overexposure and repetition of ideas, jingles, visuals? Because the human mind is malleable, changeable and able to be imprinted!

So, your takeaway from this, your conclusion from this, is not to have a hate on the advertising industry, or those 'out there' who are hogging your attention and programming your mind. Your takeaway should be to recognise that your mind can be programmed into anything you wish, so why not program it yourself for success, happiness, joy, peace and fulfillment?

Abra Cadabra

Here's an interesting idea to ponder, the phrase abracadabra means "I (will) create as I speak/I speak it and it is".

There are a few different breakdowns of its etymology, but it may come from the Aramaic phrase avra kehdabra, meaning "I will create as I speak" or "it will be created in my words". The origin of this appears to be the Hebrew words for father, son and holy spirit.

It is interesting that the phrase we have all come to associate with a magician's reveal of something magical and miraculous, is directly linked to the idea that it is the words that create the magic and miracle!

Speak it into Creation!

Understand that it is not just the words you speak but the power and intention you put behind them. Do you speak with passion? Do you speak with conviction? Do you speak with clarity and enunciation? You are speaking the unseen into the seen (abracadabra)!

It pays to give it the focus and intention of mastery, allowing what comes forth to be your creation, not the creation of your subconscious, your belief systems, other people and other influences. Yours!

Your subconscious, belief systems and the input of other people will impact your creation by nature of them influencing and impacting you and who you have molded yourself into becoming, who you believe you actually are.

Having said that, with focus, presence and empowered conviction of the words spoken you have more opportunity to create what it is *you* want and express who it is *you* are rather than continuing to meekly parrot another's opinions, beliefs and conclusions about you and about how your life should look.

Speak it into creation!! With passion, with conviction, with joy and pleasure. Understand that your words are creating you and your reality.

What are you saying? What are you creating? Is it what you want? If not, speak again! Give it your attention and focus. Give it your conviction and passion. Give it your joy and creativity – this is how you change your world!

Done with anger, frustration or annoyance, done with vindication, violence or vengeance and you create more of that energy, you create more convolution and entanglement for the self with that very experience of violence, anger, fear and frustration.

Done with conviction, joy, passion, hope and expectation of grace filled response and you create more of that in your life – grace, pleasure, kindness, love. What do you want more of? Speak it.

Speak as you wish it to be, not just the words, but the feeling and empowerment of the words – speak them with the passion and pleasure you wish to experience as life, in life and for self.

Speak the words of love lovingly. Speak the words of joy joyfully. Speak the words of creation creatively.

Speak with passion, presence and focus and behold the changes that flow gracefully and easily into your life.

Speak it into existence!

Chapter 7

Spells and Spell Casting

Spelling is the use of letters to create words that give humans the ability to write what it is they wish to express, allowing it to be in expression, potentially forevermore. Each word could then be described as a group of symbols (letters) put together into a formation and this formation is then used, with other symbols in formation, to create a sentence. The sentence is an expression of spelled words that gives the reader the idea that is expressed via the "symbols in formation".

Consider the two meanings of the word spell;

Spell as a verb: to put letters together to create a word and

Spell as a noun: a sequence of words purported to have magical powers to encourage a certain pre-dictated outcome.

If spoken words are emanations of sound, thoughts are emanations of light, and written words are expressions of symbols in formation created through spelling (spells), then bringing your desires into creation via saying them (sounding them), thinking them (lighting them) *and* writing them (spelling them) is the ultimate trinity of expression to aid you in co-creating your reality into your preference.

A very simple manifestation exercise using this concept is to write down what you want to be so and regularly read it and speak it out loud to the self.

There are nuances to this process that make it more powerful such as engaging the present moment and joyful focus by writing it as a present statement of something having already been accomplished and including thanks for its existence in your life. Take a look at the frequency statement section for more ideas on how to phrase and enact this type of simple manifestation process.

This is a very simple but potentially potent way to change your life - depending on how much resistance you have to the statement being true for you in your life, you could change everything for the self very quickly!

You already do this.

You already spell things into creation every time you speak or think.

You do it unconsciously or subconsciously and occasionally you do it consciously.

What is being highlighted here is the actual magic in what you are doing automatically. We are looking at the evolution of the idea that doing it deliberately and consciously may deliver far more synchronistic results that become obvious to the brain. Making things obvious to your brain, to your conscious mind, allows the focus to be on the result, to notice the end result and thus come into agreement with the effect. This allows you to become one with your reality and your own creation and engagement with it.

Spell Casting

You may think of spell casting as a magical practice usually involving ritual and ceremony coupled with words and actions to deliver a desired outcome. There are often actions and items involved in order to powerfully imbue the spell and create a specified outcome – but this is only one way to cast a spell!

This book is not about the spells cast by magical ceremony or wicca craftsmanship, this book is about the types of spells we create and cast every day without even realising we are doing it, or those we are subjected to via our media and marketing and the thoughts, words and instructions of others.

We do this by simply speaking and/or writing, or by taking what we see, hear and experience and deciding it is true about us or for us. We do it every day. We do it without attention to what we are saying or believing, and we do it without knowing the power of our own words (internal and external) to create not only outcomes but to actually effect our reality.

Essentially words enable the monologues and dialogues we are experiencing with the self, with others, with the news, or other forms of information we subject ourselves to or immerse ourselves in, to come into creation through our own imagination. If we think it, believe it, repeat it and take it as truth for ourselves it becomes our reality (good or bad) – this is often the way that an idea spreads fear that is unwarranted, or predictions of dire misfortune become reality.

Our words and thoughts create or lend themselves to backing up, validating and magnifying our states of mind, our emotions and our missions, direction and worth. They affect our relationships, they affect our success, and they affect our sense of self.

How often have you felt that spurt of confidence, that hopefulness about your ideas, choices or potential and then, having spoken to someone of your choices, your ideas, had them completely quashed and deflated, returning to the doubtful uncertainty of self and not knowing what to do next? From one minute to the next you go from feeling powerful, hopeful and inspired, to feeling unsure, doubtful and forlorn. Maybe you even do it to yourself – do you often tell yourself to stop dreaming and get back to reality, get back to work? Assuring the self that what you dream of is not possible in some way?

This happens when we receive other people's words and opinions and believe them to be true about us and for us. It happens when our inner voice criticises us and when we hear the inner remembered criticisms of all those in the past who have corrected us, castigated us and attempted to create us in their own image of who and what we should be – sometimes out of the most kind and loving of intentions.

These are all the obvious ways that we allow the spell to be cast, the spell that keeps us in place, that keeps us feeling small, insignificant, and unable to make any lasting change in our lives. We cast the spell of our beliefs, of our desires, of our hopes and dreams out into the world with our words every day!

When we cast the spell for a desire for something that we perceive ourselves as currently not having or that we perceive as not possible for us, it is but a wistful dream. In these cases, we are charging our spells with the understanding that this is not possible for us, so our spells, to us, appear to have no effect. In reality they are having the very effect that we have charged them with – the effect of not creating our desire, for it is not possible for us, our words, our spells tell it as so!

When we speak with decisiveness, with passion, with absolute authority and conviction, we create ripples of change in our lives! Perhaps these changes are not what we would desire, but they are changes, nonetheless. How many times has an explosive exclamation caused you to stop in your tracks? Retaliate? Cower? Or give up? This is a powerful spell! It is not necessarily an outcome you desire – but it ascertainably creates a change, an outcome!

What are your powerful spells creating? Tension? Arguments? Hatred? Bullying? Victimizing?

Consider what is possible if you used this power as passionate creation of good and kind experiences? Rather than violent creations of angry and hateful experiences? Or hurt and pain?

Feel the passion in the words without the disruptive triggered anger. It is still powerful, but it does not hold the distortion of trauma and anger to it. The spell cast from passion and love will have more chance of creating the desirable changes of your heart.

If the words in your personal lexicon are not resonating with what you want in life or truly expressive of how you feel, change them! Use a thesaurus or make-up your own. There are no rules when it comes to words for your personal creation, contrary to what people will tell you, so make up your own words. Make-up your own expressions and words that resonate more with what you are desiring from your life experience – have fun with it, get creative and expand your lexicon!

Simply put, the way you speak or think, your language, becomes a self-fulfilling prophecy of creation of your reality. The more specific and powerful your words, the swifter and more obvious your manifestation.

Casting Curses?

It might be worth considering at this point what swears you choose to use. Swears are just words, but they are interesting words in that they often come with a great deal of taboo about them and a great deal of energy behind them – you're really not supposed to say them in polite company!

In essence though, swear words are just words. It is the power imbued into the word by the swearer that takes them into a different stratosphere from other words.

How much vitriol, hatred or anger are behind the words? Or are you simply using their power for definition? Be very truthful with yourself in the use of swearing (or curse words) – there is no recrimination or castigation here, sometimes a good swear is exactly what is needed. Swears have power! It is, however, important to know what you are doing with the swear word.

If writing and speaking a sequence of symbols called letters is called spelling, you might say that using swears is then cursing. Are you accidentally throwing a curse around with the power of your spells? Or are you simply using words that have power to add oomph to your spells? Many times people think they are simply using the power of the swear when in fact they are using the curse of the swear, so, truly look at how and why you use the swears you use!

Chapter 8

Word Weaving

Extrapolating on these ideas that speaking, writing and thinking are forms of spell casting we can then posit the theory that speaking, writing and thinking are word weaves that cast spells in our environment.

Word weaving spell casting ultimately creates the reality that we experience – which can be considered in two ways:

- as a magical co-creation of our reality that we speak into existence, and/or

- as a feedback loop of other beings responding to our words, emotions and emissions (from our thoughts) and crafting their own responses to us based upon their own feelings, understandings and reactions to our words, emotions and emissions.

Keep in mind that you are operating from a self-contained pattern of beliefs and understandings, feelings and emotions, about life. The same is true for the recipient of your words, feelings and emotions.

These self-contained patterns usually go unrecognised or at least unexamined by individuals and as such seem to be set as personality, preferences, triggers, wounds and other ego type issues.

Both (or all) beings involved in a communication or experience are coming from a viewpoint that is created from and imbued with ideas about reality, about life, about humans and about possibilities, potentialities and probabilities in any given situation or conversation. Hence word weaving and spell casting can get very complicated and convoluted!

Humans are mostly doing all of this in unconscious, egotistical and fearful ways with other humans who are also communicating in unconscious, egotistical and fearful ways. Everyone is casting spells from their own perceptions, that are received by others through the filters of their own perceptions. Are you starting to see how quickly things can spiral into misunderstanding, misinformation or complete misrepresentation of truth and actual need?

The creation of your reality is a tapestry of these two effects - the magical co-creation using your words and the feedback loop of others' responses - coming together to re-weave your hologram, your reality, your external, your out-picture into a fabric of outcomes. This fabric of outcomes is based upon your input via the words, emotions, emissions, thoughts and beliefs that you harbour, loop and project in both knowing and unknowing ways.

This reality, the one we live in, is a co-creation with the external weaves of energy and the collective that aids in the formation of the hologram and it is instructed and affected by the words and thoughts we speak and emit. Not only the words and thoughts but also aspects such as belief systems, programs, emotional wounds, traumas and dramas, as well as personal self-responsibility or lack thereof. All of these aspects will determine your automatic ways of thinking, believing and speaking about life.

It's a convolution that occurs that can be arrested at any level. The simplest and most directly conscious way to do this is by starting with your words and thoughts. Self-parenting the way you think and speak will help you begin to regain mastery of your own personal emissions and creations in life.

Self-Parenting

Self-parenting is the first stage, and a very simple step, of self-responsibility and regaining of self-mastery and self-sovereignty leading to self-healing. It is a simple and ongoing effect that requires you to observe the self in neutrality and, like a loving parent, correct the thoughts, the words and the emotions that arise and erupt from you. We do this without castigation to the self for any errors, without abuse of the self and, to the best of our ability, without diminishing the self. It's ok to make a mistake. It's ok to 'say the wrong words' or to revert to old patterns of behaviour, speaking and thinking. Its ok, it happens, but it is the loving inner parent that gently points it out to self and simply says 'oops let's try that again' - all you have to do is try.

Parenting the self will become second nature. It is the act of simple self-observation and gentle correction, in neutrality. Simply observing and correcting as often as you need to. Gently, consistently and kindly course correct the self each time a deviation occurs.

What is a deviation? When you notice those 'poor-pitiful-me' thoughts, the paranoid or depressive thoughts, when you notice those angry or violent thoughts or words, when you notice those feelings of being outraged, castigated, put upon or overlooked – that is a deviation.

Any and every time you notice that your thoughts and words have become those of a bully or a victim (to the self or others), that is when your inner parent steps in and cleans up the thoughts, cleans up the language, forgives the self and makes a plan for 'next time'. "Next time this happens let's deal with it this way so that we don't spiral into old habits and thought patterns", says the loving inner parent.

There is no castigation. There is no blaming, shaming or controlling of self. It is ok, you made a mistake. It is ok. It is even to be expected. Perfection of new behaviour once the decision to change has been made cannot be instant – it would be very unexpected for it to be so!

Your system (your mind, body, emotions, ego, psyche and spirit) is dealing with a huge backlog of information or knowledge, of experiences and conclusions, dramas, traumas and wounds, that started at the very least in childhood. In some belief systems the inner backlog is a carryover from many lifetimes and experiences. You are potentially the end result of millions or trillions of individual experiences and occurrences, conversations and convictions. Each of these individually may have resulted in a decision about life, about people, about your power, about your potential and about what's possible and how to get what you need or want. Collectively these create your belief systems and your decisions about who you are and what you are capable of. What if these decisions are wrong?

When you decide to think anew, when you decide to spell cast and word weave to create your reality anew, you will come up against resistance and retaliation from within. It's ok. It's natural and normal and does not make you are failure.

Your inner loving parent is your greatest ally, your greatest friend and the beautiful one that will help you to gradually, and over time, change the foundational way you think, speak and react. Parent the self in the way you wish you'd been parented. Be your own fairy godmother of kindness and patience. Allow yourself to forgive yourself and instruct yourself with the magical kindness and infinite patience you wish you'd been afforded for every mistake you've ever made.

This process can seem never ending. It is however an evolution where you start with the broad strokes and the obvious issues, and over time you fine tune it more and more and more. You may get to the space of feeling you have done it, or you may continue to fine tune for the rest of your life. Mostly, as humans, we aim for one level which we perceive to be the level of 'I've made it' or 'success' and as we approach this level or even as we arrive there and live there, we realise how much more there is to expand into and explore and thus we choose to go further. This is not about the inability to finish or find success, it is about realising how small our definition of 'finish' and 'success' is!

Your Inner Pantheon

It's a nice idea to name your inner parent and form a close relationship with this one who you may come to know as a pedant picking you up on every little mistake. Again, this is not about criticising the self, this is about course correction and allowing you to feel the support of the inner you, so do it lovingly and kindly.

If you have a strong and powerful inner critic, recognise that this is not the inner parent. The inner critic is the one that tells you that you will fail, that you are doing it wrong, that you don't have enough information to get it right, that you are getting nowhere and foolish for trying. This is not the inner parent. This is an aspect of self that hinders you from your progress and triumph. Give it a name that is separate from the inner parent.

Give the inner critic a name that allows you to differentiate it from your inner loving parent. You can call it whatever want, call it Albert, call it Gertie, call it Marshmallow, it doesn't matter. Name it so that you can recognise it and call it out when it is interfering with your growth in whatever way it likes to tell you that you are failing.

Give it a name so that when it kicks off you can compartmentalise it from the love of self – this is not head in the sand, this is not alternate personality compartmentalising of self away from truly being you and feeling you. This is simply recognising that 'that's just my Inner Critic (Albert?) kicking off again' and when you recognise this you can see that that voice, that opinion, is only part of you, not the whole of you.

This allows you to remind yourself that Albert's voice, the voice of your inner critic, is not always (ever?) correct, that Albert is a fearmonger formed from your own sense of worthlessness and belief in the criticisms of others about you.

Perhaps Albert has the voice of your mother or father, reinforcing the failure messages you received as a child?

Or perhaps Albert reinforces the idea that you mustn't stand out, or even try?

Albert was the one formed to relay to the self all the minimising beliefs of self, or from others about the self, that you have echoed back to the self continuously in one form or another – for some reason.

Your own personal reasons may differ from someone else's, but usually, fundamentally, this is in some form designed to, or purported to, keep you safe. Albert tries to keep you safe by reminding you to stay small, unseen, unthreatening, don't reach for your greatness, don't follow your dream, allow the world, the other, those out there, to dictate your degree of success, happiness or presence. But what if Albert is wrong?

Allow the inner parent to have a different name, the encouraging and supporting one needs a different name so that you can ask for that one's help. Ask for it by name, to come forward with support and aid. Then take the time to write or speak the words that a deeply loving, supportive and wise person would speak to you in that moment.

This is the inner parent. This is how the supporting uplifting self-parenting process works. Speak to the self in loving wise tones and allow the self, like a small child who has fallen during its first steps, to rise again and do better, or at least to have the courage to keep going!

The inner critic and the inner parent are two different characters in what you might think of as your inner pantheon. The inner pantheon are those aspects of self, those opinions, criticisms, inhibitions, thoughts and beliefs that encourage or curb your behaviours. They encourage you to stay quiet, hidden, small, inoffensive and non-disruptive, or to rage, fight, be irreverent or disruptive. Perhaps you are lucky and they encourage your strength, worth, resilience and love.

Some of these voices may be entirely correct, and are worth listening to, these you may think of as your intuition, that little consideration, urge or push/pull from within that encourages an action or inaction that in the end results in something beneficial for you.

There are also other ideas, criticisms, halters and limiters in your thoughts, those ideas and thoughts that reiterate to the self that you won't make it, you're not enough and no one will love you – or some other type of self-diminishing input that keeps you in procrastination, avoidance, anger, regret and recycling through your own traumatic inner landscape. Those that keep you from connecting to your true strength, courage and kindness. These are the aspects of self that are not helping you!

There is no need to abuse these parts of the self, nor abuse the self for allowing these parts to have such a solid hold on the self. It's ok, this is how it has been for you, but now you are growing beyond that. Speak lovingly and encouragingly to the self. Speak as you would to a tiny child who is fiercely, courageously and bravely trying to do better each day.

Allow yourself to explore your own depths, your own potentials and your own abilities once more, coming at it with an open mind and allowance for all possibilities. This is, after all, about weaving your own reality into creation.

Allow yourself to at least attempt to do this from a space of no decisions, no preconceived ideas and opinions. You are already riddled with them and so even trying to do this from a place of no preconceived ideas you will have some that you are completely unaware of.

That's ok.

Allowing yourself to be as open as you can, forgiving yourself for each mistake and trying again, is all that it takes.

Keep going.

Keep going.

Life is for you, it is for giving (forgiving) and it is for growing, learning and upshifting into your own creation of day-to-day beauty and joy.

Words and Action

It is very important to make the note here that words without action have no meaning - saying saying saying, and the words become meaningless.

Have you ever chosen a word and just repeated it endlessly? You will soon find the mind questioning if it's spelt right, if it sounds right, if it is the right word, the word you meant or even if it is a word at all?

Words endlessly said to self or other without any of the emotion, action or feeling attached to them become meaningless sound drivel that have no power. This is often the reason that affirmations don't imprint and seem to have no result, they are just rote repeated and have no sensation to them. Words need action, emotion and engagement to create change!

Words without feeling, without action have no real meaning, no real sovereignty or empowerment – they are the empty promises of a philanderer to a long-suffering partner.

What are you telling yourself that you do not follow up on? What promises do you make yourself that you do not follow through on? Stop breaking your word, your promises to the self and to others. Hold yourself to a higher standard and allow yourself to shine. Expect more from the self and it will be given!

This is not about ability. If you expect yourself to be a great athlete that may or may not happen but if you expect yourself to have honour and be honourable, to be the person who does not break their word then you should not break your word to yourself either.

Expecting this honour of the self and by the self helps you to hold yourself accountable for your expressions, for your words, for your actions and for your promises.

All of this helps you to be present, to cast the spells and weave the words that inspire the actions and create the change. Life as you know it will respond.

Words about manifesting need you to take the action inspired from those words in order to make things happen! The universe, the hologram, the Great Source, the benevolent beautiful many, the inner you, the higher you, and all the other beings and aspects of self that you honour and adhere to all require you to admire, respect and honour the self just as much as you admire, respect and honour them!

You are the incarnate human. You are the one doing the job, being present and learning to heal, hence you are the one who needs to listen to you, honour you, respect you and stop letting you down. We all know life has been hard. We all know life is difficult and challenging. It can be monstrous and terrifying. It can be hopeless and disappointing, but you are the one here and you need to take care of you, love you, honour you and cherish you.

You are worth it.

Your words need to feel you.

Your body needs to feel your words.

Your actions need to honour your words and choices for you.

It is a beautiful symbiotic synchronicity that you create by feeling your words, allowing your cells to feel your own words and your emotions as you speak them.

Taking the actions that show your body, your cells, your guardians, your God that you are here, that you are worth your respect, that you are serious, that you are taking the action to move the dial in your favour such that those that witness your creation, your movement, your request will follow through with you, for you and around you. This allows the life you create to become in sync with who you are as a person of feeling, of action, of honour and respect.

You don't need to take huge action. You don't need to spend money you do not have. You just need to take the baby steps, the tiny actions in the direction of your most beneficial outcome. Do you want to be a writer? Then write every day, perhaps try to do 500 words per day, or an hour each week. Want to be a dancer? Then take a class, do the practice, move each day. What do you want to create? Take the baby steps or huge leaps or anywhere in between to show your dedication to that every day, every week.

Think you have no time to take that action? Then perhaps consider that each year you have 52 weeks' worth of time. And if you only did 1 hour towards your dream, towards your manifestation, each week by the end of the year you would have done 52 hours of effort towards that dream. If you never find that hour and let each week slip by, then by the end of the year you have done nothing towards it and you are still bemoaning the fact that you have no time to achieve your dream. Which would you rather experience the 52 hours each year and eventually you'll get there? Or never ever getting there?

Words and action marry together nicely and take you to the next level. What level are you trying to reach? Keep at it, keep at it!

Monitoring Actions by Feeling

How do you know what steps to take, to take action and create the desired outcome? Let's assume you have this kernel of an idea, something that you think would be a joyful path for you, a fulfilment of destiny in some way. How do you know if it's a fulfilling action to take? How do you know if it's related to that which is going to eventually out-picture as the life of your dreams? As opposed to an ego yearning or a blaming, shaming and retribution aim to 'get them' whoever 'they' are? Ultimately, how do you know if it's the benevolent healing path of the enlightened and returning to wholeness self or the degrading denigrating non-benevolent path of the degeneration of self?

The answer is really quite simple: the way you know is by how it feels to you!

If it feels exciting, if it feels positive, if you feel uplifted by the thought; that's an action on the benevolence-oriented path.

If it feels like retribution, if it feels like revenge, attack or 'showing them', or a vicious vindication, if the 'excitement' you feel is really a sense of being vindicated and proving something to somebody else, like scoring over somebody, then that's a non-benevolent path of degeneration of self.

This is not because the byproduct of you succeeding cannot be that others become awakened to your greatness, or your value, but because by focusing on that as the driver, as the motivator, what you are actually doing is continuing to focus on 'not you' – you are focusing on being something that they will value, respect or be jealous of rather than focusing on being yourself, feeling your excitement and following that path.

It is possible that perhaps 'they' may incidentally respect you or be jealous of you if you succeed, but that is not the focus nor the reason for the pursuit. Being a better version of you is always a benevolent focus but doing it to get back at others is the retribution-oriented power-over aspect of the domination path that is hidden in the desire to succeed in order to show 'them out there' that they had you all wrong!

Just be you and do your thing. If success comes and changes opinions about you in response to your success, then great, what a completely unnecessary bonus, but ultimately you didn't do it for that reason. You simply did it to uplift the self and heal you. Which means that your success comes with a fulness, an internal satisfaction, that is sustaining and healing, not a yearning, emptiness or never-ending striving that is unsatisfying and leaves you wondering who you are and where your life went. Your reasons matter!

Now, the thing about this is it is a self-assessment, a moment-to-moment, day-to-day self-analysis. It could be that the aspect that is important is only one part of the process. It could be that the aspect that is important is multiple parts of the process but not the whole thing, or it could be that the end goal is the part that is important but how you get there is not. It could be many things, that'll be a moment-to-moment observation and self-analysis to become aware of.

Stay in the aspect or action that feels light, bright, exciting and sparkly - the action that makes your tummy tingle and your inspiration feel high. The action that is easy and interesting to do because you find it fascinating and exciting to enact.

Analysis of why you need to do it will be important because if the why is related to telling people off, getting something over them or anything ego or retribution related then that's an abuse game you are entering. It's the flip to 'get your power back' going from victim to victimiser – that's the non-nurturing non-benevolent non-enlightening aspect of self that is determined to fight and win. For a deeper understanding of the victim victimiser paradigm that we all play and get caught up in, take a look at Word Games We Play in Chapter 10.

Chapter 9

Explorations on Words

Releasing and minimising stress and limitation is important for all of us, the human body operates more efficiently, processes food and heals itself more effectively when our stress levels are lowered or at least frequently diffused. Beyond the purely physical aspects, when we address our stress and limitations, we allow the mind to expand and find new horizons, new ways of considering the current issues being faced and new solutions and avenues, new directions for choice and possibilities.

Your words and self-talk can add to your own personal stress or limit your understanding of possibility in greater and smaller ways, they are one of the least looked at avenues for stress minimisation and yet they are one of the easiest ones to enact and integrate into your life.

Following are some lightweight explorations on words to offer alternative ways you can view them and their use – challenge your outlook and look at other potentials for what your words might be creating.

These are just ideas that may be interesting. They are by no means the only interpretation, or even a suggestion to make change. They are simply an illustration for exploration on your habitual speaking and thinking patterns.

I need to

One of the most common things we do is announce our to-do list or our intention in a way that adds pressure or restriction to said intention.

The statements 'I need to' or 'I have to' hold hidden elements of pressure within them.

The words 'need' and 'have' in and of themselves seem fairly innocuous, they describe a state of lack or non-lack or necessity or non-necessity. There are arguments around the use of the word 'need' specifically as a kind of lack word that illustrates to your system that you are without something. This is based upon the idea that if you need something then automatically you don't have it. It has become quite a castigated word in manifestation teachings, a word to avoid, due to the old teachings of speaking as if you already have what it is you desire. Hence the encouragement has been to not use the terminology 'I need this/that' or 'I need to do this/that' but to alter it to another type of statement such as 'I require or desire more of this/that'.

Now, this understanding of 'need' being a 'lack' word and how to use it in manifesting may or may not be true, because this whole manifestation principles and 'law of attraction' stuff is riddled with misinformation and missing information. It is a good idea, generally speaking, to not try and 'correct' every word you are speaking and every thought you are having, however it is worth noting some of the potential undesirable effects from certain normalised sentence and thought constructs that you may have.

In the context of 'need to' or 'have to', these words describe something that seems inescapable, not chosen and may have a limiting context to them, as in they prevent you choosing and doing what you desire.

Examples like 'I need to pick the kids up from school' or 'I need to go to the shops' or 'I have to go to the gym' all illustrate the trapped or inescapable nature of the use of 'need' or 'have'.

It is true of course that there are things in our lives that we feel we 'need to do' or disaster of some sort may occur, but when we stay in the mindset of averting disaster with the 'need to' or oppressing self-choice with the 'have to' type statements, then we can trigger a response from the body which is called a fight/flight response.

Very simply put, the fight/flight mechanism is a response originating from a stimuli (internal or external) that initiates a cycle, starting in the brain centre called the amygdala. When this fight/flight response is initiated, the body goes through a series of changes, resulting in affects to its mechanisms and processes. These changes that are initiated can affect hormones, neurotransmitters, psychology, emotions, feelings, and bodily processes. The fight or flight response of this mechanism can, for instance, draw blood away from certain areas of the body and to the arm or leg muscles, to prepare the body to fight or run.

You've probably heard of the fight/flight response, you may also know that it includes other similar response such as 'freeze' where the choice of action is no action and 'fawn' where pandering and pleasing become the choice.

Freeze is a really common response in todays over stressed human, whereby the inability to choose, to act or even to think of an appropriate action keeps you hostage to the situation.

The fawn response is often be embedded within the traumatised human who has an aversion to potentially creating any ripples in their environment that may become an argument or other form of unrest or even an attack on the self in some way.

When we often say 'I need to do' or 'I have to do' we are incidentally and accidentally adding to the stress burden in our body as we announce to ourselves that we have no choice, and we are trapped by these activities and thusly we kick off our fight/flight system in a minor or major way. The starting point is to change your mind set about these activities or things that you feel you 'have to do'. Recognise that there are indeed things that need to be done, and that's ok, that's life.

Consider thinking about this another way, understand that these are the moments that makeup your life so there is no use fighting them. If you find them unbearable, then change them. If you feel you cannot change them, then change your mind set about them and look for the benefits of them so that you can think about them, plan for them and engage in them without the sense of feeling them as being a burden, an oppression or an activity that takes you away from living your own life your way.

Maybe you could start saying 'I get to' or 'I'm going' such as 'I get to pick up the kids' (like it's a privilege you've been granted) or 'I'm going to the shops' (like it's a fun place you are going).

It all comes down to a little bit of a reframe in how you think about the 'need tos' and 'have tos' in your life.

I Don't Know/I Don't Understand

When you start to think about what you are saying as that which creates your reality, you will notice that the statement 'I don't know' or 'I don't understand' may have some deeper on flow effects upon you because when you make these statements, you are confirming that you don't know and that you don't stand under yourself (you don't back yourself).

Sure there may be situations where you may truly not understand what is going on or you truly don't know what's happening or what the answer is, but consider that instead of constantly telling yourself and others that you don't know or don't understand why not shift it slightly to be 'I'm not sure yet' or 'I don't have enough knowledge for that to make sense to me yet' or something like that?

Allow your mind to hear you state that *you are able to know more*, that whatever it is that you cannot grasp right now, is not permanent and does not make you someone who 'doesn't know anything and doesn't back themselves'. These are simply games to play with words and expressions, flip them around and experiment with weaving words in new ways that might combat any habits of self detraction you may have accidentally immersed yourself in. Aim for empowering the self with your language and becoming your best friend and biggest backer!

Information vs Knowledge

We often say we are seeking information when we are researching or attempting to gain more knowledge or understanding, but have you ever thought about what the word information is actually instructing you to do?

It can be broken down into two separate words; 'in' and 'formation', based upon this breakdown seeking information is seeking more of the same, more of the structure that exists, more of the old thinking and old news. It is seeking to stay within formation, within what is already known or thought to be known. Is this what you are doing?

Perhaps yes when you are exploring a subject or getting details for a test or exam, but then perhaps no when you are exploring for a solution or creation.

Do you want more of the same or do you want a new solution? A new way of thinking and seeking in the world? If we stay within the parameters of more of the same thinking and seeking, we get the same results as we have always gotten.

Perhaps it is time to seek knowledge rather than information? Break down the word knowledge and what do you get? A ledger of knowing! What is it that you know (or would like to know) that would enhance your life that is beyond the alignment to uniformity that information suggests? Perhaps you could consider seeking knowledge.

You could take this idea even deeper or further, do you want knowledge, do you want a ledger of knowing, or do you want to enter a wise domain (wisdom) or become lit up by something new (enlightenment)? There are so many ways to play with these words, and you can see that each word when played with and analysed is actually either freeing you or containing you depending upon what you are seeking and how your inner being responds to them. Explore it for yourself, get creative and experimental to find which way of expressing feels freeing to you – then choose it!

I Should/They Should

So often we say things such as 'oh, I should do this/that' or 'they should have done this/that' but do you ever stop to think about what really should/shouldn't happen? We are usually putting our own judgement on others when we consider that they 'should' or 'shouldn't' have done or said something. When we do this, we are not taking into account their individual needs and interpretations of what is polite, powerful, self-confident or scary for them to do/not do.

It is the height of arrogance to thrust our own ethics and morals upon another and decide what they should or shouldn't do in any situation. There may be certain situations where you might argue that it is obvious what one should or should do – a baby trapped under a car? It might seem indisputable to you that a person 'should' risk life and limb to rescue said baby, but you don't know the circumstances and personal backstories of all involved and hence cannot make the judgement. All you can say with any degree of truth is that you think you would have done it. Most situations in life are not that black and white, so it really is more beneficial to the self and the peace of mind to stay present and humble and place no judgment on what others should or shouldn't do.

When we speak to ourselves, dictate to ourselves, what we should or should not do, ('oh, I shouldn't have had that chocolate cake'), usually we are bullying, overbearing and/or maligning ourselves in some way, again, this is especially harmful to the self when considered in a healing context.

We don't learn safely, easily and expansively through abuse – and this includes self-abuse. Through abuse and castigation, we learn fear and shut down of self, we learn to mould ourselves in such a way as to attempt to not receive any more abuse.

Staying out of the 'should' and 'should not', and regarding ourselves, our actions and mistakes with compassion, is one of the ways we can minimise the cascade of hurtful responses within the body that occur from our mindset, our stress levels and our emotions triggering a fight/flight response or self-spiral downward from an abuse or domination situation.

What does this mean? It means that it might be a more kind and personally healing way to consider those things that you currently think of as 'shouldn't have done that' and reframe them into the something like:

"That was erroneous, considering whom I choose to be and how I choose to act. I back myself now and endeavour not to do that again. I recognise that it is done now and I am through it. I have noted the erroneous action. I do not judge myself for it and I allow myself to grow beyond it. I create myself now as better than that."

I know, that's a mouthful, but it is an illustration of the type of personal in depth and non-combative relationship a healing one forms with the self.

You may not need to say the whole thing each time, but the full statement illustrates for you the type of understanding a self-responsible one has for the stumbling of the self and the detours taken by actions that are not in alignment with the choices of the self for healing and improving.

I Deserve

Breaking down the word deserve you get: de 'of', serve 'service', as in the word itself is describing the act of being of service. When you don't feel like you deserve something you often activate either an over service or under service of self to the self or others. When you are aligned with not deserving, you are often aligned with whether or not you are 'doing enough service to deserve' whatever it is that you would like.

Our relationship with 'deserve' usually starts in childhood. Quite often we would be given or denied something based upon whether we were 'good' or 'bad' by the determination of those in charge (usually our parents) – based upon whether we 'deserved' it or not. How many times did you get a treat because you were good – you deserved it? On the flip side how many times was a privilege of some kind removed from you because you were bad – you no longer deserved it? You received the reward or lost the privilege based upon your deserving of it, this deserving was based upon how good or bad you had been as determined by those in charge. Very often the good behaviour was some type of service, you cleaned your room, you did the dishes, you did your homework, or you stayed quiet whilst mum did the shopping. There is learned from this behaviour a correlation of being good, of doing the service required and then deserving what is offered and/or available. This means that in some way we begin to determine what act of service is enough to get what type of reward. And this is based upon the discernment of those in charge of you and their assessment of your adhering to the rules they have laid down. If you are lucky you may have learned that very little service is required to get what you deserve. If you were not so lucky, then you may have learned that it's 'never enough' and hence as an adult you are calibrated to 'not deserving' because you've never been 'good' enough, or 'done' enough to get what you deserve.

Aligning with and calibrating to the idea of deserving something will often align you with the idea of whether or not you have done enough, been enough or know/n enough to get what it is you are desiring.

When you consider yourself in terms of whether you 'deserve' or not you are basically saying 'what have I done that could result in this reward'. That is a subjective state that rests upon your own determination of how 'good' you have been. How much effort have you put in, how much hard work or time have you dedicated to it, how skilled do you perceive yourself to be, as well as your judgement on your skillset, your intelligence, your education or your perceived worth.

All of this is subjective, and open to change at any time. It is the rare individual who can be objective about their skillset and effort – potentially no one really can, it's an ephemeral concept at the best of times. Most humans completely misjudge their own efforts and/or skillset and are either overestimating or underestimating themselves and their level of service.

Your internal belief systems and programs, the imprints from your parents, your schooling and your society all play into this by having already imprinted on you and imbued into you the parameters of what is needed to deserve the level of return you desire. If you have indeed a giant self-esteem then you may be lucky and receive large returns for little out lay and little effort, but for most folks the 'deserving' action or 'deserving' level of investment of time, money, attention, skillset or service, has already been determined by them and is too high for the outcome and return to be freeing to the individual. Their determination of what action, time, skillset etc and how much of that action, time or skillset it takes to get the desired outcome is distorted. They believe the amount of time, effort or skillset required is beyond them or not available to them, hence they never get to the state of receiving it because they don't deserve it (haven't done enough service – by their estimation – to receive it).

The suggestion is to stop calibrating to deserve, stop wondering if you deserve it, there is no question of deserving, you are human, you are here, whatever you want you obviously deserve. Who is the overlord that can tell you otherwise? Why do you validate their determination of whether you deserve or not?

Now, whether or not it will be fulfilling and freeing for you, bringing you the happiness and joy you desire? That's a whole other question! But deserve? Yes, of course you do!

The concept of deserve and what it takes to deserve something or the 'desired thing', has been hijacked and taken from you. It is not a logical concept nor a neutral concept anymore – you cannot be in complete neutrality when you are in the state of deciding if you deserve something, so it's pointless to try. Do not calibrate to it, do not justify from it and do not engage with being or becoming deserving of great things, or anything. You will fail, especially if you are humble and caring enough to consider that 'you could always have done more'; as most of us in our society are programmed to believe. Maybe you could have done more, but that does not mean that you don't deserve to have a joy filled life of ease and grace now.

Give up on trying to be 'deserving' of anything and embrace 'gratitude' for everything, not as a leaf on the breeze, but as the chooser of your own destiny.

Pretending and Imagination

Pretending and imagining are things we do a lot of as children, and then we grow up and seem to grow out of it, yet, pretending and imagining are actually powerful activities to enhance your life in a myriad of ways. Pretending and imagining are forms of mental rehearsal which is very often used by athletes, and high performing individuals to overcome performance anxiety and increase their skill level.

Mental rehearsal is a valuable tool in fine tuning or improving a skill and has been shown to have a very similar benefit to actually doing the craft as a physical practice. Mental rehearsal is pretending and imagining, it is a form of visualisation. Far from being simply a children's activity, it is one of the ways we can tangibly align ourselves with a skillset or change in our lives. When you visualise, when you see that which you wish to create, experience, or be in your mind's eye, you are imagining, and pretending that what you see is real. You are seeing it in your mind's eye as the reality you wish to create and tending it into existence.

There are multiple ways to use the word imagine and imagination to explore what these words are actually creating. Some break down 'imagine' to the idea of 'I'm a genie' (Im-a-gine) which correlates nicely with its purpose in manifestation. You could also explore it by looking at it as stemming from the word 'image' and then a word such as 'imagination' becomes 'a nation of images' – or a nation created by your own images!

When we pretend, we are pre (before) tending (tender) taking care of, nurturing, or tending to something before it exists. We are tending it into existence prior to it physically existing, hence pretending is a magnificent way to create something to have in your life to tend to.

So, we imagine something (through visualisation or mental rehearsal) and pretend it to be real (through emotion and feeling) - what is it you imagine with your imagination and pretend is real?

This nation of your images tended to prior to their physical manifestation is powerful stuff!! Treat it as such, tend it into existence with care and patience – when you first imagine and pretend it is a delicate tender thing that needs your attention, your care, your focus. Allow the tender thing to flourish, protect it from the harshness and criticism of the self or others by showering it with your gentle, consistent and joy filled attention.

The Story Technique in Chapters 14 and 15 uses the concept of imagination, pretending and mental rehearsal to aid you in creating the life of your dreams – take a look at these chapters if this idea resonates with you.

Rational

The word rational is used a lot to illustrate something that is sensible, reliable, and come to from a logical standpoint, it is something that contains reason and understanding – if you are irrational, you are crazy, out of control, talking nonsense. Some might say these explorations of words and the protocols in this book are irrational and not logical, but perhaps it is rational that is a limiting concept?

Rational, as in rational thinking, stems from the word 'ration' as in a limitation on something. Why would we want to limit our explorations and extrapolations when it comes to creative thinking and manifestation? Rational thinking ends up rationing your outcomes and limiting the possibilities, narrowing down what you can think and the options and observations that you believe are possible for you.

There may be times when rational thinking and logical outcomes are pertinent indeed, but overall, it is worth contemplating the idea that if we limit ourselves to simply rational and logical we limit ourselves to what is boxed in, rationed and sensible from a perspective of what has already been deduced to be rational. This then disallows us looking at the irrational the non-logical and allowing the possibilities that that too could be potential for us in creating the ideal life and the manifestation of our dreams come true.

Has it ever occurred to you that the avenue to your success, the pathway to your delight may be from very irrational and illogical unthought of trajectories coming out of left field so to speak? A way of thinking or behaving that is completely new to you and goes against all that you've been taught?

The quote attributed to einstein comes to mind here, to paraphrase: the definition of insanity is to keep doing the same thing and expect a different outcome.

Maybe the most beneficial thing of all is to do that which you have previously felt was irrational!

Nonsense

Nonsense is defined as foolish, absurd or no intelligible meaning, but consider this; nonsense breaks down into 'non' and 'sense', meaning 'no sense', 'a lack of sense' or 'not a sense'. We are very attached to and immersed in a society that looks at things (life, ideas, theories) and attempts to make sense of them, if you cannot make sense of them then there is no sense, and they become nonsense.

What if the sense of these things is simply beyond the senses? What if you cannot *make* sense of them because they are beyond the senses?

If you give yourself a new perspective, a new experience, a new view, you start to be able to make sense of something that was previously nonsense to you. Hence nonsense to you is sense to someone with a different perspective or perhaps with access to a different use of the senses or access to senses beyond what you have perceived to be the senses that exist.

We are taught that we only have 5 senses and anything beyond that is non-sense (as in 'not a sense') – but do we and is it?

Or is it simply the unknown? Perhaps the unknowable? How much in life are we limiting and compartmentalising because we insist on making sense of things and putting them in the order of the senses such that they are no longer nonsense? How often are you blinded to or dismissive of that which could enlighten and expand your world, perhaps bringing to your sense the very thing that would inspire and ignite the happiness, joy, fulfilment, peace or love that you are looking for?

Nonsense may not be nonsense, simply non-sense – and if this is so, all that means is that it is not something that exists in your current frame of sense network or reference. If all you believe and feel is currently within your sense frame of reference and yet your life is not what you desire and you feel the pressure the burden and the fatigue of continuing to try, continuing to push and continuing to look out there for the answer, then maybe it is time to reassess your sense of what is working and possible and take a different viewpoint. Maybe nonsense is exactly what you need?

All great discoveries come from a space of inspiration, perhaps followed by a time of perspiration, research, testing and final proofing, but where does the original idea come from? It comes from a flash of inspiration, a dream, a knowing, a crystallisation of thought, all differing ways of saying that it comes from beyond the senses, it comes from the space of non-sense.

And speaking of sense, what about the word 'innocence', we often disparage those who are innocent, or we go to great lengths to have them and/or protect them because their innocence may be destroyed by the world and yet we also smile indulgently at them with our so called inner knowing that their innocence is not worldly wise and hence they are less than us and need our protection, our guidance and our teaching. But is that so? Perhaps innocence is simply 'inner sense', perhaps innocence is the ability to operate from a place of hope and wonder, listening to and responding to your inner feelings and inner sense? Perhaps we all need a little more innocence and nonsense in our lives!

Want and Lack

Want and lack can be very tricky words and concepts when it comes to manifestation. As a starting point, if you want something you're coming from a place of lack. The old teachings would then lead to the understanding that you should 'never want' from a manifestation point of view ie, never say 'I want this or that' because you are essentially reaffirming that you lack it.

'Want' in and of itself has the definition of lack (she is wanting in social graces) additionally if you want something in your life then automatically you do not have it – so from both perspectives you are reaffirming constantly that you lack it. From a traditional manifestation point of view, this has been something to be avoided.

In terms of actual creation, using the words 'want' and 'need' tend towards aligning you with not having and continuing to not have. In terms of *desire*, now that's a different story. You're basically recognising an empty spot in your life, so wanting is perfectly appropriate. Yes, I am 'wanting' in that it does not exist in my life. I recognise that it does not exist, but that is not how I'm going to co-create it. I'm not going to co-create it by saying I want this. I'm going to say, 'in my life, I noticed this deficit and so I create the surfeit of it here now'.

The idea that when you want something you're coming from a place of lack is technically correct, but it is too technically correct because what it does is it then puts the roadblock up in your mind. So that then you think, 'well, I don't have it, and I can't want it or I won't get it, but I need it, and I do want it, yet I can't want it, but I do. . .'. It's a loop.

It would be better to refocus and repurpose that statement to deliver what it is that you actually need or desire. The framing of the request as 'I want' is not a co-creative outcome-oriented helpful understanding of the word and the feeling.

And here's the thing, remember what we were just saying; the definition of want is lack - if you are wanting in something you are lacking – when you say I know what I want, you could also look at that as saying, 'I know *where* I lack', 'I know what it is I lack', which is the same as saying, 'I see where I need to fuel myself, where I need to fill myself'. This then becomes an understanding and acknowledgement of what you don't have that you would like to create. So, the flow on from that is:

"I know what I want, and I shall fuel and fulfill it now. Awakening and opening from within with the divinity and clarity of purpose, the clear and present understanding, of what I want and how to fuel my life in the present to fulfill my dreams."

Notice there is no statement there as to what it should be nor how it should unfold? The flow on from a statement such as this is that you will then start to experience the belief systems holding you back; such as you believe you're not worthy of what you want or that you've never really connected with the emotional power of your co-creative desire, maybe you firmly believe you can co-create it but your resistance is more a question of whether you should, or perhaps you're stuck in that hoary old chestnut of whether you feel you deserve it? At these times of revelation, you need to cast a different spell for the self, such as:

"I revoke all that holds that belief system in place, and I invoke the will of Eternal Source to facilitate the changes and healings needed to gracefully and easily guide me, move me, motivate me into the harmonious life of my dreams or better with the best of the best as my only outcomes."

Chapter 10

Word Games we Play

Truth Games

As children we are often brutally truthful, telling the truth about all things we see and experience – to the degree our language can articulate what we have seen and experienced. It is over time that we become entrained into lying about our feelings and our experiences and holding our thoughts inside, potentially for the good in some cases. From there we learn how to use our words, actions, feelings and behaviours to manipulate others and coerce responses from them.

It all sounds very subversive and sinister when put into words like that, but ultimately this is how we are taught to communicate with others and engage with society. We are taught to hide certain things about ourselves and to use what we have to cajole out of life, society and other humans what it is we need or want. It is arguable that some of this hiding of self and emotions is entirely appropriate. The self-containment of one's raw or out of control emotions and responses is perhaps entirely appropriate otherwise you may spend your time delivering abuse and domination to others in your lurching about from emotion to emotion and trying to get life and others to behave as you would wish them to.

Being truthful is not about expressing every emotion and thought. It is about being present and expressing, if needed, that which is most true for you in that moment. Being truthful is not about exploding your emotions and thoughts all over the place and letting the fallout be what it is then walking away from the situation in the smug knowledge that all you did was express your truth. No, not at all.

Being truthful is about self-analysis, and observation, the time taken to determine who you truly are and where your traumas, wounds and inner emptiness have led you to manipulative or coercive behaviour through the mistaken belief that you are being truthful, acting on your truth or that you are unable to get what you want without this manipulation of the truth.

As you change your life, self-heal and become self-responsible, one of the greatest tests will be your ability to be truthful – especially with the self. Being truthful with the self about your motivations, about what you've said and done and why, is a huge step towards truly knowing who you are and what your belief systems, wounds, hurts and traumas are. It is these belief systems, hurts and traumas that you hold inside, sometimes without even acknowledging that you are doing it, that form your ideas about life, your hesitations and understandings about life, and what's possible or probable for you. These are the things that keep you mired in the place of no growth and little to no joyful changes in your life or repetition of the same sad and unsatisfying occurrences in your life.

Nobody else needs to know how sinister or stupid you've really been! Nobody else needs to know the inner machinations of why you behave how you behave – what it means to you, what your aim is, where the manipulation is in your own behaviour is yours and yours alone to know, unless you want to share it. The aim with truth is to look within the self and truthfully observe your communication and other behaviours and discern why you speak, communicate, act or engage the way you do.

What does it get you?

How does it make you feel?

Why do you believe you need to do it this way?

Does it help you feel less vulnerable, defenseless or shunted aside?

Does it help you feel more confident or dominant?

Is it ultimately who you really are or is it an expression of self designed to control your environment and others into treating you the way you wish to be treated, or prioritizing you the way you wish to be prioritized or seeing you the way you wish to be seen?

It's ok, everyone is operating from their own convoluted set up of motivations and everyone has made mistakes or been led astray by others or themselves. It is simply the healing one, the wise one, the courageous one who is prepared to look at their thoughts, motivations and actions and own them in order to grow from them. Acknowledge the truth to the self, as best you can perceive it, about why you have done what you have done, acted how you have acted or spoken how you have spoken – and then take responsibility for this and heal it.

What you think, what you say and your belief systems, justifications and reasoning behind the actions you've taken all matter!

There is no castigation for your choices, or your perceived failures and shameful actions from the past when doing this process. This is not for punishment or retribution for your badness or failures.

This truth with self is in order for you to realize how many times you have manipulated or coerced the self (or those around you) in order to have your needs met, how many lies you've told or been operating from. Once you can truthfully see the ways you have been justifying your behaviours, your choices and actions or the ways you have been blinded to your motivations, then you can see how much influence your feelings, thoughts, words and justifications behind those experiences, occurrences and actions have upon the poor outcomes and dissatisfying results you have been getting in attempting to live your life of ease, joy, love and success.

This is all about recognising the inner machinations you have been operating from. The poor-pitiful-me moments you have been expressing and using to attempt to get the love you seek, the acknowledgment you crave or the benefits you want. Recognize however that if your emanation is creating your reality, and your emanation is created from your hurts, wounds, traumas, belief systems and programs along with any of the joy, peace, ease, trust, hope and the like that you hold, then continuing to operate from the space of poor-pitiful-me, from the space of manipulating and coercing response from 'those out there', or dominating and bullying situations, self or other to get what you want, means that you are continuing to encourage the emanation of the hurt, wounded and helpless one from within you and not the emanation of the healed, happy, healthy one.

This action is tantamount to continuing to agree with the emanation of your own hurt, your own helplessness, your own status as a victim – poor me, it's been so hard, the only way I can get what I need is by being what others need me to be or manipulating them into giving it to me. This behaviour is akin to putting your focus upon the poor, wounded, helpless aspects of self, and when you are continuing to be in agreement with that definition of self you are then creating your external life as a reflection of that definition of self.

Ask yourself; are you a hurt, wounded or helpless one? Are you a victim? If not, then why are you engaging with life from this emanation? If so, then understand that this is why your life seems to be not what you desire!

There is no suggestion that the hurt, the wound, the trauma is not real and/or did not happen. There is no suggestion that it was not real or was not painful and life changing for you! The suggestion is to recognise that if that is all you focus upon, and if that is all you engage with life from, then you are continuing to reverberate the wounding in your life and the external will aid you by out-picturing your reality as a reflection of this emanation.

Your ability to be with you, in love and peace, your ability to engage with life knowing that you are entitled to the wonder and goodness that is possible, and your ability to stand tall, honour the self and choose again from an empowered kindness and joyful state, all dictate your outcomes of pleasant or less than pleasant experiences in life.

The whole premise here is that your emotions, thoughts and words reflect into or engage with the unseen and create your experience of reality as an occurrence that rings true to the emotions, thoughts and words that you continuously perpetuate from within. Go within, find the truth about the self, what wounds and hurts are you trying to cover up, or salve, with your words, engagements and communication and how helpful is that for your happiness in life?

Honoring the wound exacerbates the wound and enables its continued influence in your life. Heal the wound. Your self-analysis will show you the truth of the wound and its influence in your life. Healing the wound aids in removing the acting or reacting from it potentially minimizing or removing its impact in your life.

Know the wound is there, remember the idea of the magnification by your focus and shift your focus onto any of the more benevolent emotions that you may have. Allowing your engagements and communications to come from these more benevolent areas of self in whatever way you can. Take the time to get present, breath and switch your focus in order to stop the automatic behaviours kicked off by the inner woundings and poor pitiful me triggers. If you enact honouring 'your truth' in such a way that you are wreaking havoc, causing upset (to self or others) or in other ways creating experiences that are less than pleasant for you – then maybe it is time to reassess exactly what you think is truly your truth.

Protecting Truth

You may have experienced having your expression of truth being used against you – this can happen in many circumstances ranging from courting to court cases.

As the bearer of your own truth, it behooves you to recognise when your truth may be in peril by the circumstances and hence need your protection. It is not always appropriate or safe to share everything about the self, and all the truth about the moment you are in.

Your truth is a valuable commodity, treat it as such. What is meant by that? It means don't lie, there's no need to lie or have hidden little secrets that you're terrified somebody will find out - and if you have terrifying little secrets this is a big sign that you may be doing some things that are not beneficial for your peace of mind, for your enlightenment and for your healing. But also, be discerning with the external:

Who deserves to hear all your truth? Who does not? Who will treat your truth with respect? And who will weaponise it against you?

The Healing Truth

In the last few decades, the direction and focus for our minds and attention has been upon the stimulation and addiction of dramatic stories, click bait and shocking exposés, the sound bite meme sized click bait dopamine hit or the in depth sharing of loud, shocking and salacious stories. This has led to a state where the small sharings, the quiet stories, simple truths and solutions are often passed over, overlooked and undervalued. The search for 'something' for 'better' for 'awakenment' has been a search form something loud, flashy and instant, the expectation is that it is complicated and yet, it is actual quiet, small and simple.

The solutions are simple. The healing, the resolution, comes from simplicity. It comes from boiling the issue down to the core, the seed, the starting point and then dealing with that, directly and simply, with easy to use and do processes and focus. What you are looking for, the rescue, the healing and the release you are looking for, is simple. It is within you, and you do it for you. You can have others help you, that may feel good to you, to have the support, but ultimately you are doing it for you.

Your truth with self is where the healing starts. Be with it, obverse it, know it, and don't hide from it. The solutions are simple, it only takes opening up to the self and the exposing to the truth of self, being courageous enough to stay in that truth and knowledge, being compassionate enough with the self to admit the truth without castigation, without guilt, without admonishment. Admit it, be with it, stay with it.

How does it feel?

What does it mean to you?

Where did it come from?

Why did you accept it as part of who you are?

Why did you start to act from it?

Why did you start to be it?

Why did you cover it up?

Why did you accept it and live from it but live from it in ignorance, in fear?

Why did you agree with it, call it yours and then live from it as though it was not yours, as though it was shameful, as though it was embarrassing and sinful?

Find that truth, be with it. Acknowledge it. Sincerely analyse it and its effects upon you. Then let it go. Admit to the self the falsity of this belief, of this truth, that you have been hiding and yet living from. Let it go. Tell the self why it is not true. Tell the self why it is no longer of service to you and begin to partner with a new truth.

From the original truth, tell the self what is actually true. What is actually worth adhering to and honouring. Tell the self the new truth and from here live it. Repeat the new truth to the self often. Let the ears hear it and the eyes see it. Write it down and tell it to the self often. Understand that this is how you reclaim the self. This is how you begin to come home to the self. This is how you return to you!

Write it, read it, tell it; this is your truth. This is the real you. There is no shame to this truth. There is no fear to this truth. There is love and awaking, there is epiphany and possibly even tears to this truth, for this truth is you! This truth is deeper and stronger than the truth you have been honouring, the truth that is not truth. This new truth, this real truth, this is cosmic, this is galactic, this is universal, this is eternal thought, eternal knowing and eternal being.

You are eternal and the truth you have discovered is you. Simple.

Breathe it, be it, know it, see it. Write it, speak it, feel it, hear it. Do this many times per day. Retrain the mind, the poor harnessed duped and deceived mind, retrain it with your presence, with your knowing, with your truth. Who are you? What do you truly believe? What is there for you in the old truth, in the deception you have been living from and covering up from the self, by the self, as the self and for the self? What peace is there in that?

Have the courage, have the tenacity, have the valour, the bravery and stamina to dive deep and admit the deceptions you have been living from and honouring. Admit the deceits that you have been hiding, even from the self, for they are too shameful, humiliating, insulting, terrifying or self-defeating to admit.

These concepts that you have called truth are not your truth.

Your role in finding your actual truth is to address these concepts, to create for yourself the argument against them, to create for yourself the flip, the reverse and resolution of these so-called truths.

You are eternal.

Your mind is easily deceived into thinking other than this.

But your eternal spirit, your soul matrix, your unseen inspirational influence, your intuitions and epiphanies are all from an eternal source. The true you knows the deceptions you have been under, from the self, by the self and accepted from others.

Time to honour the true self and allow the truth to come through and be you. Have courage, have confidence, dive deep and know you are supported, protected, forgiven and understood.

You have been deceived, and you have been detoured but you are still loved, you are still cherished, you are still adored and embraced. You are still one with the One and all that is. You are a beloved child of eternity, even when you think you are not, even when you operate totally and wholly from the illusion of separation and the beliefs that are deceit and distortion. Even then you are loved, you are adored, and you are a wonder.

You are eternal, do not forget this. You are adored, do not forget this. You are a peaceful one of eternal and absolute love. Find the deceits, find the nets, find the harnessed thoughts, the looping thoughts, the labyrinth that keeps you from knowing you and being you. Find the beliefs within you that are a lie and expose them to the self with courage and with rawness. Open the wound to expel the poison. It is painful yes, but it is the only way to heal the wound, it is the only way for the poison, for the toxin, to release.

You are not judged for this, you are not abandoned for this, you are not ostracised for this. The poison in the wound is not you, it is not yours, it was given to you and taught to you. You were convinced to accept it as yours. It is not. Time to heal the self. Time to dive deep and find You now. Only you can do this. You have the power, the grace and the courage to do so. Trust this. Be brave and begin the exploration of self now.

Judgement Games

When we use words to group or categorise others as something shameful or repellent in some way – prejudiced, bigoted, sexist etc – it also may serve to bring your attention to what is within you that may be the same or similar negative feeling you are chastising or dismissing them for.

You may find that you are repelled by certain people for their bigotry for instance and have harsh words to say about them for being a bigot. Maybe you are very proud of not being a bigot and have very strong or passionate feelings about those that are - I'm not a bigot, but I hate bigots! That's the layer within the layer of judgmentalism and castigation.

If you can see it in them and call them on it whilst disliking them for it, then you hold it as a judgment about them. 'Oh, they're prejudiced, not me, but I don't like prejudiced people'. You are being prejudiced against the prejudiced, you are being bigoted against the bigoted!

It's okay to recognise their bigotry or prejudice and not enjoy being around it. It's ok to choose not to have a form of connection with them (friendship, relationship etc). They may not be the type of people you feel happy spending time with, but it is the judgment and negative feeling you have towards them that needs noting.

The negative feeling you have toward them for their bigotry or prejudice really only means you are engaging with the same feeling within yourself that you have judged them for and/or as.

This is not a 'mirror' teaching whereby what you 'see out there' in other folk means it is an unhealed aspect within you. No, that type of teaching is incomplete or diluted at best. What you 'see out there', what you 'recognise in another', is not necessarily recognised because it is within you or is an unhealed aspect of you. It is recognised because you are familiar with it, yes, and perhaps that is because it is within you or once was, but it may be that you recognise it for many other reasons. Suffice to say here that it doesn't automatically mean that being able to recognise it in someone means you have it within you.

Having said that, holding negative feelings towards others, criticising others or castigating others for their opinions, belief systems or attitudes does mean that you are igniting the judgement, prejudice or bigotry in self as well – you are prejudiced against the prejudiced.

It's worth thought, because we can very strongly think of ourselves as good people, moral people, non-judgemental people, and yet in our assessment of ourselves we have turned a blind eye to the more subversive forms of our own judgment, prejudice and bigotry.

Abuse Games

That now brings us to abuse games generally, and this is a big one, so buckle up - abuse games are rife in human society, and we are so used to them that we often don't even notice them.

We play them all the time, sometimes deliberately, sometimes accidentally and sometimes in complete ignorance of the fact that we are playing them at all. They have many differing types of names, some of which you will be familiar with, but all of them are abuse games. You may know them by words and phrases such as dominate or be dominated, victim victimiser paradigm, bullying, domestic violence, gas lighting, trolling, blaming and shaming, manipulating, triggering and so on. Sometimes we even call these abuse games being empowered, being confident, or winning, success and victory. Not every circumstance of empowerment, confidence or winning is an abuse game, but it's entirely possible that where you think you are being empowered what you are actually doing is playing an abuse game.

Our society is so imbued with abuse games of one sort or another, it can be incredibly difficult to discern where your behaviours and language are actually contributing to an abuse game, when you feel like all you are doing is standing up for yourself.

Survival of the Fittest

Our world is mired in and run by various forms of abuse paradigms. The game is played everywhere! And when you realise what the game is you will see it clearly. We live in a world that has adhered to and aligned with the ideas of survival of the fittest. This Darwinian idea of life is that only the most adapted, the most ruthless, the strongest and most competitive win. This may be true for the natural world, it may be true of the animal kingdom, food chains or even the plant kingdom, but when we apply it to human life, we are ignoring the fact that humans are a sentient form with the ability to discern right from wrong, with the ability to consciously choose compassion.

If we simply apply the 'survival of the fittest' mentality in all its variations of selfish ruthlessness for success and extrapolate it beyond the natural world we get a world which is run by callous decisions focused upon only success, money or victory as the goal. We get a world which honours, lauds and applauds those that make the most money by any means, are the most successful and who crush their competition perhaps becoming a monopolistic overlord that destroys the local flavour of life. We congratulate the winners and want to learn how they did it, failing to remember that part of being so successful is the destruction of the delicate beauty, variety and nuance of life.

There is nothing wrong with success, but the definition of success and the how tos and wherefores of attaining success may need a little analysis. This concept of win at all costs and survival of the fittest perhaps creates a mindset and a paradigm of human engagement that is nothing more that varying degrees of abuse games. Which role you play depends upon which situation you are in and what your response to the situation is. At any given time, your role in the abuse game may be victim or victimiser.

Victims and Victimisers

Maybe you think of yourself as a kind-hearted loving one who doesn't get upset, so you are not victimising anyone. There's no way you play abuse games! But perhaps you are then victimising the self by not standing up for your needs? Are you martyring yourself to the victimiser in order to not have confrontation? Are you manipulating someone else in order to get your needs met?

It's quite the convoluted environment we live in where the human dynamics get very complicated in their expressions of victim or victimiser with a subset of martyring, bullying and abuse. We each play every role at one time or another.

The human being, the human dynamic, society, family and relationships are all extremely complicated and we can, without even realising it, be playing very real abuse games with both ourselves and others during any experience, human exchange or occurrence. We can be a victim in one moment and flip straight into being a victimiser in the next. Have you ever gotten angry at being ignored or talked over and told that person off? Have you ever been in a situation where someone attempts to correct your behaviour, and you've instead shouted them down? You've gone from being a victim to being a victimiser in one conversation! Or maybe you placate and wheedle, maybe you hide your needs and hopes in order to keep the peace? Then you are perpetuating a dominating (victimising) situation through maintaining your victim status externally by victimising the self internally! You are enabling the external abuse of you by victimising the inner you and denying your needs.

It's complicated. These abuse games are everywhere, sometimes they are so complex, going back and forth switching roles many times during one single engagement. We often become completely ignorant to what is really going on and simply call it conversation or communication.

Our world honours and encourages types of communication that are aimed at keeping the peace, drawing others into your line of thinking ostensibly to help them – what in fact could be taking place is manipulation and a type of victim/victimiser game.

It is very common for a victim to accidentally or on purpose become a victimiser in order to 'take back their power' or to 'get what they need'. On the surface it appears to be an emboldened or powerful move, but it is simply switching roles and fuelling more abuse games in your life from a new vantage point.

So don't be too judgmental about abuse and bullying because we all do it! We do it to ourselves, we do it to others, we do it to defend ourselves and we do it to defend others. That is not to suggest that we should continue doing it, abuse is still abuse even if it is normalised and rife around us.

What is being pointed out here is that we have been raised on a planet that is thoroughly mired in the concepts of 'going to war to keep the peace', which is another way of saying 'dominate or be dominated', or 'violence begets peace'. Violence only begets more violence as those dominated by the violence retaliate with violence. That's the abuse game at play – and how we applaud when we see the little fella stand up and beat down the bully, because we've all been raised in, imbued by and mired in the concept of violence and victimising being the solution to being a victim.

Recognise that the victim victimiser paradigm abounds and do your very best to extricate yourself from the game! Recognise your varying roles as victim and victimiser and be truthful with yourself about your contribution to the continuation of the game and make the choices of behaviour, boundaries, words and emotions that discontinue the perpetuation of hurt from the game. Walk away from the argument, put down the proverbial weapons and perhaps hold your tongue until you can speak kindly, gently and with your boundaries in place once more.

Abuse Games and Duality

Generally, in 3D reality life we only see the duality options for a circumstance; wrong or right, win or lose, dominate or be dominated, victim or victimiser. Within a duality paradigm we only have the two choices. There are, however, many other options, we just find them difficult to see and/or choose.

We are used to a culture of duality choices (if you are not winning you are losing, if you are not a leader you are a follower – if you are not the victimiser you are the victim). Perhaps the choices are not either/or, perhaps they are manyfold, and we are just not versed in seeing it this way.

People don't like to think of themselves as being the victimiser, most normal people find the idea of being the bully, being the victimiser, abhorrent and yet they are also repelled by the idea of being the victim. Based upon a duality perception of the world if you are not the victim this automatically means you become a victimiser, and vice versa. So, if you are not the victim or the victimiser then who are you?

Many of the non-duality options to escape the victim victimiser game challenge our ego. For instance, there is the choice to walk away, to disengage, but then we are left roiling with the angst of feeling that they have won over us, or that we didn't get to say our piece. It is our ego that tells us that either of these outcomes matter. If you believe yourself having neutralised the situation by walking away, by not playing the game, then there is no win or lose. If they believe they have won, then that is their ego issue to deal with, not yours.

When we allow the ego to run us, then abuse games can act like a contagion and become self-perpetuating. When we are willing to go beyond ego it is easier to extract ourselves from the downward spiral, the whirlpool, of abuse and abuse games. The ego, however, is tricky and can lead you astray.

It is very hard for a human to not choose that which makes them feel better in the moment. It can feel better to retaliate or capitulate to the abuse in that moment, which means that many are then behaving in response to abuse as a victimizer or a victim (perhaps either a martyr or sacrificial victim) and hence enabling or perpetuating the abuse game. Maybe this is becoming hard for you to imagine, the game is very convoluted after all!

In each situation, question for the self; is it the ego that needs you to engage until you have won (victimising)? Is it the ego that needs you to correct their impression, assumption, opinion or judgement of you (dominating)? Is it the ego that needs you to hear their forgiveness and understanding of your actions (victim – why don't they love me, why don't they forgive me)?

These concepts can be hard to fathom or recognise and even harder to disengage and disentangle from, but they are worth contemplating – how often are you choosing the victim or victimiser role because that is all you know?

Dealing with the Abuser

The thing to contemplate is the concept of abuse and abuse scenarios. Abuse games are rife and are connected to abuse words and behaviours. There may very well be experiences within human relationships that feel like they need resolution or expression and certainly not allowing oneself to be abused is important for healing and soul growth BUT (and this is important) when we yell or denigrate or engage in fight behaviour (even in response to someone else's abuse of us) what we are actually doing is becoming the victimiser and abusing another.

Abusing the abuser is still abuse. You are still playing the abuse game except you are now being the bully - which is probably not who you really want to be.

It is far wiser and more healing to disallow the attempted abuse from someone else by disengaging in some way or another when we feel triggered, disrespected or unappreciated or even bullied, castigated or controlled (treated like a child).

It really is best to neutralise the conversation as best you can there and then and move away from it. Calm the self down and then assess why it was so triggering and how you can let that go (heal that) without dominating or abusing the self or the other.

You cannot change them. They will always see the world and you through their own lens, and their lens will only change through their own impetus. This works both ways, they in turn cannot change you unless you allow the change. Abuse, anger and fights rarely change a person, it's possible, but it's so very unlikely. Most abusers are not interested in hearing anything about their own abuse. In fact, often they will turn such 'revelation' about their behaviour back upon the revealer and blame them for the triggering of the behaviour. I'm only like this/reacting this way because you made me angry!

So, maybe some things need to be said between the two of you, maybe, but more importantly your peace of mind and healing calm state actually come from not playing the game in the first place. Let people do what they do and be who they are then calmly choose what's right for you. Calmly express why you do or do not agree with them, or are or are not doing what they request and do not engage in defending your position or correcting their opinions. Perhaps you need to even calmly walk away from the connection you have with the person. If your entire relationship with this person is one abuse game after another, it might be time to question the efficacy and relevancy of the relationship in the first place.

Abusing the Self

The abuse game is extremely damaging to a person and limits or (hopefully temporarily) halts the healing progress. If you are in a relationship which is consistently abusive, you may find it very hard to embody or maintain the healing and happiness you seek because the abuse game, whether you are a victim or a victimiser, is very damaging to your peace of mind, your flows of self and your inner calm and ignition of joy.

The suppression of self to keep the peace with an abuser is a diminishing of self, so, whilst you may consider yourself a calm and happy person it is not a true calm and joyful state. The hyper alertness you hold for when the abuser might get triggered once more is not predisposed to running your inner flows of peace and calm. This hyper vigilant state can sometimes feel like intuition, knowing that something will happen before it occurs, but this is not a true intuitive state. It is the fight/flight fuelled hyper responsiveness of self that keeps the system triggered and firing in fight/flight all the time. This is exhausting and can wear the body out – it's also aging.

The simple solution to this type of situation is 'leave' but it may not feel like you can, you may feel trapped, or you may feel like you are in love with the abuser. I do not profess to advise you in your personal life without knowing all your circumstances, but the observation remains, playing the abuse game in any of its forms is damaging to both the abuser and the abused.

The abuse of self, the domineering of self and the bullying of self is also an abuse game. How many circumstances do you put yourself through which are anathema to your actual dreams, hopes and wishes for your life and your happiness? Perhaps living in that abusive relationship is only sustainable because you allow the suppression of self by self and the diminishing of your dreams and hopes in order to stay 'quietly' in that relationship. You may be playing an abuse game with the self in order to have what you perceive to be a calm, peaceful or non-disruptive life with the person you are currently experiencing love for.

Empowerment and Success

Let's reiterate here that the abuse games we play, the dominate or be dominated or victim/victimiser games, are a "normal" game for humans. Normal in this usage does not mean acceptable, agreeable or even appropriate, it means common and everywhere, it means usual, typical or expected. It does not mean right or okay.

Even though these games are everywhere, most people don't realise that that's what they're doing or, at least, don't want to admit it or simply can't see that there is any other alternative. They think they're being empowered. They think they're taking control. They think they're winning. They think they're being successful. In fact, what they're doing is dominating others.

A lot of people think in terms of, *"well, if s/he's yelling at me, I've gotta step up and take control of that situation and yell back,"* with thoughts and justifications of *"if someone's attacking me, I'm gonna be fight back, they're not gonna get the best of me"*. That's a victim victimizer game again, but in our society, it is sold to us as a self-esteem game, as a self-worth game, as an empowerment game.

It's not. It's a domination abuse game.

What our society teaches us constantly is that as long as you are the dominant one, as long as you are not the victim (almost by whatever means) you are the winner, and you've played the game correctly. Now, of course, that doesn't include obvious abusers and bullies and violence, right? Because even though they are clearly the dominant one, we clarify by saying, *"well, they're pushing people around, they're using their fists to make their point. That makes them a bully, and that's not ok"*. And, in many ways, you would be right, in these very overt bully and abuse games it is obvious that 'this is not right'. But we forget that there are also much more hidden games, many abuse games are played subversively, in ignorance, or hidden from plain sight, and most people don't even realize that they personally might be quite the bully – they may just think of themselves as persuasive, confident or forthright.

Abuse games are so much the norm in our society that it's really only when it's expressed in distortion that we notice it. That is when there's yelling or there are fists or there's obvious physical abuse such as domestic violence, war or something similar. But it is everywhere.

So yes, you've played it, of course you've played it, it's human to play it in this day and age. And you've played it really, really strongly, you've been a master at it! But that doesn't make you a standalone amongst everybody. We all have been a master at it. It doesn't make you a bad person, a person that everyone can point to and denounce for being wrong. It doesn't make you any more or less than anyone else. No. It makes you human. You are a human mired in the systems of life that we are working through and healing, and the fact that you can recognise it in the self actually gives you the advantage, the opportunity to move beyond it. That's a helpful healing space to be in. You are ahead of the curve.

Abuse and negative talk get you nowhere when it comes to beneficial states of mind, joyful thoughts and feelings and happy trajectories in life. It is worth considering that bullying, victimising, and being the victim or martyr are all the same energy. They are simply on opposite ends of the spectrum. The bully has the same energy damage as the victim – both of them are an abuse of power. Both of these situations, the victim or the victimiser (bully), are not centred in absolute love and neutral self-responsibility, both of them are damaging and diminishing to those involved.

There is no castigation here, we all choose to do what we think is the only option available to us or what we have been taught is the way to get ahead. Mostly we are oblivious to our own role as an abuser or a victim and our participation in the abuse game, but now that you have more knowledge about it, you may be able to see it in the self and in your life more clearly.

Inner Bully

It is quite common for the victimising bullying behaviour to come not from an external source and directed towards you, but from within – directed towards the self. You are your own oppressor; you are the one telling you that you are not good enough. You are too fat, too thin, too stupid, too shy, too short, too tall, too something or other that you deem to be not perfect enough for the good results in life, whatever that means to you. One must directly confront the internal bully in order to be a good steward of self and take responsibility for mastering one's life trajectory.

Negative self-talk and destructive ideas are the inner bully trying to keep you small. Name them, in order to call them out and disallow their subversive insinuations of your powerlessness.

It starts with the baby steps of recognising what you are doing to you and continues with the self-parenting of *"shhhh I no longer speak like that to myself"*. Then it expands out into the external over time as a more and more sure and certain sense of self. It continues with kindness for self, with courage and patience for self.

As you make the changes and hold the line for the self you get better, you get stronger, and you get wiser. Nourishing the self with kind words, strong ideas, backing of choices, and using the techniques such as in this book will empower the self with better ways of thinking and speaking about the self, about life and about your potentials and possibilities.

The sovereign one, the present one, the healing one, the self-responsible one notices the thoughts and feelings and questions their origin. Where did they come from? Are they even mine? And cruises through them to the truth of and for self.

There are many mechanisms here on earth that influence your state of mind, and emotion is contagious. Just as you can feel when someone is angry, and it may even make you feel angry yourself – emotion is contagious. Be careful and circumspect with yours and be aware that what you think, and feel may not really be yours.

Abuse language comes in many forms, it comes as overt yelling and spitting in your face, cursing your very being, and it comes as quiet manipulation, as little pokes and prods that when you are confronted by you hold up your hands and say I didn't do that I didn't mean that you are so mean to me to say that about me, see there is the evidence that I am a poor little innocent victim and you are bullying me.

The hardest thing to do is to get truthful about your style of communication and the words you use. You do what you do because you have believed it is how to communicate, it is what needs to be done to get what you want, or to dominate the situation, to not be victim to someone else, but it may be a perversion of communication that actually keeps you in the dominating role and victimizing the self and others without you ever recognising it.

Triggering Language

When we experience being triggered or triggering someone else it can feel very overwhelming and may even shut down our rational thinking and intention to be kind, to speak kindly – we may feel a knee jerk response to castigate, blame, shame or shout at the cause of the trigger. When this occurs to us, perhaps the best action we can take is to pause and be silent, go within and, to the best of our ability, remove ourselves from the situation and spend some time contemplating what we were feeling and focusing on the 'why' of the triggered response.

What did the situation remind you of? What were the emotions that surfaced and what did they remind you of?

These types of questions to the self will actually show you that, in most cases, it wasn't the current person or situation that was the problem. The reason for the triggering, the reason for the sudden and perhaps disproportionate response in that moment, is actually rooted in a past person, relationship or occurrence. This would then lead to the conclusion that this past person, relationship or occurrence has had some type of deleterious effect on you, your psyche and personality such that it needs healing or resolving in some way to mitigate or prevent the triggered responses exacerbating the abuse in your life and the deliverance of abuse by you to others or self.

Wise ones remember that when we speak, those words are out there forever more. What is said can hurt, wound or escalate into a very unpleasant situation. Perhaps it is best to just not say anything.

Do you want to contribute to the abuse language and the raging shouting and blaming that is 'out there' or do you want to be a new generation of peaceful ones, calm ones and gentle talking ones, those who listen and respect others and do not feed the flame of violence with abuse talk?

When you feel triggered, when you feel attacked it is not time to attack back. It is time to stand strong in who you are and firmly say 'no' to the attack – perhaps verbally, or perhaps metaphorically through action or behaviour. Shouting and blaming in return is adding to the victim victimiser game and spewing more negative violent abuse talk energy into the world. Remember, what you flow and stream of you and by you creates the next moment in your life. So, shouting at the shouter? You are aligning with the language and energy of abuse and creating more of that in your life.

Anger, vitriol, violent words and actions could be considered like a contagion, perhaps a virus – when one person is carrying the virus and spewing forth their anger, their oppressive speak and domination tactics, the receiver of those tactics is triggered to fight back or capitulate. Both actions are enabling further transmission or exacerbation of the virus. The shouting back is like being infected by the virus and then running that contagion as part of your flows and streams, you are now stuck in the violence and aggression virus. Yet capitulation and molly coddling maintains your victim role and enables the angry one to continue to spew their vitriol as and when they feel is their right. An abuse contagion can only continue if there is a transfer of infection to the other or an enablement of continued infection by the other.

This doesn't mean that it is your role to help them heal from the anger contagion. That is their job and their job alone. They will only come to the conclusion that they need to change or heal if their anger is not working any more. How is it not working? It is not continuing to infect and feed off other people and/or be enabled by others.

It is, on the surface, a very difficult thing to not react to an angry person, to not be triggered by them, and of course it seems normal to fall into the downward spiral of being triggered when it is specifically directed at us. We've all done it. But the rescue of self, the healing of patterns that are emanating and creating a rocky life of discomfort, are all enhanced by you letting go of the anger contagion. Responding with silence, or quietness but strength, and holding your boundaries, walking away from the triggering abuse, and choosing again from a space of peace, aids in not perpetuating the contagion's life and infection cycle.

Some abusers never come to the realisation or choose to change, and that's ok, that's their choice and their path. Your job is you. Your job is your safety and peace of mind. Your job is your rescue and self-responsibility. You are the most important person in your life, and you need your attention. Let the abuser make their own choices and you make yours to heal the self and not enter into the abuse game nor perpetuate the abuse contagion.

If you choose to spend time with angry people, volatile people or abusive people, then know that you will be affected by this and confronted by this often. It's ok, you can choose that, but truth with self means that you must recognise that this is *your choice*. You are then not the deliverer of the anger, of the triggering statements or actions perhaps, but you are the enabler of its continuation in your life by staying in the situation.

Recognise that enabling the abuse, enabling the vitriol and triggering language by continuing to allow it in your life, enables the abuse game to continue to exist, to continue to be a source of power and domination in our societies. If you wouldn't allow a certain type of behaviour or way of speaking to happen to a small innocent child or animal, then perhaps it is time to draw the line and disallow it for the self.

If you can truthfully say that you hold a competent degree of self-love and you know that you are not too sensitive and yet you find you are triggered regularly by a certain situation or a certain person, then you are in an abuse game that you are in some way enabling and/or perpetuating. There is no castigation or blame here, there is just encouragement to recognise the truth of your situation and your role in perpetuating it.

Your life is your choice, and whilst you may feel stuck and whilst you may feel like you have no choice, there is always a choice. It may not be the choice you dream of, the choice you want or even the choice you thought you'd have when, as a child, you envisaged your life, but there is a choice. Out of all the choices available to you in that moment, pick the best choice, and do it, then let things settle. From this there will be another set of choices, pick the best one, then let it settle. Keep repeating this process and you will find that soon, and before you know it, life starts to look a lot more pleasant and joyful for you. It's a process of movement, even tiny baby steps but movement, nonetheless.

Reverse Bullying

When our words trigger another, we cannot in the eyes of the receiver, without knowing their history, dramas, filters, wounds or traumas, we cannot define for them whether they should or shouldn't feel abused or dominated by the words. You can apologise and rephrase it and try again but you may not get the result you wish – this may or may not be based upon what you said and how you said it but based upon their own filtering and personal history as to how they received what you said and how you said it.

When you decide that you have done no wrong and call someone too sensitive because of their reaction, recognise that this is a form of abuse in and of itself – you do not have the history and knowledge of what is going on in their inner convolution of self, called personality and identity, that is causing the response. It is very possible that they are being too sensitive. It is very possible that they are actually using the hypersensitive reaction to control the situation and dominate you. Recognise this without entering the abuse game that is being played by the sensitive reaction.

They may even be trying to abuse you and dominate you via manipulation and a victim's retaliation to a perceived victimiser by turning the tables, calling foul and have everything stop to deal with their issues thus creating themselves as the centre of attention. As such they become the dominant person in that moment and potentially move from being victim (which is how they think of themselves) to victimiser (which is how they think of you).

If you personally want to create your world as harmony then buying into their manipulation games by antagonising and dogging them with exasperation or dismissal of 'you're too sensitive', 'toughen up' or 'it was only a joke' is peppering your own language, life and creation with the language of abuse.

It is better to just not even try to engage with a reverse bully like that and with those that are truly non-manipulatively sensitive and sometimes a bit triggered or cowed by very innocently worded and intended statements, then you can view those exchanges as learning experiences in how to rephrase, how to reword and how to speak with clarity and kindness.

Gossip Games

There is a long-standing tradition amongst humans of exchanging information, sharing ideas, and experiences between each other. Traditionally the exchange of information, stories or experience could be used for simple things such as ensuring that the appropriate people knew where the fruiting trees were or where the good game could be found right through to keeping culture or spirit alive by ensuring a living history of the society.

We don't share in the same way or even for the same reasons anymore and quite often our habitual sharing actually devolves into sensational gossip and vitriolic oversharing about other folk who are not present during the sharing.

When the dissemination of information that keeps others abreast of the experiences of the community or those they know of, but whom are not present, turns into gossip, you are playing an abuse game.

The salacious and vitriolic sharing of 'did you hear what he/she did' or 'did you hear what happened' with the intention of creating sensation and making judgment upon another is gossip. It helps the sharer feel important and it aligns the humans in a game of 'us against them' where we like to align with the gossiper and denigrate and shame another so as to fit in and be acceptable. It can form a sort of tribal experience where aligning with the gossiper keeps you in the inner circle – a position of importance where you are 'in the know'.

Gossip is an abuse activity. It is a sharing of sensational or personal details of another person in order to judge them, shame them or embarrass them. Having said that, it is a social activity to share information and stories between each other, and some of the stories will be about those that are not present. There is no gossip in catching others up with the details of another's life when there is no intent to shame, create rumour, sensation or outrage. Just be careful about crossing the line into gossip when sharing exchanges of information – consider, where does sharing experience of another end and sharing intimate personal details that are not your own with intent to shock or outrage begin?

Blame Games

Blame games are everywhere, and in many ways could be considered a subset of abuse games – it may be more correct to say that all of the word games that have been mentioned here are abuse games of one sort or another. We separate them out to clearly illustrate some of the more noxious ways we use our words to release self-responsibility, to distract from presence and mastery.

The blame game is a significant game we play regularly, especially if we have felt in any way bullied, hurt or minimised by life and the people in it. If we have felt powerless, or unacceptable, in some way we may have developed a propensity to shift focus to 'that out there' and see it as the reason that we feel bad, that we cannot succeed, that we have explosions of temper or are hyper critical or castigating.

The blame game is a very succinct and swift way of removing oneself from self-responsibility, from presence, sovereignty and mastery of life. It is an acknowledgement, perhaps subconsciously, or even accidentally, that you are a victim of 'that out there' and if only you could control 'that out there' you could be happy, successful, kind, caring and even-tempered.

Blame continues one on the path of sorrow. It can be confronting and feel exhausting to realise how often and how much we are mired in, immersed in and operating from the varying forms of abuse games that are entangled within our communications and engagements throughout our lives and relationships. It can be far easier to point the finger in one way or another and seek fault elsewhere.

There is no suggestion here that external input is not of consequence or does not have impact on your success, your situation or your direction in life – of course it does. What is suggested here is that the more you focus on the external as the reason for your attitude, mood, success and ability to live the life of your dreams, the less likely you will actually be able to live the life of your dreams.

There is no mastery, no self-sovereignty, to blaming. There is no kindness and compassion to shaming.

Yes, the external impacts our lives, and sometimes it can be shocking and limiting, sometimes it can be unexpected and abrupt, closing doors of opportunity in our face suddenly or unreasonably, being confronted by bullying and aggression without warning and without any provocation. These things happen. They are shocking, upsetting and discombobulating. They are from the external and impact you, yes, that's true, but relinquishing sovereignty and self-mastery to those situations means that you have now aligned with the external having mastery over you, your choices and your emotions.

Mastery entails not only co-creating your direction, your external situations and circumstance by redirecting your focus, your flows and your emotions, but also taking that unexpected, perhaps shocking experience, and reframing it, growing from it or learning from it for the self to mitigate, diminish or negate its influence on you and your direction. Choosing again for the self, not to perpetuate the flows of the abuse game that you accidentally, incidentally or unexpectedly became part of.

It's ok, our world is mired in victim shaming, as well as victim glorification and blaming of the victimizer, all of these are abuse games of one sort or another. There are countless ways the blame game becomes part of your day and experiences, for instance how many times have you become involved in salacious details of someone else's downfall? How many times have you cheered at the exposure of their lies and deceit?

It can be a healing action for people and society to root out the lies and the manipulations of those in power. It may even be healing to know some details about it, potentially disallowing the same avenues of deceit to occur again, but ask yourself the following question:

Where does exposure of wrongdoing, explanation of action and illustration of untrustworthiness stop and the blame game, the abuse game, the salacious sharing of shocking detail to whet the appetite of the listener and denigrate the wrong doer begin?

This is just one of the many ways that we use words and feeling to assault others and dominate situations along with losing not only our sovereignty but our mastery of life, of our emotional state and our own success and happiness in life. By taking responsibility for self and self's feelings we are bringing ourselves back to centre. We bring ourselves back to ground zero, the creation point. In being present here, in being mindful of our own emotions, our own feelings, our own responses and actions, we become the master of our domain, of our lives and our potentials for a happiness that we seek currently by blaming others in the hope that they will change their behaviours and make us feel better.

Give up the blame game and ignite the mastery game – you will have far more success at creating peaceful moments when you realise you get to choose to enact them rather than waiting for 'those out there' to adjust their behaviour or acquiesce to your requirements of them to make your life better.

We can use a form of the blame game for ourselves for personal healing and positive benefit by recognising that we have within us many differing aspects of self that sometimes speak very loudly to us of our failures, our hurts and our unlovability. We also have within the voice of calm, of peace of loving delight. That voice is quiet and less boisterous than the voices that point out our failures.

The voice of our doom, the one that doesn't back us and points out our ineptitude, points out why we should be denigrated, unsuccessful or are unlovable, has been suggested previously in this book as the voice that we should name and call out. This naming and calling out is not a self-castigation exercise; it is a self-compartmentalization exercise.

By compartmentalizing the self in this way, we offer ourselves the opportunity to see that there is the ability to disagree with the negative self-talk, to neutralise the inner castigator if you will. When we use the compartmentalizing technique with ourselves, what we are really doing is taking the natural propensity for blaming and using it to distinguish between the inner dominating bully and the inner loving parent or angelic being. Thusly we can then see that the inner dominating bully is 'to blame' for the negative self talk – it is not all that we are, it is not even true of who we are, so we can disagree with it.

Blaming in this way can be a very effective technique for self-healing - compartmentalizing to distinguish what is the 'loving source-connected inner encouragement and inner parent' and what is the 'castigating, dominating paranoid and pushy aspect of self' that is trying to keep you small and stop you pursuing your dream life. Having said that, when blaming is used to dominate self or others, when it is used to ridicule or force apology or in some other way manipulate or dominate a situation, a person or self, it is an abuse game.

You Own Your Feelings

Your feelings stem from within, you make them within, you own them. They are not made by another; they are made by you and as such you are responsible for your own feelings. They are your creation.

You create your feelings from within, your feelings are a chemical response within the body that are created by you, not the other. An explanation of your state of being to the other, an explanation of why you responded in a certain way, or of your feelings is perfectly valid. Blaming someone else for your feelings is lashing out and abusing the other. For instance, when we say "I felt this way and that's why I did that" it is very different to saying "you did this/that and made me feel this/that and that's why I did this/that". One is an explanation; the other is a blame statement.

Recognizing your sovereignty, recognising your personal creation of your own feelings and state of being is vital for your healing and your growth beyond being the victim and beyond turning your victim status into a domination game with another, perhaps seeking their contrition for whatever hurt you feel they subjected you to. It may be that the other did hurt you. It may be that the hurt was inflicted deliberately but in terms of your healing and happiness, that is of no consequence. What is of consequence is how you deal with it, react to it, work through it and heal it within the self.

You are a sovereign being. If you have been hurt, then deal with your emotions as a sovereign one – heal what it is that triggers you into displays of unfortunate exchanges and engagements. Deal with what it is within you that needles, blames and shames another in an attempt to get attention, or be understood. Heal that which provokes you within resulting in your sense of impotence, sadness, hurt, anger, frustration or aggravation with 'that out there' or 'those out there'.

Why not choose joy and peace, and spend time with those that choose the same? Choose to spend time with those that understand you and do not attack you. Then you will find that feeling misunderstood or in need of restitution becomes a thing of the past!

As said previously, we are all immersed in abuse games. We've all been abused, and we are all abusers, it's just a matter of degree, and a matter of how present you are and how truthful you are with the self about your role in the game.

So, the question becomes how will you stop it?

Will you call the abuse game to a halt for the self?

Will you choose presence, mastery and peace? Because a master of self does not abuse self, nor anyone else.

A master of self chooses the high road of forgiveness, choice and the best of the best outcomes for self and all – even when those outcomes are not yet clear.

A master of self trusts to peace, to loving thoughts, actions and behaviours and chooses to enact those loving thoughts, actions and behaviours to self first.

A master of self disallows the martyring or victimhood of self by self or other – thusly coming into any situation as a self-loving one, fully nurtured, loved and restored by self and choosing from love beyond any abuse game.

Forgiveness

Now that you've been immersed in the thoughts, concepts and ideas of the many and myriad abuse games that are part of our society and relationships and perhaps you've seen a few abuse games that you play, it's probably time to have a small word on forgiveness.

Forgiveness of others does not mean you condone their behaviour or even need to have a close relationship with them. It does not mean that you return to their side and do life with them again – unless you want to. It simply means understanding they too are dealing with their own internal and (perhaps to them) mostly hidden, convoluted markers, traumas and knee jerk opinions, responses and protective choices. These may play out as abuse, domination and control attempts of others and their environment in order to get everything and everyone behaving in a way that is appropriate (by their definition) and hence makes them feel internally calmer and safer.

This is what practically everyone on the planet is doing. Sometimes the inner convolutions encourage fight behaviour, other times flight, freeze or fawn behaviours – all of these responses play out as various actions or reactions that are ultimately designed to make the world feel safer and more navigable to the perpetrator of the behaviour. The simple recognition that this is what everyone is doing and understanding some are doing this whilst consciously acknowledging they have damage that needs healing, perhaps even attempting to heal it, and others are not, makes forgiveness easy.

We understand that everyone is doing the best they can with the damage they are harbouring and the convolutions of emotional response that has formed within from this – in the same way that we are. Sometimes we get it right, sometimes wrong. There is no castigation on the self for getting it wrong, in the same way that we do not castigate others for not even trying – who are we to judge that they should even try? Our focus remains upon ourselves and our journey.

Everyone does the best they can to be as happy as they can given where they are at with their own understanding of life, self and healing. Knowing this, you can choose to embrace them back into your life, understanding that there may be turmoil again or, if the behaviour is too much of an assault for you, too much of a deviation from the loving peace that you desire in your life, then let them go and love them from afar. Allow them to be who they are without judgement and continue on your own inner journey of peace.

Holding onto unforgiveness ultimately only harms you because it keeps the resentment circulating within. This internal looping then spirals you down into further darkness of self. The holding onto of your anger towards the other and the repetition of the unforgiven action in your mind and in your system, to justify why forgiveness is withheld may ignite other abuse games within – such as trying to prove that you were right, and they were wrong.

It doesn't matter who is right and who is wrong. It matters who is happy and who is suffering – and you have the power to choose your path, your engagements, in such a way as to step off the path of sorrow and suffering for the self and move into the cool clear streams of peace, calm and joy.

To do this, first you must overcome your propensity to maintain connection with the abuse (internally and externally) that steers you into the path of sorrow again and again. Then release all unforgiveness, allow the other to be the forgiven one and choose your direction without the burden of the festering anger, guilt or sadness over the unforgiven one.

Once the other is the forgiven one, remember, you do not need to have a relationship with them again or any more, the forgiveness is for you, the forgiveness is your healing action for the self, allowing you to go forward in peace and find the life you desire.

Chapter 11

Manifestation

Truthfully, there is no real manifestation in the way that most of us have thought of it. There is simply alignment with the flows of the universe and the flows of the self, being truthful to who you are at the core of your being – not the created self you have become to hide your embarrassment, because of your shame, to fit into society, to be popular or acceptable to someone or something. We're talking about the true you. The kind, loving, eternal seed of peace that you are.

Listening to the true guidance of the self and surrendering to the universe; not a let-go-and-let-god attitude of 'god will take care of it all' and not an 'I must take action for anything to happen', but an alignment with self, true to self, a trust in the universe and flows of life and then a let go and stop pushing. Stop trying to make it happen.

What you feel enthusiasm about, spend time doing. What you feel joy for, spend time doing. What thrills you, interests you and uplifts you, spend time doing. This is your action. This is your inspiration from the flows of life that will somehow, in some way that is usually beyond your ken, align you with the actual physical appearance, materialisation and/or unfolding of what you desire and need in your life.

This is the process of manifestation and it's actually very simple.

It isn't focusing really hard on something. It isn't positive thinking, manipulation or domination of your environment. It isn't doing a special meditation, binaural training, imprinting or attending workshops.

It is focusing upon, attending to and healing the self and all the distortions and deviations to the true flow of who you are and the peace, love and presence of being who you are.

MANIFESTATION

It is continually sifting and shifting through all deviations of self away from Self. Sifting through, dissolving or resolving all layers, masks, personalities, aspects and overlays, all reactions and flip comments, knee jerks and ambushes we hand out to others, and all veils we have agreed to include or install as part of us and that we keep firmly in place so no one, not even you, sees who you really.

It is neutralising all of this in an effort to remember and return to the Self as much as possible. Your Self (big 's'), as opposed to your self (little 's'), is the loving one, the peaceful one, the replete one, the fulfilled one, the joyful one that is who you truly are. Some would refer to this as the divinity of Self, the truth of you, the God Self or Higher Self – it doesn't matter what you call it, it's still you, hence it's the Self.

When you move through these layers and overlays that mask the Self, when you come home to who you truly are, life moves with you and supplies you without you even focusing on it. There is no need for pressure, domination or powerful input. There is only a need to heal the self and remember who you are and what presence feels like. Being in love with the self and allowing the flows of absolute love to fuel you and fill you, brings you to the moment of now, and all else just falls into place.

It doesn't fall into place through your demands, nor through your urgencies, and doesn't fall into place necessarily in the way that you dictate that it must, but it does fall into place, nonetheless. Offering you what you need and allowing the best of the best and the creation of your highest joy to unfold as reality in your life.

You will try and manipulate it to be what you want, and that's ok, we all get distracted by the outside noise that encourages our success to look a certain way. Ultimately though, if you focus on the inner, if you focus on the healing of the self and the bringing of self to the peaceful state of true loving presence, not martyring, not sacrifice and not loving presence designed to look and be a certain thing as dictated by another, but the true loving presence of self and the peaceful knowing that you are who you are and you are ok, then you are in the manifesting zone.

MANIFESTATION

When you bring yourself to this state you resonate with the flows of life and the universe, which is, at its core, a creation of love, from love. All things are created from love, bubbling up through attention and focus to eventually become a manifest object, experience or outcome. When you heal the self to this state, you become aligned with the loving outcomes of life and the flow of life supports you into the loving outcomes of life whether you know what they are or not.

You may be distracted from the simplicity of the loving healing of self, the continual sifting and shifting through all the distortions and deviations of self that led you away from the loving flows of life, and that's ok. When you notice you have become distracted, draw your attention back to now, back to self and allow the self to once more pulse the love and focus on you and heal the distortions one by one by one.

You may fear that this will take forever! You may fear that the process and progress is slow and thusly you will never have your dream, you will never reach your personal summit. This is the fear of the ego. This is the fear based upon the outside parameters of success. As you heal, as you become You through the process of loving attention on self, you naturally alter your engagement with life. Its flows then immediately begin to offer you the peaceful resolutions from the pain and harm you have been operating from and the best of the best outcomes become a natural occurrence, a natural result and begin immediately in many forms. Miraculous and unexpected solutions and resolutions may just become your new normal.

The healing of self is a personal journey. It is a peaceful loving journey of no castigation, no blame, shame, guilt or humiliation of self. It is the kind and gentle discovery of where you have been led astray or led the self astray. There is no domination of self. There is no bullying of self or abuse of self. There is no pushing the self to be a certain shape or say certain things or fit a certain mold. These too are activities of abuse, to the self and by the self, and these activities of abuse deny the flows of love and life.

This is a journey of pondering and wondering, of looking at your life, your experiences, and your thoughts, words, actions, inactions, fears, doubts and blockages, and asking the self:

Why do I do that?

Where did that come from?

What is going on here?

Then lovingly allowing the self to tell you the story of self without any judgment contributed by you about you.

Simply, in neutrality, look at what you are doing and why you are doing it. Recognize that if it is anything other than loving to the self, others and humanity, then it is distortion and all the reasons that it exists represent your trauma, your drama, your wounding and your justification which represent your armor from the traumas and wounds.

We are complex creations of original purity dirtied by wounds, hurts, traumas that we try to cover up and defend against others knowing about or further hurt exacerbating. Thus, we become beings of scars, sores and scabs covered in armor, deflection, and resistance. It's ok, everyone has this combination, just in different ratios.

We are faced with so much harshness and judgment that it becomes unsafe and sometimes unwise to truly expose who you are at the core, beyond all the wounding. When you do, the regret that sometimes (often?) comes with that decision can be something overwhelming and can ignite and encourage the donning of further armor to defend against the vulnerability that was just created.

These complex creations that we are, are all that stands in the way of us working with, engaging with and streaming with the flows of life and living the dream of dreams where all that we want and need presents effortlessly in our lives delivering the best of the best to us, in known and unknown ways. This is what manifestation truly is. It is complex and also very simple. It is doing the same thing every day without cause for concern of having to get it right or take any specific action. What is the same thing we do every day?

We heal ourselves, with peace and love, with truth, grace and trust, and from this process we come to recognise and rely on the flows of life being the support, the guidance and the backing that engages with us to direct our trajectory into the true desires of our eternal heart.

Action, Change and Manifestation

There is a process that occurs as you manifest or co-create your 'new reality', the process involves shifting, lifting, moving, removing, dissolving and resolving or neutralising that which is currently part of your emanation or your psychology and belief systems, that would be contrary to the creation of your outcome. Part two of this book presents a few differing ways you can use words to co-create your manifestation such as frequency statements, stories and prisms. You can find out more about these techniques by reading part two, but for now, let's look at the action of co-creation and its effects that can be kicked off by using any technique to make change to your life.

The statement, the prism, the intention may seem like a small thing, but it can have huge consequences. And to see the results of this small thing as the grand outcomes of differing, upshifting or uplifting your reality you need to have a small understanding of the processes of co-creation, manifestation and change.

In order for things to change towards (and remain in) the new trajectory, your frequency, your belief systems and programs, all need to be on board with the new reality and reflect the vibration of the new reality in order for the feedback loop of 'reality check' or 'vibration and frequency match' to occur and continue to deliver the 'like to like' match that co-creation and manifestation operates with.

In other words, small actions and statements, frequency statements, prisms, even affirmations (done right!) do not work in isolation. They work with the focus, attention and engagement of you and your self-healing responsibility.

To change your life, to change your trajectory, to upshift your reality, you need to not only take the action of doing the prisms, frequency statements and the like, but also to take the actions, the intuitions, the inner nudges *resulting from* these and act upon them, making the changes that occur to you, because this will be the avenue to bringing your desire to fruition.

Some of this will be uncomfortable. There is no way around this, because you cannot keep doing what you do, believing what you believe and not doing what you are not doing and yet expect a change to occur – *change in action, creates change in circumstances which creates change in reality.*

Sometimes we have to make changes that are very uncomfortable such as walking away from a situation and/or people in our lives. Remember that the changes you make are usually associated with letting go of all impediments, beliefs and programs that you hold to, that are delaying or preventing the reality you desire.

The Clean Sweep

When you start a process, such as working with frequency statements or prisms you can tend to get a little overzealous and believe that 'all things must change – none of my life is working' and so cut yourself off from everyone, break off your relationships and do a sort of clean sweep of your life.

You may feel compelled to take up exercise, shift to all organic food and increase the super supplements, as well as quitting your job, dumping your partner, changing your friends, moving house and so the list goes on – in most cases this of course is an overreaction. It is akin to making a new year's resolution and not being able to maintain it, at some point you will find yourself alone and lonely without any of the support that you would have had had you not done a clean sweep.

There are occasionally times when a clean sweep is required, but this is not common unless you have led yourself (or allowed yourself to be led) down a path of great degeneracy such as extreme drug or alcohol addiction and all the life changes this entails. The problem with a radical clean sweep is that it usually cannot be maintained, and at some point, your old habits, behaviours, associations creep back in. Which opens the door to a personal sense of failure and a feeling that nothing has changed, and it wasn't worth it. Then you continue on in your quiet ways of sadness and destitution of self, critical of self, believing that you fail at everything, that you are not worth or deserving of changing your life, or worse, that it is simply not possible.

There is also the flip side of this where you know that something in your life is the 'reason' that you cannot make the change you desire – maybe you are in an abusive relationship, or maybe you are in a friendship group that is always partying, doing illegal things or criticising you or others and you know it is not part of what you want in your life – and yet you choose to stay there. There is no judgement on that, what is required for self-growth, for upshiftment and for co-creating a new outcome or trajectory for the self, is to see these impediments clearly and to understand the choices of the self to continue them or finish them.

Knowing that you chose 'it' and you chose to continue 'it', even when you have the understanding that 'it' is what is limiting your ability to create the life you desire, is an empowered stance. Even as you stay in 'it', you have the personal clarity that this is a choice, that you are choosing to accept this limitation – 'it' will impede your ability to create life as you desire it, but you have the sovereignty of choice, and you are choosing to stay in that situation.

Within the parameters of what you choose to heal and change, and what you choose to accept and allow, you can make many changes, you can have many shifts, but you may not be able to co-create the outcomes to their greatest potential given the limitations you are choosing to maintain. Again, there is no judgement on this, this is the human free will choice – and, yes, EVERYONE does this! Even those who walk away from a relationship, friendship or job to allow the new into their lives, will still be holding onto habits and internal dramas, traumas and wounds that will in some way limit their outcomes. Sometimes humans feel so defined by their internal dramas, traumas and wounds, or those they cannot forgive, that they simply do not want to let them go or heal them.

All is ok, it is simply important to own who you are and what you are willing to and not willing to change, release or heal in order to claim the life you desire.

All of this is the complexity of the energetically and psychologically entangled human – and we are all energetically and psychologically entangled with something or someone to a greater or lesser degree. Some people are just better at their coping and compensating behaviours. Some are better at moving through the healing process and some are less convoluted having been exposed to less drama, trauma and wounding in their lives, but all humans are entangled with and effected by the dramas, traumas and wounds they have personally experienced or that they have witnessed or been associated with in their community, society and/or country.

The way forward with these things is quietly, quietly, gently, gently. Make the changes as they seem appropriate. Don't resist them, but also don't go severing great swathes of your life. You may find it was your enthusiasm and misunderstanding of what was actually in your way – which is a bullying, blaming and shaming (of others and self) activity – that led you to destroy some very real and beautiful friendships, relationships or resource supplies (like your job!).

All of this is to say; there are influences, beliefs and programs within, psychological attitudes, emotions, feelings, past dramas, traumas and wounds within you that dictate your frequency and emanation. Every human has them.

There will be a lot of internal convolutions to your own system (energetic and psychological) that will disrupt, interfere, mitigate or alter your hoped-for outcome. Some of this will result in delivering something better than expected. Some of it will result in delivering that which is a smaller version of what you hoped for.

That's ok. It's all ok. This is why we assess, adjust and reissue our words, statements, protocols, as we go along. Manifestation and co-creation is a dynamic activity. Both you and life are dynamic. Your thoughts, feelings, actions and non-actions, your beliefs, programs and emanations are subject to change at any time.

Your environment will sometimes bring you back to an old belief, an old fear and you will operate from this for a while. Then you will have an empowered moment and notice that you have been operating in fear, from an old belief, and you will say 'no more!' When you experience a 'no more!' moment, you are emanating the powerful life changing emanation for co-creating the desired outcome of change.

You may feel like you have conquered 'it' whatever 'it' is, but then a week later you are feeling 'it' again. This is so normal. It happens to almost everyone. There are very few humans who have the 'empowered moment' and stay in the energy – the energy is usually too high frequency to maintain. Not that the human can't maintain it, but often the 'empowered moment' is such a drastic deviation from your system's habitual frequency that holding it is anathema to your system. It will gently revert back to its habitual frequency.

This is why this process is gently, gently, quietly, quietly, because gradual osmotic and constant upshifts of your frequency are the upshifts that reliably stick with the system and maintain you at a higher or upshifted frequency of flow.

Quite often when a human does have the empowered moment, the energy they are in is not actually an empowered energy. It is a bullying controlling oppressive energy, oppressing the old self, bullying the self out of the old behaviour and into this conquering energy - that is not a space of love and empowered presence, that is a space of defiance! Maybe that's what you need for a short time whilst you pull yourself up by the bootstraps to understand your true trajectory, to get over the pity party of self and the idea that you are a failure and unable to 'get it right' or 'not deserving of good things'. When we stay in this 'domination of self' energy though we become a bully, we become a tyrant and a victimiser, except we are victimising the self!

This domination of self is, perhaps, sometimes helpful in order to move through a situation or stop a habit, but when we stay in this energy, it is exhausting, and it is damaging to the psychology of self and the emanation of self. You become aligned with the energies and ideas of 'everything takes effort and control', 'nothing is easy' and 'the only way I can make anything happen is fighting (the self)'. This encourages the controlling and bullying of self into the desired behaviour, aligning with the idea that using your energy to create an outcome only comes from force and effort rather than from the natural flow of pulse that gracefully and easily changes your reality.

When you set things in motion and follow the natural flows, you can observe what comes up, what thoughts and/or feelings come up, what seems to need healing, what inspirations occur, or actions need taking and what epiphanous understandings spring to your mind that might need pondering and processing. This is the self-healing process of moving through the dross that is standing in the way of the actualisation of your outcome in reality.

Changing Your Life with Words

Words said with intent have focus and direction. They have power and utilise your own inner power and conscious focus to give instruction to chi, the universe and your mind to change frequency and create the stated change in your life. They rely on you being the apex being of your life and taking charge with making the changes you desire. You are your own lead protagonist in your life, so take charge!

Words spoken or thought contain focus and power – used as part of a protocol as presented in this book in the next section (frequency statements, stories or prisms), they attempt to build momentum, force and feeling in the stating of them.

The crafting and saying of words in formats, such as frequency statements and prisms, is designed to use your words and your presence to pulse out a vibration, a frequency, that has the ability to change your reality. These protocols are said with intention, with presence, with personal empowerment as a command to the universe, to the reality, to the very cells of your own being, an instruction to upshift and change into the vibration of the statement.

What does this do?

It attempts to alter your personal vibration to match the frequency of the statement, of the emission you put into the statement, and in this attempt all that is contrary to the frequency being attempted and all that blocks it or stops it from being your present now frequency, will come to the surface for your attention, neutralisation and/or healing. This offers you the opportunity to move through the dross and mire of convolutions that you hold that are not allowing the statement to come to pass and be the actual reality that you live.

We must remember that the idea here is to bring about the changes that can be brought about, progressively and gently. The aim is to not alter your entire reality at such a rate that your life becomes chaotic, unbalanced and overwhelming as the shifts and changes occur, for if this happens you may begin to feel that it's not working or that it is having the opposite of your intended effect and give up on it.

When you experience the rapid effects of changing all that stands in the way of your desire in quick succession or all at once – it can feel chaotic and tumultuous. If you're up for the ride, then go hard, use the tools herein that bring about great swathes of change - this too is the journey towards your outcome (as dictated by the focus of the tool you choose), it just may be quite the ride! Otherwise, embrace the graceful progressive change by using the graceful loving tools (such as the Golden Shining One or Returning to Pristine Prisms) or altering the frequency statements to suit you and slow things down for the self.

There are a couple of basic issues that you may experience in your attempt to make a change in your life via frequency statements, prisms, or any manifestation action, and they are the roadblocks thrown up when one attempts to change beliefs – which is fundamentally what you are doing when you are attempting to ignite a new frequency state or co-create a manifestation in your life. When we attempt to override, change or in other ways alter the influence of a belief system or program you will find that there are two main pathways of resistance.

The first is that the conscious mind immediately rejects the frequency statement or prism or even the visualization, dream or hope as absurd – that is just patently not true/possible in my life. This is often the first hurdle to overcome – why is it not possible, why do I believe that?

Your mind looks at the outcomes of the past, the present situation and the current beliefs or understandings of the self and projects to you the idea of what's possible for you. It informs you of details about your personality, your abilities, your life, life in general, the people in your life and what's possible and allowable for you given all these factors.

In other words, you have already made decisions about what's possible for you, so when you start to create change in your life using tools like frequency statements or prisms often the first point of resistance is the undoing of these decisions such that the conscious mind's rejection of the content of the statement AND the power of the statement does not impede it's out-picturing in your life.

To counteract this propensity, it is important to start with statements that don't immediately feel absurd to you – ie, as a simple example of this, you may want to increase your wage or abundance level hence start with a frequency statement such as "I always have more than I need" rather than "I easily make $10,000 a week".

This helps prevent the immediate rejection of the idea by the conscious mind, especially if your current income is vastly less than $10,000 a week, giving it more of an opportunity to penetrate to the subconscious and evolve into a natural frequency state for the self.

It is also important to work on the conscious mind to help create a conscious mindset of faith, hope, expectation and belief in miraculous, rapid and radical change so that the conscious mind becomes more accepting of the ideas and possibilities of profound change and big leaps forward.

This change in conscious mindset can be done with any of the holistic frequency statements or using prisms such as 'Returning to Pristine', 'Reality Bubble Buffer' or 'Shining Golden One'. The idea is to train the mind into believing change is possible, encouraging the self to think in a more positive and expansive way.

An easy way to overcome this immediate rejection or questioning by the conscious mind is to start your statements in a credible way, making statements that can be consciously, cognitively and logically seen as possible in one way or another. You will find that this applies most to using Frequency Statements because Prisms are already designed to overcome this natural resistance that occurs during manifesting change.

Over time you can expand on your frequency statement and gradually move toward your ultimate goal – rather than going for the brass ring straight away. As mentioned before, it's perfectly fine to start with a statement that is going to radically change everything in your life but get ready for a rough ride and keep in mind that the conscious mind's resistance to it may impede its initial effect.

The other common impediment to changing a belief system lies in the subconscious conditioning of your own mind. The subconscious does not know the difference between reality and imagination; hence the belief patterns it currently holds are based upon judgments and information you have deduced to be, or accepted as, correct. They will appear to be reality even if reality could be something different to or for you.

As an example, if you have a belief system that you 'can't afford' then you will play out a reality of 'can't afford'. Money opportunities will not come your way. When you have money, you will suddenly have a big unexpected expense. You will not notice the opportunities that are available until too late. You will get sick or exhausted and hence be unable to take advantage of opportunities that exist. You will procrastinate, make excuses and just plain delay in order to create your reality of 'I can't afford' – but it will all feel real. It will all feel like that's actually how it is.

Your job is to continue to see the positive reality you wish to create and keep pushing past, dismissing as incorrect, or healing yourself through, all of the limiters that the Universe throws up around this.

Life is dynamic. Your response to it should be flexible and dynamic to get the most out of the ever shifting, responding, upshifting and changing hologram you live in. It is a usual outcome that when you make the placement for your manifestation through a frequency statement, through upshifting your language, through a prism or in any other way, the hologram, reality or world around you starts to bring you opposition, or perhaps the opposite of what you desire. This is normal and allows you to clarify what it is you actually want – it is a form of increasing your discernment as to exactly what you want, allowing you to reframe your statement, reframe your communication with self and others, and thus put yourself in alignment with and calibration to the actual result you are after.

When you begin to experience the opposite to what you want, or experiences that are non-reflective of your desired outcome, this can also be an exposition to the self of the impediments to the desired outcome that you hold inside. You may just be seeing your belief systems, your programs and your resistances or limitations playing out in front of you.

If this is the case then consider it an offering of the universe, Eternal Source, your Eternal Soul or whomever you believe is the bringer of such opportunities, for you to recognise the limitations or impediments within and heal, neutralise, or dissolve them in order to be able to fully resonate with and align to the frequency of the statement and create your desired state of being or outcome.

You could think of these limiters as a gift from your Soul. It loves you so much it will present to you every block, belief, limiter and misalignment you have that is currently preventing you from achieving your goal. It wants you to achieve your goal to the highest degree possible because to do so feeds the Soul and brings you closer to your own form of the life of your dreams hence it will throw up every lesson possible so you can keep clearing and clearing, bringing yourself closer and closer to your own zero point, the matrix field of creation, the place of no resistance – where all things are possible.

Belief Systems and Frequency Statements

Using any manifestation method focused on statements can result in a feeling of a rush of energy or perhaps shaking or tears the first few times you state it to the self. Then you might feel a doubt around it, and begin to question its holistic coverage - but what about in 'this case'? But what about when 'that happens'? But I haven't addressed 'this idea' or 'that idea' hence it's going to fail and be ineffective.

Those are all valid thoughts, but remember, they are likely the belief systems internally attempting to convince you of the ineffectiveness of what you are doing. If you genuinely believe you haven't covered off all the aspects of the belief system, then add more detail to your frequency statement or prism, but if you have covered it all off then you know that the inner belief systems are encouraging the sense of failure.

It is entirely possible that one of your base belief systems is that of 'I'm a failure' in which case every action you take to change your life into your deepest desires will be stymied by this belief system. What does that mean? Does that mean you'll never be able to do it? Not at all! It simply means that before anything else can be significantly successful, you would do well to face the "I'm a failure" belief system itself with a powerful frequency statement or prism.

Why would the belief system internally kick off and stymie you when it is clear that what you are aiming for is an upshift of being, an upshift of feeling and experiencing? Because the process begun will eventually eradicate the belief system itself – perhaps the belief system is fighting for its own survival? Whilst the belief system exists it holds power over you to keep you in the state that is diverting you from the life you desire.

To use a typical example, if you are aiming for wealth, or a cessation of destitution in some way, the belief system may actually be keeping you in the poverty zone. Why would it keep you in the poverty zone? Because part of your inner workings, part of the make-up of you, is keeping you safe by aligning you with the state that is being dictated by your belief system.

As previously discussed, belief systems are formed to keep you safe in some way, to protect you and align you with the state of being, the experience of life, that is calibrated to the personality, the occurrence or the outcome that is deigned acceptable, safe and reliable for you. In the example above the outcome of the belief system would be to keep you in financial struggle. If you cannot remember where these belief systems come from, or what they are and how they work, we explored these ideas in the sections on the human, the minds and belief systems (Chapters 2 and 3).

Turn the inner resistance felt towards the effectiveness of your action, frequency statement or prism, the doubts about whether its working, the doubts about whether you can do it yourself and all the other ways your mind and worries convince you that it cannot be done or won't work, turn these from a monologue, from an inner castigation of self or an inner domination of self, to a dialogue and begin to question; 'that's interesting that I doubt that, why do I doubt that?

Where does that come from?' This dialogue with self will help you discover the root cause and enable you to begin the healing of it.

If the doubts are simply clarification exercises, illustrating where you haven't been thorough in covering off some aspects in your word protocols, then shore up your statement to cover off any loopholes you become aware of.

If your frequency statement or prism is a masterpiece, then the doubts are likely to be the inner resistances and limitations (belief systems and programs) attempting to keep you stationery and reject the change power of the statement.

Ultimately the negative that surfaces, the doubts, worries, fears and procrastination that surface are all telling you something. They exist. They are showing you that there is inner resistance to your statement, there are belief systems, dramas, traumas, and wounds that detract from this being effective or 'coming true' in your life.

Recognise them, question their validity, and if you can instantly dismiss them – great! If not, then the question about the doubt is, 'why would I believe that' – add to your statement some wording that dissents against or removes consent for the power of the doubt/belief system.

Alternatively, go deeper, and deal with the underlying belief system that prevents you from making changes to the current belief system you are focusing upon. This may mean a temporary change of focus, but this will save you time and energy in the long run by dealing with the underlying impediments to your desired outcome or state of being coming to pass.

In the example above this would be a change of target from the 'poverty' belief system to the 'failure' belief system. This change of target may be temporary and after dealing with the failure belief system you could return to the poverty one – or you might find that the change of target to deal with the failure belief system (which is probably a doozy!) automatically cascades into neutralising the poverty belief system.

As with all of this work, it is a journey of constant checking in with self, monitoring of feelings and truth about your own progress that allows you to identify if you need to do further work or if you have the result you desire.

Mistakes are Part of the Process

This is a pondering and wondering exercise, a philosophical investigation of what some words or statements may trigger in you or others and how to upshift your thinking, speaking, words and expressions.

If you have previously explored or been associated with the concept or use of affirmations and other self-help tools based upon thinking and speaking differently, you may currently hold some rigid ideas around what should and shouldn't be part of a successful affirmation or word manipulation to co-create a different outcome in life.

These very rigidities can bog you down when it comes to creating and using highly successful and personally empowered words, affirmations, frequency statements and the like because they will hold your focus so strongly on whether it has been crafted 'correctly' or 'incorrectly'.

One of the fastest ways to lose friends, become annoying and also to feel like a failure of the self is to get way too hung up on exact phrasing, getting the perfect word to use and correcting the self and others constantly regarding word choice.

You will use the wrong words now and then. Accept it.

You will notice your thinking and speaking are not expressing precisely what you would like to create. That's ok, that's normal and human.

Don't get too hung up on yourself as a failure, simply correct as you go and be kind to the self and others about the nuance and deviations from perfection. What is perfection anyway? Your idea of perfection will grow and change as you do, so don't get too hung up on it.

Take it easy on yourself, you will make mistakes. It's what we do as humans – remember this; humans don't tend to seek improvement of a situation unless they are in pain, unless that situation is lacking in some way. Which means that the mistakes (pain) are the impetus for continuous improvement, the mistakes are the way you stay on the journey and remain dedicated to the upshift, to the healing, to the self-love, self-responsibility and self-sovereignty journey.

You're not supposed to get it right all at once. You're not supposed to make one right move and from then on nothing goes wrong – that's stagnancy, that's not evolution and movement into better and better and better.

Mistakes are part of the process. Mistakes are the human learning process, the human seeking process and the human upshifting process. It's all good. Make mistakes and learn.

Victory and Triumph Journaling

One of your greatest allies in the self-healing journey, in the upshifting and return to self journey, will be your Victory and Triumph Journal.

Get yourself a notebook, perhaps keep it by your bedside so you can make notes in it as the day ends for you (or as it begins). Note all your victories for that day, or from the dream state or from the day before.

Note everything from the teeny tiny (oh I managed to take 5 minutes to myself today and it made me feel . . .) to the huge (wow I stood my ground when someone was trying to dominate me, and I didn't argue with them or raise my voice and it made me feel . . .). Note the actions, protocols or practices you do each day, how they made you feel and the experiences you've had.

This does a few things:

- It brings the victory to your present attention, allowing the mind to see that things are changing, allowing your brain to note that and align with it

- It shows you the results of any protocols or processes you have undertaken and

- It reminds you of your progress.

The brain will forget that you are changing. It will forget how you used to be, unless you remind it.

As you change you become just more of who you are, and it happens osmotically, naturally and gently. There is often no lightning strike that leads you to a massive change whereby one moment you are one way and the next you are another. These types of radical change are easy to remember, but when the changes occur osmotically it becomes such a natural and graceful change that you forget who you used to be, how you used to feel and how you used to react. You start to wonder if anything is changing, if it's even working at all.

Your journey is a return to self, and you will begin to believe that you have always been this way – your conclusion might be that there is a lack of progress, and no change is occurring.

Journaling your victories is a way to create a timeline for the self that shows the progression that you have gone through. Write down your experiences, your victories, small and large, and include all the emotions and sense of magical action or synchronicity that occurred for you, because, again, you will forget these, it is natural to forget them.

You can also write down your dreams because they too will show you the level of, and progression of, your healing, they will give you insight as to what is lifting and shifting, and what is still there and needs attention.

This is not a gratitude journal; this is a victory journal. A gratitude journal is a lovely thing to do, it does draw your mind and focus to the joyful and happy things in your life. It helps to realign your attention to the 'what else', to the joyful and beautiful things in life, but it doesn't specifically address your individual healing journey.

What you really need as you heal is a timeline of your progress. You need to create something that you can reference back to and see that you are changing, you are growing, and you are having magical and mystical transformative experiences.

When you have a moment of doubt, when you have fear that it's all for nought, or it's not working, grab your victory journal and flick through it, see your progress and/or be inspired by what's possible – then begin again working with the self to heal and grow beyond where you've been or where you're stuck.

Words for Power and Creation

Words hold frequency and emanate power, flowing with the potential of creation.

How will you use them?

What will you create?

Look at their origin. The origin of a word.

Mix them up and use them in different ways.

Look at ancient words, words that have left common parlance. Why have they left? What power did they contain?

Words of power.

Words of might.

Words create states of being; hearing them, speaking them, thinking them, planning them.

Play with them.

Your mind thoughts are words – how do mind thoughts become things?

The vibratory frequency of them as mind thoughts creates wave patterns of attraction and repulsion drawing or expelling things in your 3D matrix.

On a deeper level the sound and light emissions created from you, by the DNA vehicle's response to your words, though read, spoken or heard, weaves a fabric in a dimension by emitting the decision of you, about you and what you are, who you are, what you are capable of, where your weak points are and what you deserve and will or will not allow.

WORDS FOR POWER AND CREATION

This gives the unseen all the information and permissions it needs to begin working for or against you, with you or not.

This then helps or hinders the movement of the waves and strands of energy that weave reality in 3D and creates manifest outcomes of what you desire or don't desire.

Done 'the right' way with expansion and opportunity as the aim, they even create new things, things you've never thought of before, that have never existed before, on Earth, in humanity nor in your soul lineage possibilities, but that are better than anything you could imagine.

This is the power of words – especially the words you write and speak for yourself.

Write and speak it into reality.

You are your own mage and sage!

Play with words.

Create with words.

Words create worlds.

Words and worlds

So intense and interrelated the forgotten power of words is time to reignite.

Words for worlds.

Speak it into reality.

Write it into reality.

Using frequency and sound to change your world, the world and humanity.

What will you write today?

What will you speak today?

WORDS FOR POWER AND CREATION

What will you think today?

And how will that change your world?

What information are you giving about you to you?

And who are you giving permission to help, or hinder?

What and who is listening to you?

You are!

Speak of love.

Speak of forgiveness.

Speak of welcome.

Speak of homecoming.

Speak of peace and integration.

Of the self.

To the self.

Becoming one.

Become one.

Become whole.

And rest.

Forevermore complete now.

Whole in the now.

So, what are Word Weavers and Spellcasters?

You are! We all are!

We use our words and thoughts to weave our reality.

We cast our spell over reality by the use of our words and thoughts.

What are you weaving into creation and casting as your spell on your reality?

PART TWO

Words for Co-Creation

Chapter 12

Affirmations and Frequency Statements

Affirmations

Affirmations have been very much a part of the new age and personal change scene for a long time now, but if you don't know what an affirmation is, it is usually a short statement about the emotional state, or life state, that you would like to create for the self. They are usually expressed in the present tense with a positive bent to the statement, such as "I am calm, I am happy, I am peaceful" or "I am abundant beyond measure, I am lucky and happy".

Affirmations are often used as a sort of trite expression of what someone wants to be so in their experience. Most often it is considered that if the affirmation is repeated regularly, the words will somehow magically become true. Affirmations are oft repeated by rote and have little to no impact, mostly because they are not performed with presence, focus and intention, not performed with positive emotion to fuel them into existence and because their power, their process, is misunderstood.

Affirmations generally are seen as lightweight, ineffective or hippy dippy, and those who use them often see them as something to be done by rote using simple repetition in order to align the self with the statement being made.

AFFIRMATIONS AND FREQUENCY STATEMENTS

This way of performing affirmations will rarely have any effect because there is no true power to anything that is said as a simple and ineffectual repetitive wish. Repeating of a statement in the hope that the endless repetition of it will offer up some miracle of change that we need is kind of absurd, right? It also has no self-empowerment to it – it casts you as the leaf on the breeze, ever hopeful that the breeze will blow you in the direction you want to go.

It's possible that the simple and repetitive focus or verbal repetition could change your mindset or experience of life, but it's unlikely. The action does not take into account the rest of your personal reality bubble and/or the rest of the environment you live in, nor the influences that are held there. It also does not account for your soul's choices for you and your life. Which means you're not dealing with the dramas, the traumas, the wounds, the deviations, the belief systems, the programs and all of this accumulation of self that may collectively be steering you away from or in opposition to what you are focusing upon. These aspects needn't be an impediment, but they require your focus to clear, neutralise or heal them, in order to open the pathway for the affirmation to be a present reality for you. When using affirmations, this part of the process is often not actioned.

Affirmations are a way to train the brain into new thought patterns, new neural grooves. They are a way to change the habit of being you and the habitual way that you think, thusly allowing the habitual way that you think to become aligned with the desired state of being, thought or emotion that the affirmation contains. The problem with affirmations is the misunderstanding of the way that they work.

They work using the frequency of the words themselves, the structure of the sentence, yes, but they actually only really gain power when used with intention, focus and emotion. This is when you really pay attention to the state you are in when you say the affirmation and feel its value, its recommendation, its new state of being, within the words as you say them. How many people do you know who say affirmations in this way?

Perhaps you've now come to the conclusion that adding your desire to the affirmation, adding your emotion to the affirmation will fuel it more strongly? Yes, it will! There is, however, a caveat here, and that is that the type of emotion added matters!

It is most common when doing an affirmation, that the type of emotion added is a sort of deep yearning, a sadness, desperation, or even a type of anger or urgency, for what is being stated as true via the affirmation (remember that affirmations are often said in present tense about the self). This type of emotion is not going to fuel anything except a stronger sense of not having it!

Overall, simple repetition and yearning will not bring about the positive change you desire. Fundamentally it just doesn't address the way that change comes about in material reality. Material reality is responsive to you *and* your emotions as a whole!

How Does the Change Come About?

The change from an 'affirmation' done correctly, comes about through several mechanisms, each of these mechanisms is important, and they work wholistically to create the outcome you seek – or the closest facsimile that is possible for you, given your internal landscape.

There are fundamentally three mechanisms that will play a role:

- The frequency and power of the words themselves,

- The changing of the neural pathways to create new habitual ways of thinking, emoting and emanating and

- The drawing to your attention of the habits, beliefs, wounds and thought pattens you hold that impede the manifestation of the affirmation as a truth in your material reality.

So, if you are not paying attention to the resistance you hold to the statement, if you are not paying attention to the movement and reaction in your life that occurs in response to the affirmation, paying

AFFIRMATIONS AND FREQUENCY STATEMENTS

attention to your thoughts, your emotions, your dreams, the experiences in your life as you begin to apply the power of the affirmation to your life, if you are not processing them, understanding them, healing them, then you are missing the fundamental offering from the affirmation. That offering is the suggestion to make the changes and take advantage of the opportunities that will bring about the material transformation in your reality that aligns with the affirmation statement. This is part of the journey of manifesting the affirmation as a material reality for the self to experience.

Taking all of this into account and observing how affirmations are used by those who use them then, you may be able to see that as a repetitive rote saying in an attempt to create change in your life, an affirmation is unlikely to have much of an effect. There is a better way to do this though, and that is by upshifting your affirmation into a frequency statement.

A frequency statement is not simply a statement in the positive of what you wish were true. It is a statement of power expressing what you are creating in your life! And what is power? Some think power is violence, anger, loudness, but we are not talking of that here – that is domination, not power. Power is presence, focus, precision, intention and bringing all of you to that one moment as you make the statement. That is power. Thus, affirmations said with focus, presence, emotion and power become frequency statements and this is where change can occur!

Spiritually and energetically, affirmations are sound frequency statements that can change everything. The frequency can break down various impediments in the human energy grid allowing a higher consciousness to be accessed. They can also reprogramme the subconscious brain and balance out the frozen spots or crystallisations of light in the energy/light body. These frozen spots in energy play out as behavioural issues, emotional issues or experiential issues in the human and their life.

AFFIRMATIONS AND FREQUENCY STATEMENTS

If you consider words as light packets of spells delivered to you about you, or to the world about you and your preferences, you may now view affirmations in a different way, understanding that, said with power, focus, presence and determination they become spells creating new frequencies, new thoughts and new outcomes in your life.

Affirmations are not things to just rote repeat and take lightly, they are spells of frequency and focus. Said from this state of being they are in fact frequency statements that can aid in altering your life via changing the way your automatic thoughts work, reforming belief systems and thought patterns.

Done with presence and focus they have a potency that encourages your emanations to upshift, making you a frequency match for something different and allowing your world to change.

It doesn't just take repeating the same mantra, it takes empowering the words and becoming one with the statement such that you feel the words, feel the meaning of the statements and emotionally connect with the expression of them into your world as a creation spell.

Frequency statements, done correctly, are mini spells.

We have been taught that it is the repetition of the statement of positive outcome that has the power when it comes to our words – and this is not wholly correct. Repetition has an impact, yes, but ultimately it is the retraining of your focus, your thought patterns and your emotions that is intended by the frequency statement that creates the change in your life.

These changes, these retraining activities, usually only occur with any degree of permanent success when we move beyond the rote and trite repetition of an affirmation and into the empowered personal focus and presence of a frequency statement. As with everything, words and actions need to meld to have any degree of meaning and permanency in your life.

AFFIRMATIONS AND FREQUENCY STATEMENTS

Affirmations as Frequency Statements are said with presence and intent, be with it and feel it, then it is like a spell that you are casting, and it comes to pass. Every cell, nerve, muscle and fibre of your being must be powering it. Clear the mind and do it, don't do it whilst thinking of what you will be doing next, don't do it whilst driving or as an addition to another task - do it as ritual with present minded focus.

Giving your frequency statement your attention and present minded focus encourages the universe to bend to your will – the Universe is literal and unconditional, it will do as you ask, you just need to remember that you are usually asking for what you don't want!

Being present with an empowered statement of what you desire to be so, is giving the instructions to the universe with the explicit force of focus and intention. Done right, and it will be so!

You think it, you say it and it is. Abra Cadabra.

This is why Frequency Statements and prisms are often more successful at rapid or even instant change, because they take the time to elicit the emotional state needed to truly imbue the self with the power and resonance of the words you are saying.

Crafting a Frequency Statement

There are many teachings around manifestation and the framing of affirmations or co-creative prayers/statements for manifestation. It seems that manifestation and manifestation techniques, especially for increasing abundance, have been quite the thing over the last 20 or 30 years!

A lot of the teachings will very gravely tell you to use or not use certain words or phrases, so, let's take a look at some of the suggested upshifts in language for manifesting and some of the theories behind them.

Take it to your own internal judgment as to whether the words work for you to create your desired state or not – there are no overlords of

AFFIRMATIONS AND FREQUENCY STATEMENTS

words and grammar that can dictate this to you. You are in charge, and you get to choose. If something isn't working as you would like, then choose again!

Frequency statements needn't be long, but sometimes it is easier to generate the feeling and focus you need to fuel them when they are longer in form. A sentence or two is generally a good length but a paragraph or two might be what you need to feel truly present and engaged with the statement.

They are best said slowly, as the focus of what you are doing there and then, disallowing distraction. This need only take a few minutes but is best given full attention when you are doing it.

Breathe, get present, focus on the frequency statement and repeat it to the self out loud. The ears need to hear it, the body needs to feel it and the mind needs to focus upon it as you say it.

Your mind, especially your subconscious mind can be a bit like a 3 year old with its distraction and disruption, thus keeping your frequency statements and decrees simple and easily understandable will help you believe in your statement (or decree). A decree is a statement of 'this is so', from an empowered point of view with an expectation that it has already come to pass, hence a frequency statement could also be thought of as a personal decree of an expected outcome without any disputing.

You could also use a frequency statement as a type of prayer. Create a simple phrase that is your expected outcome (this would be considered the answer to your prayer). Follow this with a simple expression or statement of thanks, thus making it a Frequency Statement Prayer. Take a look at the example Frequency Statements for illustrations of this type of prayer.

With regard to actually crafting a powerful frequency statement for the self, it might be worth considering the following explorations on words to consider in order to assemble an effective frequency statement for your needs.

Choose and Want

When it comes to manifesting, it is often said about the words 'choose' and 'want', that they imply the 'lack'. You are choosing or wanting because you lack it, hence choice, choose and want all denote a lack.

In manifestation theory the idea of stating or thinking in lack is the attracting of more lack hence the words 'choose', 'choice' and 'want' can seem problematic. This seems quite a resonant concept for the word 'want' because 'want' also has the literal meaning of 'lack' as in, 'she is wanting in social graces', so, 'want' could be a good word to avoid when framing a prayer, affirmation or statement.

'Choose' could be viewed either way, often you 'choose' it because you don't have it, which is a lack concept, but you also 'choose' it over something that you don't choose which is an empowerment concept! The ability to choose is a freedom and empowerment concept, so, it is perhaps best to take a look at your own personal association with the word 'choose' and decide for yourself if it is the right manifestation word for you.

Consider also the concept of the choiceless choice, in our societies, the places where we think we have choice, and hence freedom and power, perhaps we actually do not have choice because the so called 'choice' we are offered is between this or that, not between all potential options.

Ponder your own ideas around choice, is it a freeing word for you? Or is it a choiceless choice and hence constraining you within tight parameters?

Other options that you could use instead of the words 'want' or 'choose' are:

It is time for...

I am ready for...

I declare that...

I embrace. . .

I calibrate to/align with. . .

I allow. . .

I consent to. . .

I dissent from. . .

I experience now. . .

Ownership

Another theory that is helpful in manifesting practices is to understand the personal nature of the manifestation. When you are choosing or announcing readiness for, or stating the time is right for, something, remember that whatever it is, it is yours! Thusly, we want to include words of ownership such as 'my' and 'mine'. For example:

It is time for my *prosperity.*

I allow my *loving relationship to bloom and prosper.*

I consent to my *success and happiness.*

My *life is peace-filled, joy-fuelled, fulfilling and prosperous.*

I experience now my *life of joy, ease, happiness and prosperity beyond* my *mortal mind's comprehension and limitation.*

Specificity

Certain types of specificity are very important to co-create instant, strong and powerful results. When we are not specific, we still get results, but they are vague, have little potency, and may or may not be a 100% match for what you are trying to ignite in your life.

Other types of specificity will actually limit your potential outcomes, bearing in mind that you only know what you know. You can only imagine and visualise coming to pass what it is that you believe is possible for you and/or for the physics, the mechanics and the

AFFIRMATIONS AND FREQUENCY STATEMENTS

structures of the world. If you do not know about an avenue or pathway of manifestation or materialisation existing, then you cannot envisage it as occurring for you. In these instances, being specific in your 'how' of the occurrence, and in your end result and how it looks specifically, is not going to aid in bringing forth the materialisation of your manifestation in the millions and trillions of unexpected ways that it may occur.

The basic principle is to be specific in your statement but not on the actual outcome or process of the outcome coming to pass.

Allow specificity to work for you in terms of the actual focus, emotions and statement and then let go of the specifics of how it turns up and the avenues, mechanics and people involved in its appearance in your life. Just remember that once you set it in motion, it will occur, so be ready for action, be ready for responses from the world around you and be ready to dynamically change and adjust your expectations, actions and statement of manifestation on the fly and as you go. As parts of it unfold, the original statement may become redundant to what exists and what is coming, so be ready to change.

So, how do we be specific and non-specific at the same time? Well, that is the art of it all!

Being specific with your command, request, statement or affirmation is key. So, decide what it is you want to change;

How is it that you would improve your life, and what would that feel like to you? If you had what it is that you desire, how would you feel?

From this place of knowing what it is you want and how it makes you feel, then you can, with specificity, craft your manifesting frequency statement and adjust your personal communication and self-talk to reflect the feeling.

What if I know I want something, but I don't know it with specificity? I know I want abundance, but I don't know specifically how much. I know I want happiness, but I don't know what would bring me

AFFIRMATIONS AND FREQUENCY STATEMENTS

happiness. I don't even know what I want but I know I don't want more of what I already have!

Ok, so, sometimes it is hard to be specific when we don't know what would make us happy or what we really want or need. In these cases, it's perfectly fine to come at this concept of specificity from another angle – we don't need to be specific about the outcome, or the amount or the details, we just need to be confident, assured and specific in the asking or commanding of this outcome.

"I experience my life as the best-of-the-best with beneficial win-win outcomes all round"

This statement on the surface appears non-specific, and yet it allows for all forms of upshifting of your life to occur. A statement such as the one above will help you to refine what it is you do want because it is so overarching, so wholistic, that as things change in your life you will get more specific about what you do want.

For instance, the statement above may bring about a change in (or cause you to focus upon) the occurrences in your life that are not the "best-of-the-best" and this attention will remind you of what you do want. So, your love life is still rocky and yet you are focusing on and using the frequency statement for the "best-of-the-best"? Well then, what are you fighting about, what is it that is rocky in your love life? Looking at this specifically will bring you the area that you would like to change/correct and thusly you can now create a more specific frequency statement to address that area of your life. Alternatively, it will draw your attention to the misalignments in your love life and allow you to delve into the ideas of why you would choose to have a relationship that includes these types of misalignments, and/or how can you heal these misalignments within the self or the relationship?

Specificity is important, but let's reiterate here that specificity about outcome, what it will look like, who will be involved, what will occur and when, will actually limit you from the success that is possible, but that you do not currently see, or the success that is possible but your limited perception disallows you even understanding is possible. Allow for all the ways that are beyond your knowing to be part of the manifesting process and do not specify outcome in terms of whom/what/when, simply specify how it feels to you.

Ultimately, it is worth remembering that the idea is not to get it perfect – it is unlikely that any statement will be perfect for everyone — the idea is to get it calibrated to *your* focus, *your* desire and *your* need, as well as attempting specificity to the extent that you can in creating your outcome.

Present Tense

Often when we craft a frequency statement or manifestation statement, we accidentally use unhelpful negations that could create a stress level or blockage to the free-flowing appearance of the manifestation. Examples of these are when we word our desires using words such as 'stop being' as in 'I just want to stop being so unhappy' – what you really want is to 'be happy', which is a little unspecific in itself, but if you look at the opposite of what you want to 'stop being' you are looking at what you want to 'start being'.

'Stop being' is a very blocking and abrupt expression in and of itself, if you 'stop being' you die, right? So, don't 'stop being'. If you have to, then 'start being' but it is more optimistic and present to 'align with' or 'calibrate with' or 'allow absolute love to override all that is a deviation from'.

Remember that adding in what you are experiencing without negating it is actually asking for more of what you are experiencing, so, "I just want to stop being so unhappy" is basically asking for you to 'stop being' (die) and then announcing the opposite of your outcome 'so unhappy' not 'happy'. Do you want to die 'so unhappy'? Or do you want to align with, immerse in, experience and emanate happiness?

It gets a little pedantic and can be a bit of minefield to get 'totally correct' – though as mentioned previously, totally correct should not be the aim. It is of course almost impossible to get it totally correct but it is worth considering that it's a good idea to use present tense, specificity, and positively oriented words.

If you don't know what you want to experience, if you don't know what would make you happy, or you don't know what it is you want to align with, then look at what you don't want, flip it to its opposite and craft your wording, your statement or your manifestation oriented towards that. The table below lists some ideas for flipping an emotion into its opposite status.

Negative State	**Potential Opposite State**
Unhappy, Sad	Happy, Joyful, Content
Depressed	Joyful, Hopeful, Excited
Helpless, Weak	Capable, Powerful, Strong
Hopeless	Happy, Optimistic, Joy-Filled, Hopeful
Discontent, Angry	Content, Happy, Peaceful, Satisfied, Replete, Fulfilled
Poor, Destitute, Struggling	Prosperous, Profitable, Ease-Filled, Affluent

Examples of present tense frequency statements are as follows:

"I experience, feel and revel in happiness in all its forms, expressing and experiencing my life in joy filled happiness and ease".

"I allow absolute love to bubble up and overflow, overriding all that is a deviation from my joy filled ease fuelled fulfilling and happy life".

"I am peaceful, satisfied and replete easily releasing all inner urges to turn from that which would continue this in my life. I do not consent to the inner turmoil that encourages my focus away from peace, kindness, happiness and successful fulfilling experiences in my life. I easily see the healing solutions needed to calm myself and hold myself in presence and joy-filled ease-fuelled peace."

Aligning with the Emotion

After all that analysis of how it can go so awry when crafting a frequency statement, you're probably terrified of getting it wrong and accidentally manifesting what you don't want – right? It's understandable!

Maybe let's flip this now and make it easy; all you really need to do is craft your statement or upshift your language to more optimistic, positive and present statements of what you want more of in your life. If you don't know with specificity what that is, you at least do know with specificity what it would feel like! So, you can use very simple statements such as;

"I experience more happiness and joy filled occurrences that ignite the sense of love, connection and peace within me".

"I am a happy, peaceful and fulfilled person and I create more of the peaceful, joy filled moments in my life everyday".

"My life is an easy experience of beneficial outcomes, I am lucky and always supported, buffeted and cushioned from the vagaries of life. I am aligned with and experiencing the best of the best in outcomes every day in every way."

Personalising a Frequency Statements

A frequency statement is usually a present state verbal expression of a desired outcome or state of being, it is more powerful if it is:

- explicit consent for something,
- dissent against something,
- removing of consent for something, or
- an invocation of a desirable something.

Now they all sound like very highfalutin words, but essentially all you need to say is a statement that directly deals with the belief system or resistance you are targeting. So, for example:

Let's say you've identified a belief system that basically says:

"I believe I don't deserve to be abundant because of the religious program within me. The meek shall inherit the earth. The poor are the ones who are not corrupted, the rich are corrupted".

Taking that belief system and its statements about you, you can flip it around and that gives you an idea such as:

"I believe I can be wealthy because there are some really awful poor people as well, right? So, poor can still be corrupted. It's not humble and pure, just to be poor. I can be humble and pure whilst being wealthy, or at the very least provided for."

This shows you your argument to the self against the belief system that is holding you back. From here you would instil and your argument against the belief system with a frequency statement that does not consent to honour the lie inherent in your original belief system of 'the meek shall inherit the earth' and 'the nobility and purity of poverty'.

AFFIRMATIONS AND FREQUENCY STATEMENTS

This might look something like this:

"I do not consent to honour the lie that poverty is the only noble state. I claim the nobility in wealth or prosperity. I invoke the purity of wealth for myself and ignite within my divine right, my birthright as a human here now in 3D, of affluence and prosperity of self on all levels including financial. I allow myself to feel it, know it, emanate it and experience it now. I am a wealthy prosperous one of humility, kindness, joy and ease."

This process thusly creates a personalised frequency statement for the self that you can use regularly and addresses the issues that most stymie your success and happiness.

Chapter 13

Practical Frequency Statements

Experiencing More

"I exist and it is time for a new experience, I choose to experience more of..."

"I release, let go, heal, dissolve and resolve all that I have adhered to, held to, operated from that defines me as wasteful with time, money or resources, or debt-ridden, destitute or perpetually break even in money, time or resources. I am a wealthy individual. I am prosperous on every level of self, and I allow myself to see, understand, heal and transform all that which holds me in any state that is other than peace, joy, affluence, prosperity and the empowered state of personal presence in love and compassion for self and others."

"I exist, I am here, and I am ready for more. It is time for me to experience more affluence, more abundance, more prosperity of self and benevolent outcomes. It is time for this to start now, accelerating and expanding into my future. It is time I experience profit and prosperity through ease. I am more of that experience, more of the experience of profit, prosperity, happiness, joy, success, fulfilment, through easy and joyful activities, doing the things I love."

PRACTICAL FREQUENCY STATEMENTS

"I exist. I am here. I experience more of the happiness, prosperity, joy, ease and peace of life now. I experience more of the totality of me, the success, delight and prosperous joy and abundance of living my ideal life now. I am this now, it is so.

Everything to the contrary, everything that belies this, is not me and has no part in my life now. I release it now and attach to it no more. I revoke all the contracts involved and dissolve, resolve, neutralise or heal as appropriate all the beliefs, permissions and programmes perpetuating all that is not aligned with benevolent outcomes and the best-of-the-best for me now. I affirm clearly now that you no longer have any power over me.

I am free, I am prosperous, I am financially profitable, autonomous and living my grandest, happiest, preferred and most fulfilling life now. All is well and getting better every moment. And so, it is. Thank you."

"I easily attract income not attached to my physical output. Time and money are not interconnected for me - it is easy for me to make money without exhausting myself or depleting all my time. I do not consent to the linking of my time and the creation of money, nor the linking of my energy levels and the creation of money.

I am abundantly supplied with ideas and energy for the co-creation of my prosperous life. I have plenty of time for my desires and chosen actions whilst being abundantly supplied into a state of financial independence. It is obvious to me what actions to take and where to put my focus in order to create an ongoing supply and resource inflow whilst maintaining my experience of freedom and sovereignty.

I am blessed with all that I need to create this in my life now."

PRACTICAL FREQUENCY STATEMENTS

Creating Peaceful Ease

"I release all attachment to (and any beliefs, programmes or permissions that perpetuate) the idea that the creation process is long, arduous, fraught with wrong turns and pitiful outcomes, that I am incapable of co-creating the changes and upshifts I desire to transform my life into a flowing graceful and joyous experience of the best of the best."

"I, in this moment of now, as the apex being, dissolve, resolve, neutralise and heal, as appropriate, all that keeps me in a rinse repeat rerun process of poor, upsetting or disappointing outcomes and experiences in life.

I step forward now as the sovereign one, the apex being of this incarnation, and in my sovereign power, which is my birthright, I affirm that all is well, and getting better!

I affirm that I am the co-creator of my life and I am here to experience the best of the best in every way every day. I see this, note this, experience this and affirm this now."

"My life is a sequence of joyful present moments recognised by me as the most helpful and healing in every moment. I pay attention to me and my thoughts feelings and emotions.

I breathe deeply to go within and recreate anything that is not currently expressing in my out-pictured reality as the ease, joy, peace and affluence that I prefer.

My out breath creates anew in each moment the peace and ease I prefer. I see it, acknowledge it and share my gratitude for and with it in every moment. Thank you thank you thank you."

PRACTICAL FREQUENCY STATEMENTS

"Everywhere I have ever attached to or believed, lived out or pretended that I am the poor one, that I am the small one, that I am the unsuccessful one, that I am the struggling one, that I am the one to be pitied and taken care of by the family or others, that I am the one that doesn't do well, that I am the one that doesn't shine brightly or stand out, that I am the odd one, the strange one, the one that lives in a delusion, the sad one, the bereft one, I allow myself to release all of these limiting beliefs now.

I adhere to and ignite from within the understanding of who I truly am and what is truly possible for me. I allow the glory of me to rise and fuel me and fill me bringing with it the true alignment with my potential and possibilities."

"I consciously choose to detach from, no longer held by, influenced by, connected to or fed by all the memes, miasms and collective unconscious grids that don't serve my choice for and desire for; awakenment, empowerment, affluence, ease and true eternal love. I experience more joy, happiness, fulfillment and ease every day in every way."

"All things are possible for me. It is very easy. I am at peace, blessed with grace and grateful for all that is. I follow my passion, and life unfolds with effortless ease and joy! I know, understand and follow my guidance and direction. The Universe always provides abundantly, and my life improves in big and small ways every single day."

"I allow myself to be blessed at all times. I return myself to me, to my present state of innocence and heartfelt loving of me and life. I recognise myself as a true one, a loved one, and even when I have not felt loved, have felt neglected by or disconnect from love, I see now that I did that, that I chose to harbour the thoughts of unlovingness and made them right about me. I chose to return to the situations and people that were unloving towards me, punishing myself with their company again and again. I am worth more. I see that now.

I am a cherished one, a loved one of the universe and myself. I am deeply and profoundly loved, and I allow the love to glimmer and shimmer in each of my cells growing brighter and brighter every day. Fuelling me and filling me with the profound exploration of and emanation of eternal love that I am.

Every day I acknowledge the love within growing stronger and showing me a better way. I allow the love to be my fuel, and my discernment, leading me to the places and spaces, the people and experiences, that fuel more love and peace. My life becomes an experience of love, loving and being loved, by all things. I am a Lover of Love living a life of Love."

"I am light. I release all imprints and implants that are not mine or that do not align with or actively impede my desire, my choice and my experience of a life of ease, peace, prosperity and happiness. I release all beliefs that are not of my original concept, those that have been given to me and accepted by me from others in my tribe, family, country, world, government, military, church, schooling.

I release all psychic connection I have held with the church, politics, military in any direction of time or space and any reality I have every existed.

I allow myself to be free from negative aspects of the conditioning of society. I deny the fear and worry that has been imbued into me or triggered from me that which keeps me small and stationary in my life. I do not consent to fostering it nor honouring it any more any further.

I am free, I am light, and I am a sovereign one supported by and guided by my eternal soul and eternal source to be a loved one of prosperous ease here now."

PRACTICAL FREQUENCY STATEMENTS

"I release all vows of poverty, pain and suffering for God, for family, for country or for karma. I do not consent to honouring these old conditioning patterns, I am a free, loved and prosperous one and it is time for me to experience my life as a glorious journey of ease and fulfillment on every level. I am here.

I release all decisions, vows or agreements to work through or pay for karmic debts not of my own instigating nor directly related to my actions in this life. I am free. I am lucky and blessed. I appreciate all that I am and all that I experience. Thank you."

"Everything in my life is unfolding in beautiful perfect expected and unexpected ways.

I am divinely guided into the best of the best with swift and easy resolutions into win-win scenarios, even when I can see no way out.

Everything just gets better and better from here as I create my life in the direction of my highest and best outcomes, igniting my light from within and healing into the expression of peace and love that I came to experience.

I direct the dissolution of all bonds, cords and attachments that hold me in any experience that is unfavourable, unpleasant or elongated in its inconvenient intensity drawing me away from my desire for peace, ease, prosperity and joy.

I am freedom, love, abundance and fulfilment.

And so it is. Thank you."

PRACTICAL FREQUENCY STATEMENTS

Realigning With Eternal Mission

"I choose and align with my original uncorrupted unpolluted mission contracts for this lifetime."

"What did I do that allowed this lifetime to be the most transformative, the most enlightening? I choose to overcome my brain's limitation in knowing this or remembering this.

What did I do in this lifetime that transformed it, that allowed us to be more of who we are at an eternal level, enabling this to be the most upshifting, uplifting and transformative lifetime propelling my eternal soul into the next evolution of me? I allow myself to know this now."

"I choose to honour and align with my mission, the mission of my eternal soul and my eternal family for this incarnation, the original unpolluted and uncorrupted contracts for this lifetime that are aligned with do-not-harm and honouring the evolution of my soul into the lighted one I am.

I choose and align with embracing allowing and flowing with the eternal contracts that this incarnation is designed to further and master.

What did I do in this lifetime now that honours, embraces and furthers my mission, our mission and the mission of light that my eternal soul acknowledges, embraces, honours and chooses? It is time to remember and enact that now."

Holistic

"The voice of my true heart speaks clearly.

I am no longer limited by controlling it all and having to know how it happens or what happens.

I am no longer limited by the how, why, where and when.

All things are possible, and I see evidence of positive change every single day.

Thank you thank you thank you."

"Reality conspires to bring me all that I desire, faster than I can imagine.

Relax, it's super easy. I am magnetic to good, and my presence, love and joy is all it takes.

I am joyfully blessed, and my life is a series of benevolent blessings.

I see that now.

Thank you."

Chapter 14

Story and Stories

Your Personal Story

Humans have fantastic brains; they can easily convolute their experiences and attribute meaning and motive to them whether that meaning and motive was there to begin with – and even whether or not that meaning or motive is important, helpful or necessary. Each person knows their own meaning and motive, their own story, inside out and back to front. You may not think of it as your story, you simply think of it as you – this is who I am, and this is why I am the way I am.

On the surface, this understanding of self appears so relevant to who you are and why things are as they are in your life. It seems so important and relevant to express to others why you are who you are in one way or another. It seems so important to share yourself in this way so that others understand you, or so that you can get what you want/need or so that others know that you understand them.

All of these motivations are very human, and seem necessary to form connection, and to share understanding. We tell our stories to ourselves and others all the time, advertently and inadvertently solidifying them within us, as us, and reinforcing the emanation of us as the story we have told, shared and repeated about us.

The more you tell your story, the more you recreate it as a reality in your life. The more you tell your story, focus upon your story, act from, think from and engage from your story, the more that story creates your life and dictates the experiences, occurrences, thoughts and emotions of your life.

Consider for yourself what your story might be. You may have a long history of certain types of experiences, you may have experienced things in childhood that were tragic and painful, you may have been bullied or beaten, and this is now your story.

I cannot love because I do not trust.

I do not hug because my mother never hugged me.

I am lonely and bereft, but I cannot open up to anyone because being vulnerable leads to humiliation.

I was bullied as a child, so now I try not to stand out.

I'm sensitive and fragile, no one understands me, so I'm quiet and accommodating to others.

I keep myself small and insignificant so as not to draw the abusive attention from others.

The above are just a tiny example of the types of stories and conclusions about us that we adhere to and continue to tell and recreate in our lives. The stories are not necessarily wrong, they are perhaps telling of experiences that really did happen and have shaped you in some way. They may even be creating a safety of self that has been sorely needed, yet they can also inhibit our success and limit us, and we don't even know that it's us that is the inhibition.

Conclusions about the self, such as the above, often come from the experiences of the self in childhood but sometimes they can form later in life through a traumatic or disruptive experience.

These experiences then lead to the decisions of the self about the self that become the thoughts, habit patterns, love patterns, and personality expressions of self all culminating in the story of you.

Ultimately your story about the self to the self or others is that which emanates from you and dictates your actions, your relationships, your choices and your experiences in life. Your story about yourself creates your life. Do you like your life? Is it fulfilling, peaceful, loving and successful? No? Then begin telling a different story.

When you start telling the story of you from the past, it's a way of expressing who you are to other people. It's a way of giving people history and context. It's really normal. We seek understanding from another and so we tell our story to the other. Because we all tell our story so much, we're addicted to the idea of helping other people understand why what happened happened and why we are who we are or do/did what we do/did. It seems to be some way of explaining ourselves and excusing our behaviours or seeking understanding from the other, seeking to understand from the other if they 'get you' if they are a kindred spirit. For all of these reasons and many more we continue to tell our story to others. For who are we without our story? Ultimately, we are free without our story! But that is a difficult state for the human to rest in. We desire the knowingness of self, and that knowingness comes with a history, a context and a story.

All of this is the game we're playing, the game of engagement, friendship, relationship, happiness, success, and the seeking of the same. You can get the most out of the game by aligning with ease, peace, love, joy and choices that make you feel lighter and brighter and more uplifted and upshifted.

You can get the most out of the game by rising above and choosing higher, telling the story of your triumph wherever possible. The alternative is to just repeat the same tale of woe about how your history, your context means you cannot do this or have that. In doing so, you're just hurting yourself constantly by retelling your tragic story and thusly recreating it in your life daily and experiencing it again and again.

Ask yourself about your story in order to figure out which parts of your story are actually holding you back:

What is my story?

What is it that I always tell people about myself? Why?

STORY AND STORIES

What is it that I always tell myself about myself? Why?

What is it that I use as an explanation for any failure or inaction on my part that is really just an excuse based upon a story about myself that I have aligned to and perpetuated?

Where am I recreating my own personal pain and not taking mastery of my life by the re-telling of the same story of me over and over?

It's time to tell a new story - begin telling the story of your triumph and victory.

Do you find that some challenges in your life have been there a long time? That they just keep resurfacing in different ways? Maybe you can never get ahead financially? Maybe you end up in one relationship after another with cheaters or liars, egotists or narcissists? If a challenge has been with you for a long time, if a repeat pattern has been with you for a long time, it is part of what has not only formed you but re-forms you each time you stay in that story.

It may be that you have something that needs healing, it may be that a story you tell about the self needs to be adjusted, healed or let go. An ongoing challenge, a repetitive challenge in your life is telling you that a part of your true self is suppressed or has been hidden within, overlayed perhaps with a drama, trauma or wounding that is currently unhealed. Isn't it time to face it, heal it and move on from it?

Your life is about you. Your life is about your soul's evolution and rising up to be the most joyful being you can be in the human body. Not joyful in a defiant way, bombastically laughing in the face of tragedy, but truly, peacefully and easily running the flows of joy within, feeling the calm and ease of true mastery of self and life. This only comes from truth with self and healing that which impedes the peaceful joy flows of a healed heart, such as grasping onto your story.

Perhaps you have become addicted to your story, your suffering and being the victim? Perhaps you are feeding the 'poor-pitiful-me' agenda to get the attention and love you think can only come if you are broken?

Then maybe it is time to deal with the aspects of self that do not believe you are worthy of love as your healed self. Perhaps it is time to address your inner trauma and that which formed you, the experiences of your childhood. Perhaps it is time to clear the traumas, dramas and wounds, the inner insistence upon victimhood, or domination, that you have become so adept at expressing as self in one way or another.

Claim your insight, your self-responsibility. Claim your mastery of your emotions, your mind and your life. It takes tenacity and discipline to start forming the habits of the new being that you wish to become as an embodied experience on Earth, but it is really the only thing of worth doing here.

As you heal the self of the story, as you become the innocence and love that you truly are, you will notice your world 'magically' transforming into a place of love, peace, ease and success beyond your ability to ken when you are wrapped up in your personal story of woe.

Tragic Back Story

We are a community obsessed with back story, we are obsessed with profiles, histories, artifice and making our story sound compelling and interesting, but is it the truth of who you are? Because the story you are telling is what you are creating and recreating over and over again!

What story are you telling, that is actually a limitation? What story are you telling, that is actually some type of excuse to limit your success? Your ability to succeed? Or are you using it to elicit sympathy, or gain attention from others? What exactly is your tragic backstory? And how are you using it to control the opinions and engagements of others, and the self and life itself? How are you using it to keep yourself from being your own victorious hero in your own life?

The tragic back story gives a human uniqueness whilst also being a reason for attention and sympathy – perhaps even opportunity!

We as a society appear to be going through an era of valorising the victim, of pedestaling the tragedy and focusing on tragic back stories. We seem to be exclaiming the victim as worthy of sympathy, love, opportunity and attention simply because they are a victim, and yet, they are surely of value for other reasons.

This valorising the victim could be because we are going through a type of regaining of balance between victim and victimiser, calling out the victimisations occurring in our society by pedestaling the victim. It could also be related to other aspects of society becoming so important such as the hyper focus upon back stories and biographies in order to prove expertise or relevancy for many reasons ranging from getting a date through to getting a TED talk. This results in a focus upon what makes you interesting, sensational or an expert and worth listening to. These back stories are told over and over again to validate the expertise of the individual and may come to define one within a very limiting concept of who you are.

Let me be clear here with regard to valorising the victim, there is no suggestion that the victim does not deserve or need help. There is no suggestion that the circumstances of the victim are not potentially truly reprehensible, and that the victimiser did anything that wasn't abominable. It is simply that the act of valorising the victim and the glorifying of the tragic back story and circumstances of the victim deny the victim the opportunity to be courageous and rise above and beyond what the external or the other may have inflicted upon them. This denial of opportunity for the victim to become self-accountable and embrace mastery of their own lives and choices leads to a loss of purpose, potentially igniting the apathetic behaviour of blaming and shaming others for their circumstances or lack of success. Offer help, offer support and option but glorifying the victim and encouraging the victim to constantly focus on their tragic circumstances and inciting them to rage and fight against the supposed perpetrator of the circumstance is different to inspiring them to take accountability and use the opportunity to rise above.

Offering the victim the opportunities to do more, be more, be safe and have more is a laudable and wonderful community oriented caring and sharing thing to do. We should all help our fellow man and support each other into win-win scenarios. But the glorification of the tragedy and tragic back story, the valorising of the victim actually only holds that being in the victim status.

Pointing out the circumstances to the victim and expressing to them that they should be blaming others, blaming circumstance for their lack of happiness, lack of friends, relationships or success takes away their self-responsibility and accountability. This external locus of blame is a form of avoiding doing the self-healing work that could help you find the success, joy, love that you seek.

How many times have you told someone that they ruined your day because they did one thing or another? Did they ruin your day? Or did they do something annoying frustrating or even reprehensible, and yet you took on the emotions of that and stayed in that emotion thusly ruining your own day.

What story about you and your tragedies in the past do you dwell upon, blame for your behaviours or circumstances and share with others repetitively? This is your very own tragic back story. How different would your life be if you told yourself a different story? How could you change your life if you spelled it differently by changing the story you tell?

There is no suggestion that your story isn't true, maybe it is, and maybe it is more dramatic and tragic than most, but what is being said here is that the continuing of the tragic back story as the driver of your life and choices, as the causes of your situation and your inability to change the situation, could be the reason you have not achieved all that you want to achieve and become that whom you desire to become.

We all tell our stories in so many different ways – is your story filled with woe and hardship? Outrage and unfairness? Things that happened and happen to you that make your life the picture of destitution and

STORY AND STORIES

difficulty? That make it so less likely that you can succeed and prosper? So why even try? Are you seeking explanations and research out there to explain why you cannot or do not succeed, without then using this to teach the self the truth, heal the self of limitation and change your outlook, your mindset and your actions and behaviours in life to bring about a different outcome?

Why spend all your time explaining and justifying to self and others why exactly you can't or won't succeed? Why exactly you fail and/or won't even try? It's not worth it, feel sorry for me and understand that what makes me unique and special is my tragic back story. I've had it so hard, and by telling myself this I excuse myself from trying for success, and by telling others this I get them onboard with sympathy for me and not expecting anything from me.

They are all perhaps true stories, they are perhaps things and experiences that did happen, and perhaps you were greatly victimised and perhaps it was unfair or uncalled for, but in the end, it happened and now it is not happening. It is simply the story you tell the world and self about who you are.

It is your story of failure, of why your situation has been so unfair and why you cannot expect to succeed. Why 'they' should just stop expecting it of you, or why 'they' should feel sorry for you and give you a break, ease up and let you get away with something or perhaps get away with doing less than others to get the same opportunities.

The stories we tell about ourselves, about our tragic circumstances and how unfair it all is, are all put in place by us to keep the status quo and often also to excuse the self from even trying. They are related to the blaming and shaming abuse games we play. There is no suggestion that at one point these stories were not true, there is no suggestion that the stories are not dire, and the circumstances were not tragic or unfair or that the actions were not outrageous and abominable. Not at all, but it is also true that the more you stay stuck in the story the more you continue to create the destitution of self as created by that story - in its original expression and in its many and myriad retelling experiences that you have ignited, installed, fed and nurtured throughout your life with every retelling to the self and to others of your very own tragic back story. The more you create and recreate those very same experiences or echoes of their damage and limitations on a repeat loop in your life.

Isn't it time to change the tune? Isn't it time to spell a new story of the self to the self and to others? Isn't it time to create and recreate your life anew as an experience of happier pulsing dancing and exciting energy of creation?

Creation of a Hero

It's ok, everyone has a form of tragic backstory. Our world teaches us that the tragic back story is heroic, but the creation of a hero, whilst needing a tragic backstory, also needs that tragic backstory to be overcome, moved through and recovered from on some level in order to rise as the hero in the third act of your own life.

There is nothing heroic about staying in the tragic back story and repeating and reverberating it throughout every atom, angle and direction of your life, perpetually keeping you stuck in the limitation of that tragedy.

It is time to rise from the ashes of your tragic backstory to overcome your impediment, your very real and very painful impediment. You seem to be stuck in the mire of your own tragic history. How could your life change if you could change your adherence to your own tragedy? How much of your identity do you attach to your tragic back story?

Is it possible to be seen as a success and get attention and accolades for that success rather than excuse the self (oh, I can't because. . .) and attempt to elicit sympathy, attention, understanding (or whatever the ultimate aim of your personal tragic back story is) from others in order to keep the status quo of repeating the same tragic backstory circumstances in your life?

Often, we don't even realise we are stuck in our own backstory. We don't even notice that we are using it to excuse ourselves from changing our lives and becoming better or to elicit some type of sympathy or attention from others.

If you change your story how would your life change?

If you stopped focusing on how hard it has been, how would you feel?

Would you feel that people might not see you the same way?

Would that matter? Why?

Would they expect more of you?

Are you afraid of not being enough? Of failing?

Are you afraid of being unimportant?

Are you invisible without your tragedy?

Are you staying in your tragedy to keep from attracting attention?

Does it keep you small enough to feel safe whilst also delivering the limitation that prevents the happiness and joy you truly seek?

Does it allow you to act in ways that are hurtful or dominating to others or the self, whilst also excusing the self because your tragic backstory damaged you so much you can't trust others or life or even be kind, vulnerable and generous to others?

Staying in the tragic backstory means you never become the hero in and of your own life! It can mean you never have true and loving connection or fulfilment in life. Recognising your tragic back story, the story you tell yourself and others about yourself and your life, and growing from it, healing through it and growing beyond it, is how you become the hero of your own life. It is how you embrace and walk the hero's path, enacting the superior action of the upward trajectory of eternal soul's incarnational success, fulfilment, joy and prosperity of self on all levels.

How can your wings lift you high if you allow your feet to remain in the mud and suction of the old stories of you? Time to spell a new story of the self and to the self and embrace being the risen one, overcoming the tragic back story to fly high above the petty vicissitudes of the life lived from being stuck in the muck, mud and mire of your old story!

What story of self could you create and recreate as a joy-filled ease-fuelled expression and experience of life if you were willing to change your current story and re-spell your life into ease and joy, into comfort and success, into happiness and fulfilment?

Your Hero's Journey

We all live in a story of our own creation. Sure, there are other players in our story, those who may affect certain outcomes in our lives or are affected by our actions and outcomes, but it's actually your story. We may even feel that we are subject to the other players in terms of them getting to dictate the outcomes of our story, yet it still your story. Your life is your story. Others may be bit players in your story in the same way as you are in theirs, but your life is *your* story, not theirs.

You could be the hero, the victim, the villain or even a bit player in your own story. When you are not being the hero of your own story, you are designating yourself to being a support character and allowing another, or several others, to be the creator or even the dictator of the story that you are living.

What story of yourself, about yourself, are you telling the self and others over and over again?

What is your story? What is your role in your story?

What is it that you repeat to the self and/or others as an explanation for who you are and what you can expect from life?

Oh, I was raised a catholic, and so I cannot do this or that.

Oh, my father committed suicide and so I am this or that.

Oh, my childhood was terrible, I was unloved, I was traumatised, I was neglected, I was bullied and so I am this way or that way.

I didn't have the opportunities that you had, and so I am destined to fail.

Whatever the story you tell, over and over again, it is the story of you. In many circumstances the stories we tell are actually truth at some point in our lives and then they just become the story of who we are, and what we want other people to know about us. We tell the story over and over, recreating ourselves over and over, as the person in the story we tell about ourselves.

Being the hero in your life begins with how you speak your stories. Are you telling the tales of your victories? Or are you telling the tales of your tragedies? Are you focusing on the things you have overcome? Or are you focusing on the difficulties in your life? One is a hero's story, the other is a victim's. We speak from our own flows, our own history, our own wounds and traumas and how far we have healed from them or whether we are still stuck in the muck and mire of them.

You are either the hero of your life or you are not. The hero's journey is one of self-responsibility and overcoming odds and/or oppression. It is the journey to fulfilment of desire, the journey towards becoming more than you were and better than you have been.

When it comes to your individual life, the aim of being the hero in your life, the hero's path for the 'regular Joe (or Josephine!)' is the path of presence, of empowered choice, of leaving victim or victimiser status behind and claiming personal sovereignty in kindness, compassion and absolute love. It is the journey of self-healing, of self-evolution and self-accountability. It is the journey to becoming the greatness, the kindness, the compassion and caring that you seek in others or out there. Don't wait for it to arrive, know it is within you already and claim it, live it, be it and respect the self enough to allow nothing else.

In kindness and compassion, with courteousness and respect for self and others, allow only that which aligns with your personal hero journey.

Remember who you are and be the hero of your own journey. Self-accountable, self-responsible, respectful and courteous to all – including self. If you consider yourself reliable, if you consider yourself a person of your word – then why are you letting the self down with disrespect of your own word to the self? How many times do you say 'I won't do that again' or pledge that you will eat better, be better, do better, and then forget and go back to old habits? Does a hero let people down? Being the hero means respecting your word to yourself as well as others. You may still forget, you may change your mind, or you may go back to old habits, it's ok, but the hero would recognise this and gently encourage the self back onto the path of self-respect, self-accountability, self-care, self-responsibility and personal sovereignty.

Shifting from the Story

How do I move on from my story? How do I stop telling it as my recreation of self?

The first step is to consciously monitor your thoughts and words, to self and others, and to stop or correct yourself each time you notice yourself telling it to the self or others, using it as an excuse to the self or others and even just revelling in it, falling into it or feeling sad, hopeless, dejected or rejected by it.

It happened, whatever 'it' is, there is no denial of that, it happened.

The truth is 'it' probably didn't happen exactly how you remember it, not because you are wrong but because the human brain doesn't always see things objectively. The human usually sees and remembers things much more subjectively. What this means is that even if two people see and experience the same thing, they will both come away with having experienced it differently in terms of what parts affected them the most, how it affected them, what emotions imprinted upon them about it and how its ongoing effect occurs/ed in their lives.

So, the experiences of this story you tell will be different to all the other players in the same story. Your siblings will remember it differently. Your parents will remember it differently. Your school friends, teachers, colleagues etc will all remember it differently. Some of them may even be surprised that it has affected you so much, they may express emotions such as 'but it meant nothing', or 'it wasn't that bad, why does it bother you so much' etc denigrating your emotional experience and ongoing effect from the story that means so much to you.

It doesn't matter what they thought it meant or how it affected them. It doesn't even matter if they firmly believe you are being too sensitive or that 'it shouldn't affect you anymore' – your fact is that it does, and that's ok. It's ok that it affected you, its ok that it is not understandable by others that it affected you so much. That's ok.

There is nothing to fight here. It happened. It affected you. It is subjectively true for you in that you had the experience, and your mind has continued to feed that experience to you as the foundation of your anger, your hurt, your sadness, your difficulty in having the successful life that you desire. It's ok. Don't fight it by denying its effect. It happened and the effect is real.

Some may argue that objectively what you are affected by is not true, but feelings and trauma are not objective, so even if the effect is not the same for everyone involved in the issue/incident, the effect and outcome is still subjectively true for you and has had real consequences for you and in your life. That's ok.

The only issue here is that this story, this experience, this demarcation line between pre "the story" when you were able to succeed and post "the story" when you are not able to succeed, is the thing keeping you from inhabiting yourself as the successful one, as the joyful one, as the peaceful one. So why are you continuing to feed that story? What are you getting out of it? Why are you not moving on from it or nullifying its effect? The answers to these questions will tell you how much you value your story or whether you are ready to heal it and grow from it.

When you are first starting to 'shift from the story' you will find that you notice it all the time. Your habitual ways of thinking, speaking and acting will all be informed by this story that you keep repeating to the self, and the world, about the self and the world. This is normal. This is where your self-parenting is very important. There is no castigation of the self. There is simply partnering with and nurturing of the self.

Each time you notice the words, thoughts, actions, behaviours that are informed by the story, stop yourself and gently encourage yourself to say it differently, to act differently, to think differently. No abuse of the self, no castigation, just gently lovingly and kindly correct the self, forgive the infraction and move onto the new way of thinking. One day this will be so seamless that you won't even notice it anymore. Then it becomes the natural way you think and there is no need for the gentle self-correction.

If you find yourself continuing to repeat your story, or if you find that you need to tell your story for work, or family or when giving speeches, or even just when rehashing your day with your spouse or friends etc you may like to use some neutralising statements such as:

It's over now and I'm just telling you the story, so you understand. . .

I'll tell you for context and history, but it's not true anymore, it's not present now. . .

I'm through it now and victorious so I'm just telling the story now, so you understand. . .

It's over now, I'm victorious but I'm telling you the story, so you are informed. . .

I'm telling the story, but it's over now and I'm victorious. . .

Announcing your victory over the story you are telling, or the difficulty you are relaying, can be very uplifting, so do consider how you can feel any sense of victory enough to incorporate it in your statement.

If you don't feel 'victorious' (remembering of course you can be victorious just by having gotten through something – not only by your definition of winning) then simply say:

I'm through it now, it's over and in the past, so I'm just telling you the story of it now.

These types of statements effectively reinforce the idea that even though you are expressing an old story, you have moved through it, and this is not a story that you are imprinting to live by, this is something that you can easily move through and past.

You can still talk about your life and share your experiences with others without it becoming defining of self as a failure or exacerbating any remaining old opinions of self as 'less than' and unable to have the life of your desires. That's how you negate it, to the best of your ability until you find one day that you're not actually telling the story anymore.

If you are having trouble even recognising when you are wrapped up in your story, look for your actions, words, thoughts and behaviours that seem to be coming from a place of neediness, a place where you are doing or saying something to get something from 'those out there', the external world.

What is it you do to gain acceptance, attention, sympathy or any other inclusion or recognition that is not behaviour aligned with your true needs, wants and desires?

Where are you saying things like 'I'm so bored with this, I'm so tired of this, I'm so sick of this' about a circumstance or behaviour?

These are all signs that you are in some way coming from your story.

Your life is your choice. Are you someone who keeps their word to themselves? What can you do now that will ease your way forward into an empowered state of sovereign mastery? What part of your story can you drop today and pledge to the self to never engage with in that same way again? Make that small pledge, engage with the self as a team and keep your word.

Story Manifesting

Story is an ancient teaching technique. It is an ancient memory technique. It reminds the flows and the cells of what's real and true and who you really are. And it's also an ancient manifestation technique, because you can tell the cells and self the story of where you're going and what is going to occur.

You can do that verbally to the self. You can do it with writing, or you can just do it with a visual journey projecting yourself into that future point and seeing what it looks like for you and to the best of your ability feeling how it feels to you. This is often called visualisation or mental rehearsal.

That's the story you're telling yourself. The visualisation is the story you tell yourself about your future. What do you daydream about, what do you dread, what do you worry about? What do you hold to as your personal story, perhaps your tragic back story? That is your mental rehearsal for the future. That is the story you are creating in your now for your future.

By using the story, to others or self, you are weaving together the strands of a fabric created into an expected outcome. When we repetitively tell our story about ourselves and our tragedies, we are, in the now moment, weaving the fabric of that into our reality. As we retell the story through our words, thoughts and actions we are weaving it into the future moment to out-picture in our lives as still occurring and real for us until we change the story in the now.

Visualization and mental rehearsal change the story in the now. The story technique for manifesting is based upon mental rehearsal – remember, the mind does not know the difference between reality and non-reality.

If we are watching a movie the mind is responding to it with the same emotions and tension as though it is real. Using story for the self and on the self creates a similar sensation. It allows the mind to see the future projected story (mental rehearsal) and feel it as real thusly creating the emotions and tension in the body in the now moment that are aligned with the intended visualisation.

When this is done consistently the body literally changes its biology to align with and calibrate to the visualised reality. Your frequency emanation changes, your mental expectation changes, your literal hormones and cells change to align with the visualised future, meaning that you have now come into alignment with your visualisation, and it expresses as an out-pictured reality in your life.

Chapter 15

The Creation Statement and Story Technique

The story technique for healing, changing or manifesting is based upon the idea of mental rehearsal or visualisation. It's a way of telling yourself the story of what you wish to create in your life as your experience. It is a visual process involving the use of words to engage with the higher self, the universe, eternal source or whomsoever you believe has the understanding, knowledge and knowing about the future and/or the creation of the future for you.

This technique uses visualisation, questions and specific tense to frame the journey as a future outcome but takes the journey as a present moment-to-moment experience of unfolding. The question opens things up and creates the opportunity for the universe to step forward and show you the steps to take to be who you choose to be and experience what you choose to experience.

The imagination is the precursor to reality and physical presence. It's been proven many times that envisioning an action over and over again improves your ability in that action in a similar way to actual physical practice and repetition of that action. The Story Technique is designed to work with this mechanism of the human mind.

Maybe you think you cannot visualize strongly enough to do mental rehearsal? Perhaps you've tried visualization techniques before and you just can't get that picture clearly in your head? It doesn't matter. If you can't see it in your mind, it's ok – intention still works. The idea behind the Story Technique is that the questions and state of presence work perfectly well even if you don't feel like you've been able to clearly visualize what you are desiring to create. Even if you don't actually know what you want to create, it still works!

Future You and the Question

Understand that your future self knows who you are and what you've been through/are going through/will go through. You could consider this not just as the future you from this lifetime, the one on the deathbed looking back at the life you've had this time, but also the you that is many lifetimes ahead of this one, and remembers all that you went through in this life.

Even if you don't believe in multiple lives or reincarnation, just for the purposes of this technique, consider that the You who is looking back at the life lived is the You that is far smarter and more knowing than the you that you are now. This You is looking back at you and you cannot hide from this Future You.

Future You knows what you did and who you are. Future You already knows what you did for the rest of the life before Current You has even done it. You can use this as a type of foreknowledge and premonition, as suggestion and guidance, for what you need to do or would benefit from doing in any situation.

Consider Current You and Future You as a team and ask questions to gain more insight and intuition about what actions to take. You can use the following as a type of immediate prayer to engage with Future You and the higher knowing aspects of self:

> *"You who know me, you who remember me, you who have been through what I am going through and remember the outcomes, the importance, the journey, those of you who know the higher outlook, bigger picture and remember being me, I ask you now for your input."*

You can then ask various questions of Future You, such as:

What is it that I did that resolved this current issue?

THE CREATION STATEMENT AND STORY TECHNIQUE

How did I let absolute love override all my difficulties and create the best of the best as my outcomes?

How did I create the out-picturing of the highest and brightest life for me in this incarnation as this I AM?

How did I serve?

How did I thrive?

How did I have the most desirable outcome for me in my human incarnation that also serves my eternal soul? Remember that serving your eternal soul's needs can be done in many ways, some of which are unpleasant to the incarnate. Do you want to do the unpleasant if it serves? Or do you want to serve in incarnationally desirable ways? It's up to you; you have freewill choice.

What did I do to create that?

What is my highest choice for us now?

What did I do here now that led to our brightest future self outcomes?

Future You is not just an ephemeral concept. It's also a very credible one, just look at who you are today and remember who you were 10 years ago – the you that you are today was Future You to the you that you were 10 years ago. How much have you changed? How much more do you know? In what ways are you better? How much could you have soothed and guided Past You of 10 years ago? Just contemplating this you can see that Future You will have guidance from a place of more experience, more knowing than Current You.

You might also consider other ideas such as; in what ways are you more cynical, closed off or angry? In what ways have you given up on your dreams? Perhaps past You can also teach you how to recapture your optimism, hope and joy!

As a side note, you can also use this concept of Future You (as well as Past You and Present You) to help in your daily healing and process, to aid you in making personal progress. Consider when you are doing anything, how much are you leaving for Future You to deal with? How much of a backlog of work or unnecessary activity are you creating for Future You? Perhaps you could do Future You a favour and deal with some of the issues in the Now as Present You? Perhaps you could fold up your clothes and put them away, or do those dishes now rather than leaving them for Future You to deal with? Viewing it in this way helps you to stay present and stay on target rather than pushing things to the side to be dealt with at a later date. When you know that Future You will have to deal with it, and you now have a relationship with Future You, then you can do Future You the courtesy and favour of dealing with it in the now.

The Use of The Question

Asking questions, allows the Universe to align with showing you how it happened ie creating the circumstances that led/lead to 'it' thus creating 'it'. We're not interested in dictating to the Universe how 'it' happened – that's limitation – we are interested in conversing with the Universe and allowing ourselves to be shown how 'it' happened. Future You is showing you how 'it' happened, which means Future You is telling you what you did and what steps to take. When you ask a simple question such as "How did that happen?" prior to something happening, you are opening the door to being shown the steps to take to get to the outcome.

For instance,

Asking a question such as: "How *did* I create my life of ease and joy?"

The question is in the past tense, you are asking to be shown how you did it, which means that even though you have yet to live the life, on some level it is already done. This type of question is designed to open the door to you being shown, daily, the steps that lead you to feeling ease and joy. Therefore asking; how did... as though it has already happened actually creates or manifests it.

The Story Technique

The basic format of the Story Technique is as follows:

1. Get Present

2. Ask the question – how did. . .

3. Ask for the story – show me Universe, show me the story again. . .

4. Clear the impediments as they occur using Frequency Statements, prisms, self-healing, counselling, energy healing, or whatever processes work for you.

5. *Optional*: Input the positives to counter the impediments – again using Frequency Statements, prisms etc. This is a voluntary and optional step, because the clearing of impediments often automatically fills the void with something of higher vibration, but inputting your chosen positive can direct you into the trajectory you have chosen.

6. Ask the question again – how did. . .

7. Ask for the new story (if there is one, or the same story again)

8. Clear the next impediment

9. Repeat as necessary

Get Present, Visualise and Feel

Get present with your breath or intention, you might like to spend some time in meditation or do a breathing exercise to bring yourself to a state of calm and peace.

From this calm and peaceful state, visualise going to the end of your life, or past the event/healing you are working with. Look back as though you lived the life of your dreams, were healed or achieved the result you were after.

Witness it all. To the best of your ability, see, hear, feel and know your amazing life and how it all ended up so perfectly. If you feel like you can't visualise it, or feel it, spend some time 'knowing it', attempt to generate within an absolute assurance that your life was the life of your dreams. Try to envisage how you might feel at the end of your life (or past the event that is currently problematic for you), envisage and elicit the love, triumph and satisfaction you might feel.

What if I still can't see it?

It's ok, the seeing is optional, if you can see it, fantastic, but if you can't, in some ways you actually have an advantage because you won't be bogged down by the outcome looking a specific way!

So, it's ok if you can't visualise it, just take a moment to centre yourself, attempt to visualise but mostly stay focused on generating the feelings of what it would be like for you to have your desire. How it would make you feel happy, secure, joyful, peaceful, calm, safe. The feelings matter more than the visual.

What if I don't know what I want to create?

That's ok too! Again, this is possibly an advantage because it keeps you from being focused upon and narrowed into certain parameters of what the outcome should look like and be and who should be involved. None of that helps. None of that allows the millions of other ways that the outcome could be attained that you currently know not of.

So, if you don't know what you want, you don't know what the solution is, that's ok, simply focus on the emotions you wish to be feeling. For instance, if right now you feel sad, depressed, hopeless and confined, then focus on feeling expansive, joyful, replete, supplied and fulfilled! See yourself spinning around on a mountain top (yes, very Sound of Music, I know) feeling the wonder and joy at the beautiful, supplied and safe life you've got/had. Feel that, imbue yourself with that, breathe into that, the expansion of it, the freedom of it, the joy of it. You don't need to know what it is exactly that has led to that joy and expansion, that's what the next few steps in the technique are for!

Ask For the Story

Whilst there, in the feeling of having passed the event or at the end of your life and feeling victorious, triumphant or fulfilled, ask the question 'how did ...' – ask the Universe to show you, to tell you the story of how it came about.

Consider the Universe as a beloved grandfather, grandmother or elder of some type sitting you down by the campfire and, in their wise and comforting voice, telling you the story of you and how you did it – despite all that appears to be happening little one, look how amazing it all turned out! Just allow yourself to be told an inspirational story about you, and your happiness.

If you can't envisage the story, or the storyteller, just allow yourself to revel in the feelings of victory, love, peace or satisfaction and fulfillment – generate them from the feelings you have had watching movies of great and triumphant characters and circumstances if you need to.

See if you can envisage some type of story that involves you as the primary character, the triumphant one, the glorious one, the loved and successful one. Remember that the idea is not to see yourself as the victor who squashed all competition, or the one who got revenge on those 'bad people' - that's abuse!

THE CREATION STATEMENT AND STORY TECHNIQUE

What you want to do is see or hear the story of how all the 'badness' was irrelevant, and you rose to shine in the glory of you without hurting anyone else and whilst living your grandest happiest and most fulfilling life. See your story as akin to coming off an amazing ride and thinking "wow, that was glorious!"

Example:

(Viewing the beauty and affluence of your life – ask with wonder and excitement)

"Grandfather Storyteller,

How did I get so rich and happy?

Show me that story please, the story of my life and how I became so rich and happy, show me step by step, day by day, moment by moment starting today.... thank you thank you! What an awesome life I led! Wow!"

Then observe the stories, ideas and visions that are shown to you until you've feel you've received what you need.

Return to Presence

Now come back to the present and bring with you the joy and wonder of how you did that ie, how you got so vibrantly healthy, wealthy, happy etc.

Celebrate the gratitude of it happening – see, feel and know the peace, beauty and gratitude of it. Like feeling the joy, nostalgia and hope felt at the end of an awesome movie or the joy of sitting down to hear an ancient shaman tell you the story of your awesome life.

Feel the amazing joy of it, those powerful positive feelings are imprinting states that will input new information, new belief systems, new ways of living your life. There is no need to know how it happened or to remember anything that was shown specifically – but if you do, that's great, write it down in your victory journal to remind yourself later that the process has begun!

Clear the Impediments

Once you set this process in motion by mental rehearsal, visualisation, the question and feeling, what you are doing is triggering a process, a cascade of change within your life. This is designed to align you with the visualisation experienced and the answer to the question out-picturing in your life.

In order to create this out-picturing as manifest reality for you, there will need to be changes internally to you and externally to your reality. This means that you will experience certain movement in your life to rearrange your reality to resemble your desired outcome – that which you asked the question about.

You personally may see and experience this in many ways. You may even find that you suddenly start to feel very tired, start procrastinating, avoiding taking any action or feel stymied or blocked in any action you are taking. These are illustrations of impediments to the outcome.

These are that which you would then look at, delve into, go within and dialogue with the self to attempt to understand what it is within you that is triggering a resistance to the change you are attempting to bring about. This could be due to many reasons, but fundamentally ask the self;

Is it a resistance to the change, or is it a signal to the self to reassess the desired outcome?

You may find that there are belief systems, programs, dramas, traumas or wounds that currently disallow your alignment with the desirable outcome, that which your creation question is attempting to bring to pass for you. This is really common – logically, if you did not have these resistances or impediments to your desired outcome, you would already be living your desire outcome!

So, when you begin to feel these emotions or experiences, these impediments, celebrate! They are clear evidence, that what you are attempting to bring to pass in your life has begun working in your life. If you are kicking back against it, then your subconscious has recognised the shift in desire, the subconscious has recognised the input of new frequency, a new focus and new information and it's now attempting to steer you back to the old energies, the old focus and the old decision.

This is because the subconscious is your guardian and friend and is trying to keep you safe by realigning you with what has been previously deemed acceptable and safe for you BUT the subconscious often has limited, stunted or warped ideas about what keeps you safe. So, when you notice that you feel the resistance, when you notice that you are delaying or procrastinating, then you know that the subconscious has been kicked into action to keep you in the status quo. Yet you also know that the status quo is not what is needed right now. So, celebrate!

Dialogue with your subconscious and give it the reassurance that the change is beneficial. Take any action you possibly can in the beneficial direction, allow the self to move forward in any way possible to help the subconscious to gain the understanding that the movement is not life threatening.

Celebrate each small or large victory to imprint the feelings, the energies and frequencies, of the joy in the changes. It sounds ridiculous, it sounds futile, but it really works. You simply have to think of the resistance, the subconscious and the procrastination as those parts of you that are afraid of the unknown and flip that fear into a feeling of excitement. Remember, butterflies in your tummy could be from fear, but they could also be from excitement and anticipation of something wonderful!

Your aim here is to consciously decide that the procrastination, avoidance, blockers and stoppers you are experiencing are not fear but excitement. You may find that consciously changing your mindset about them is all you need in order to overcome them and find yourself productive once more, or it might take a little more effort to overcome them.

THE CREATION STATEMENT AND STORY TECHNIQUE

Everyone's journey with impediments is different – and it is important not to simply bulldoze through it, but to be present with it and gain clarity as to why it is occurring to heal it and clear it from your system where it may trigger again.

You may also experience occurrences such as the external fighting you in the creation of your desired outcome. Maybe you suddenly get very busy. Maybe those around you suddenly fill you with their concerns about how you're changing or how your dreams are impossible. Maybe you feel within yourself a doubt, or even a sense of futility. These too are impediments thrown up to roadblock your success.

These roadblocks can be considered pause points where you can assess if you truly are going in the correct direction, or if you have the clarity and determination you need to achieve what you are aiming for.

Impediments are basically signs and illustrations of where in your life you are not aligned with your desired outcome. Are you hanging out with naysayers who don't support you? Are you a pessimist who doesn't support the self? Can you find a way to view your life as a burgeoning experience of joyful outcomes or are you stuck seeing everything as crumbling and failing and constantly disappointing?

All of these types of situations are various forms of impediment to your desired co-creation out-picturing in your life. Some of them are clarifying experiences, there so that you can refine your direction, refine your choices, refine your action. Others are there for you to go within and heal the drama, trauma, wound, belief system or program that disallows the desirable outcome to come to pass for you.

Sometimes we even have to make changes in our external, such as leave the job we are in, leave the friends we have aligned with, perhaps even strike out on our own and recreate our lives from the ground up with new friends, alliances and experiences.

It is rarely this radical, but it will depend upon what you have aligned with thus far in your life. If all of your friendship circles, your family dynamics and work experiences are aligned with a life that is very far from what you wish to experience, then you may be in for a radical shake up in order to co-create the life that brings the joy to your heart and soul that you are looking for.

Always remain discerning, considerate and neutral, in your assessment of what is needed, how you may need to change your external or heal your internal when in the process of a manifestation unfolding. There will be triggering situations and there will be false starts, detours and side tracks. That's the nature of the manifestation journey. As things change, as you change, there will be nuances to the resistance. There will be occasions where you are blinded to the truth of what is going on and where you feel so charged and excited by the changes that you neglect to see the 'fine print' of the change and perhaps end up going in the wrong direction. That's ok. That happens. We can sometimes think one thing is going on and then become ignorant to the other influences internal and external that hijack the situation to lead you astray again or bring you back to the turmoil that is so comfortable to you as an experience.

The turmoil is not your desired destination, but it is what the system currently knows so well and hence the system sees it as the place of comfort, the known place. The unknown is terrifying to the system, but sometimes we have to leap empty handed into that void to co-create something new. As long as you stay present with the self, as long as you observe where the discomfort is coming from and what it really means, and as long as you nurture the self, stay truthful with the self and continuously monitor and course correct – you will get there!

It's about self-love, self-trust, self-accountability and recognition that perfection is not the aim. The aim is truly nourishing and guiding the self through the maze of life. Doing this you will find that the outcome you seek, the life you desire, is attained faster than you currently think possible.

Your current thinking is based upon the negative entanglements and convolutions of the subconscious mind. The dramas, traumas and wounds within have created the Self up to now and have designated the emanation of self as a frequency match for the current unsatisfying experiences of your life. Your current thinking and emanation is what has created the life you are trying to change.

It is not to be afraid of this disruption, these impediments or the shake up that could happen as you begin the manifestation process of change. They will occur, sometimes greater, sometimes smaller, but they will occur. They are to be celebrated. You can feel joyful when you notice them because they are a sure sign that what you are doing is having an effect. There would be nothing to impede if no changes were being made, so, recognise them, and nurture the self through them, with discernment and clarify why they are present and what you need to do about them.

Do you need to make a decision in the external, to stop or start doing something? Or do you need to heal something internally? Do you need to grow beyond that which is triggering the impediment? Do so!

Then you will cruise once more, until the next opportunity for clearing more impediments. It's a joyful journey of healing and refining as you go. Then one day you are there, living the life you visualised as your out-pictured reality. You made it.

When you do the story technique, in fact when you do any manifestation technique, it is a dynamic process of being present, reassessing, and making the changes required as you grow, as you evolve and as your life unfolds. Within the story technique is the suggestion that the question you began with could be asked again and again or could be updated to suit your evolving external.

As you remove impediments and heal into being the true you, your story will change, so asking for the story again allows you to witness/create the nuances (or major changes) that you are now capable of believing are possible for you to receive/experience.

Ask the Next Question/s

When you feel that it is time to ask the question again, see the story again, or ask the next question, return yourself to the state of presence and emotion by repeating the 'Get Present, Visualise and Feel' section and asking for the story again.

Ask the next question whilst filled with the wonder of how amazing it all was;

"Wow! How did I do that? Show me what I did today that led to that – thank you!"

It is a good idea to daily ask the question above, or a version of it and make the choices that present. This keeps you in the presence of the suggested actions that occur from asking the question.

Each time you ask, clear the beliefs and impediments that may come up around it – you are being shown what is standing in your way of creating the story you desire. You can clear the impediments with frequency statements, prayer, prisms or any sort of energy, counselling or body work that seems appropriate and applicable to you.

When asking the question, remember to choose the action, expression, or activity that seems related to 'how you did it' by choosing the action/activity that seems to have the most excitement attached to it.

What action today makes you feel the most excited, the most hopeful, the most anticipation and joy? The activity that, out of everything available to you in that moment, holds the most interest, excitement and joy? Choose that action.

If you believe that everything in your life is a bit yuck, then choose the action/activity that holds the least yuck, by default this will be the action that holds the most interest, excitement and joy in comparison to all that which appears available to you right now.

Allow the process to happen by going with the flow; the path of your truest destiny is the path of no resistance (but because you are human it's probably the past of least resistance – there's always resistance, right?). Be aware, however, that the path of least resistance may actually be the path of avoidance. Consider; it's easier to go to the movies than to find a moment to do some self-development work like meditation. So going to the movies may, on the surface, appear to be the least resistant path because it has fun, ease and joy attached to it, but it could actually just be the path of avoidance where your resistance to the change kicks in and detours you.

This could be the inner mechanism of the subconscious safety reactions kicking in to steer you away from what the subconscious has determine to be the change that 'takes you away from safety'. Sit with your choice of action and determine with clarity whether it is the path of least resistance or the path of avoidance. Going to the movies may be exactly the inspiration you need, or it may be procrastination and avoidance – only you know, so be truthful with the self about this.

At any time, you may have a new question, or you may want to re-experience the beautiful life you had; ask your new question or re-ask your original question by taking yourself to the relaxed state of joy and wonder, through going back to step one and talking to the beloved Storyteller again. It's simple!

Story Technique Considerations

Your Old Why

Generally, the old why for your situation (Why is your life like this? Why is your relationship like this? Why can't you do this or that?) doesn't matter when you decide to enter the Story process. It is the past and if you continue to feed it, it will be your future, but all it has done so far is create your life up to this moment now. It may be interesting to you as an understanding of self. It may be interesting for your brain to understand it, but if you want a different future, then the old 'why' does not matter anymore.

You do not want it to be creating your future by staying in it and focusing upon it, agonising over it and exploring it incessantly without any actual moving through and beyond it. If you do all of this what you are really doing is recreating the same or similar outcomes in your life by remaining in the frequency of that which has created your present now moment.

Remember that your present now moment is an out-pictured reality created from all your past moments. You are looking at the past. Your life now and everything going on in it (the good and the bad) is an expression of the thoughts, focus and feelings that you have had up until now. So, leave your old 'why' in the past.

The Minutia of the How

The nitty gritty of the how doesn't matter. You are not looking for explicit moment-to-moment blow-by-blow explanations and illustrations of exactly how your desire comes to pass. You are asking the question of 'how did. . .' as an open-ended question to the universe, as a show of trust that it has happened, will happen and does happen. All you are doing is allowing the universe or Eternal Source or God or your higher soul to understand that you trust that it will/did happen because it has already happened. Now all that you want to do is live it in real time allowing the universe to deliver the steps day-by-day moment-by-moment.

You are opening the door for the expression of inspiration to come directly from Source or that ephemeral inspirational place that delivers the knowing of what to do. You are not asking for the explicitly set in stone exact how of the process. You are not even asking for the express set in stone outcome. You are asking for the desire, the feeling, the experience, not the specific person, or home or car or what have you.

The idea here is to feel it, to immerse yourself in the feeling of the joy, the affluence, the happiness, the fulfilment, the peace and ease, then ask how did you come to that feeling, that space of being. Following this question allow the universe to guide you step by step, through each inspirational moment, through each moment of focused attention you deliver to the most exciting and interesting option in that moment.

Trust and Discernment

Trust is really important with this but couple the trust with discernment. Trust that you will be shown, guided and supported as you take each step and action. Taking the most interesting and exciting step or action that occurs to you in that moment but use your discernment as to whether you are getting distracted, procrastinating or in delusion.

Your present state of focus and presence in the now, whilst trusting that each step is leading you to where you desire to be coupled with your discernment of when you are veering yourself off path with delusion, procrastination, rationalisation or even hopelessness is what keeps you on the path. We can lead ourselves astray with both 'head in the sand' optimism and 'rationalising' pessimism.

Staying present with self, partnering with self and talking yourself through your moment-to-moment helps you to defeat any clueless ignorance to reality and any 'realist' dismissal of spirituality.

THE CREATION STATEMENT AND STORY TECHNIQUE

Story Questions to Consider Working With:

How did I do that?

What would it take to...?

How did I get to feeling so loved, so adored, so trusted and trusting?

How did we create such a beautiful life together?

How did I get so fearless?

How did we find such love together?

How did everything change so instantly and positively?

How did I get so lucky?

How did I find him/her/them so quickly?

How did that happen?

What else is possible?

How can I create more beneficial change from this?

How can I use this to create joyous change in my life?

How did I get so easily financially independent?

Chapter 16

Prisms

And so, we come to the idea of Prisms - if frequency statements are a tiki torch and stories are a backyard fire, then Prisms are perhaps a bonfire.

What are Prisms?

A prism is a document, a type of personally empowering long form prayer, that is designed to be said out loud. They comprise varying components, being part prayer, part revocation, part invocation, and part mesmerisation or uplifting self-meditation.

P – Prayer

R – Revocation

I – Invocation

SM – Self-meditation

Hence: prism!

Most prisms will contain all components within them, but some will be more focused on one component more than others. They all orient towards personal empowerment and healing using your own sound and light to reorder, heal and/or recreate your life.

Words repetitively spoken and/or thought become part of who you are, part of your foundation belief systems, base line mind patterns and part of your auto response to situations and experiences – how many times do you say the same exclamations and explanations when put on the spot? These reflect your foundation belief systems (or one aspect of them).

To summarize some of the concepts investigated so far in this exploration on words and being:

- Words are written by putting symbols we call letters or 'the alphabet' together.

- The putting together of these symbols to form words we call 'spelling'.

- Words are combinations of symbols created by spelling.

- What you read and speak could then arguably be thought of as a form of spell.

- Words have a sound component when spoken and a light component when thought, thus, words are sound and/or light projections that emanate from you in one way or another.

- What you think and speak, both its format and its content, is intimately entwined with and reflective of your inner landscape made up from many things including your belief systems and programs resulting from your experiences in life both good and bad.

- Thoughts and words create reality and/or your experience of reality by various mechanisms including their alignment with your inner landscape, your belief systems and programs.

Words might be considered a container of frequency; they contain the frequency of the emotion they have been thought or expressed with. Sentences could be considered the presentation or structure of that frequency.

When you are reading something that has been written, you are not only reading the meaning of the words, but you are also reading a container of frequency which holds the frequency of the state it was written in.

What this means is that when you read something that has been written in a spiritual flow, a flow of inspiration or truth, an altered state or awakened epiphany, what you are actually offered is the reigniting of the healing flow of the original download of the creation each time you read it. That original frequency is still contained in the words and ready for your ignition or integration should you wish it.

Prisms are documents created in spiritual flow designed for healing of the self by the self. They are a type of long form prayer or self-meditation for helping your mind, body and personality shift and lift the impediments that hold you immobilised in the current experience of your life. By using prisms for the self, by the self and on the self you encourage the movement, the lifting and shifting, of that which holds you in its thrall; the thought patterns, the belief systems, the programs, the markers, the traumas, wounds and dramas that you operate from, that you reimagine, reignite and reinstall with your unconscious, subconscious and sometimes even conscious day to day manoeuvrings, thoughts and talks.

Why do Prisms?

Prisms are a gentle consistent healing tool for the self and by the self. They will help you to re-empower the self and fortify your personal boundaries. They bring you back to presence and work with the power of your own intention, your own voice and your own personal autonomy to bring your attention to the now, and to your personal sovereign choice in the now, to create life as you choose. The time and focus taken to say them builds frequency, force, presence and empowerment and works as a type of filtering device, a boundary or border in the unseen.

The presence and focus given to a prism also works as a persuasion to the mind to allow it to believe and understand something is changing, something is happening from this there comes an alignment with the words and choices of the prism and the creation flows into reality – speaking it into creation.

A prism works using the age-old concepts of chant, affirmation, prayer and repetition. There are many aspects to them, and they are layered with information, some of which may trigger you or feel 'stupid' – including the act of saying them out loud to the self. They are designed this way for many reasons including to help you cover all of the mind's objections, queries and rejections, along with igniting within you the understanding of what your limitations might be. The aspects, words or ideas of a prism that trigger you will show you what you are avoiding in yourself, what your belief systems are and whether or not you are able to open the mind and work with them.

Outlook, mindset and emotional change mechanisms, practices and protocols have been around for a long time – affirmations are probably the one you are most readily familiar with. These types of practices and protocols have the aim of bringing about personally beneficial changes in a person's life via several mechanisms, such as repetition, toning (sound) and focus.

These mechanisms work as a trinity that helps you to change your mind set, emotions and emanation (frequency) by imprinting the words of the affirmation as the conscious and subconscious flows of self. All three of these aspects, the repetition, the sound, and the focus, combine to eventually create new neural pathways and a change in mindset, as well as a change in frequency emanation of the self.

The trouble with affirmations for most people is that, by their very nature, they are often announcing something that the conscious mind sees as demonstrably not true in the now. This leads to an immediate kick back from the mind of 'but that's not true' and hence a resistance to the affirmation. This can create a situation where the affirmation is stated without any passion, without any belief, without any hope that it will work or come true. It is done simply as a rote exercise. Yet passion, focus, feeling and presence are essential for imprinting the power of the affirmation!

Prisms take the time to address the disbelief and the potential, or real, impediments to your affirmation being a truth statement for you in life.

To do this, prisms are long form and often go through a process, which is kind of like a lapping wave on the shoreline. They state a removal of that which prevents what you desire to align with, then an alignment with that which you desire to align with. Or they may state an ignition of a feeling that is a resonance for that which you desire to align with. This is often followed by another form of revoking that which prevents the alignment and an invoking of alignment with the desire again, and so on.

This process is often repeated throughout the prism, creating a sort of pulse and self-mesmerizing state of being. This process is hypnotic and allows you to imbue yourself with words of great change, with ideas of upshiftment and upliftment. Done regularly with focus and loving attention they will change your mind set, your personal presence and your empowered state, bringing about positive changes in your life.

The Layout of a Prism

A prism is a self-healing tool and often is also a teaching tool. It contains peaks and troughs; it has a sort of pulsing rhythm and will lull you into a meditative and empowered state where you are hypnotizing the self into a powerful positive and victorious or peaceful state of being.

The prayers, revocations, invocations and self-meditations within a prism lift and ignite your frequency, slowing the mind and body down, allowing change. The power of your voice and the intention of your words can literally change the way reality functions on the energetic layers of you.

Read Them Out Loud

Prisms are designed to be read out loud. They are designed for the eyes to see the words, the ears to hear the words, the brain to process the words and the cells to feel the words. This allows cognition on many levels including getting the cells and energy bodies to recognise and understand the boss's (you) voice and instructions. This process of reading them out loud also provides less chance of a wandering mind and the instructions to the unseen become clearer, partly because you are focused on what you are saying and what you are asking for, dissenting from or consenting to.

Read at a normal to slow pace so you can hear your words, and your body can hear your own loving voice. Try to resist the urge to read too fast, to 'just get it done'. Read slowly with presence, savouring each word. As you do this you will feel the energy building and the pulse of the document unfurling.

The aim is to not go into a 'quick I just have to read this' mode; you want to be actually listening to and absorbing what you are saying. Sometimes over pronouncing the words helps the mouth and mind to feel the words and be with the words there and then. This is not a task to get done, this is a prayer to be present with and feel the power of, allow your own voice to mesmerize you.

Talk in that voice where your own body can feel your love and stay with it, feel it as you speak it. Try not to do them in a monotone, this may happen when you lose focus or when you are reading something that you find you cannot relate to or resonate with. If this happens consider choosing a different Prism until you find one that you can stay present with, focus on and put feeling into. Alternatively, take the time to research the words and concepts so that you can relate to it and understand it, then try again.

Allow your voice to take over the room, not with volume but with presence, passion, resonance and reverberation. This brings you to the eternal moment of now and changes the dynamic of the room to peace.

This may be the first time you have ever actually been present as a sovereign one, it may feel unique! Put your heart and soul into it, say it out loud with projection. Say it often and it has the power to change your life, bringing you back to You. It is not about being loud, it is not about shouting it, it is about feeling it! You can say the most life changing thing quietly, passionately, fervently and purposefully with conviction.

You do not need to do a prism with fight or aggression because coded within the words are a myriad of ways of saying "I do not consent..." to anything and everything that may be your limitation and inhibition from a glorious life of joy and ease.

The best way to ignite this state of being is to stay calmly present, breathe and speak from power not domination. Prisms are designed to speak from power, to remove consent for deviations from joy, peace, prosperity of self and ease in life. There is no need to fight, there is simply a reclamation of self and birthright.

Do them with loving intention. None of this is violence and vitriol. What existed, existed. What you chose, you chose. What you honoured and repeated, you honoured and repeated. Then you woke up, released the self, changed perception, drew your attention away, broke the spell, dissolved the thrall, however you wish to believe it occurred, somehow you became aware that your perception was faulty, incorrect, unhelpful or misleading. Then you chose differently by starting the journey to healing the inner perception that needed rectifying. So, there is nothing to fight or castigate, including the self, there is just the recognition of 'now is the time to journey home to you'.

How Often and For How Long?

A suggested time frame for doing your self-healing spiritual work would be to do it daily. You could consider doing it for 6 days and then, if you wish, give yourself a break on the 7th day. This is not about punishing the self by forcing constant repetition, this is not a self-flagellation exercise; this is a self-love process of ease and consistency. Repetition is important, consistency is important but so is time off to relax and integrate the changes occurring.

The most benefit will be obtained using prisms regularly and consistently for a period of time. Take the time to be present with them when reading and read them slowly. Do this every day for a period of time and you will begin to notice changes and results. Generally, it is recommended doing a prism consistently for a period of maybe 14 to 30 days, this consistent repetition allows the energy of the prism and the changes it brings about for you to have a sort of snow balling effect, a cumulative effect compounding its action in your life and your unseen world.

It is beneficial to do at least 30 minutes of spiritual practice each day, but you will often find you get swifter results from a longer timeframe such as 1.5 hours per day.

Prisms are only one aspect of your spiritual practice, so you don't need to be doing only them for 1.5 hours per day unless this really feels good to you. Any activity of presence, focus, calm attention to self and peace would be considered 'spiritual practice' for the self. This could be anything such as walking in presence, meditation, prisms, activations, prayer and so on.

Doing something is better than doing nothing, so don't fret if you aren't doing 1.5 hours of spiritual practice per day! It is often very hard to find that much time each day to do some spiritual practice, just remember that your intermittent focus throughout the day on affirmations, frequency statements, present empowerment, breathing, monitoring your thoughts and speech patterns etc all count as spiritual work.

Any combo of peaceful present state healing action you are taking (especially that which is done alone or unfacilitated by another or a group) all counts towards your daily practice. You may actually be surprised by how quickly and easily you achieve 30 minutes or more of daily spiritual practice, and how quickly and easily it changes not only your state of mind but also your enjoyment of life.

The idea is to become so consistent with doing your chosen spiritual practices and so enamored and immersed in doing it that your natural way of thinking begins to reflect it – this is the autonomous sovereign state where you are changing your foundational thinking habits and beginning to emanate the sovereign present and empowered state of peace, ease, joy and love. Immersed to this degree, your every moment of every day becomes a form of spiritual practice, then there's no trying to do it, you are just doing it naturally. It becomes a part of who you are.

Chapter 17

Specific Prisms for Healing

On the following pages are a select few prisms for your use in aligning with differing states of being and/or clearing the self of impediments that may hinder your ability to co-create the life you desire. You can use any of them for any issue as these particular prisms are wholistic in nature, but you will find that some of them are targeting specific issues such as nightmares or personal guidance.

If you want to understand the particular focus that each prism is best suited for, you will find, listed over the page, their general focus, or you can read the About section at the beginning of each prism.

Even though some of them seem to focus on something particular, each of them will have a great deal of benefit in bringing you to a peaceful state of presence and clearing or silencing the scattering disruption of self. What this means is that you don't need to find the specific prism that suits your purpose unless you want to, you can just choose whichever one resonates with you.

If you feel overwhelmed or fearful of choosing the 'wrong' one, do not worry, all of them are gently and benevolently oriented in order for you to have a graceful and peaceful experience with them – so just choose any one and try it out. You cannot get it wrong!

If you still doubt which one would work best for you, perhaps start with The Audit for 30 days and then consider if your mind is clearer and decisions are easier. If not, try it for another 30 days and consider again.

You should find with each usage of The Audit that you get clearer and clearer, stronger and stronger, if not, then perhaps you may need to engage with outside help in some way to help yourself feel stronger, more present and decisive, perhaps seek a counsellor, an energy worker or an allopathic practitioner to aid you on your healing journey.

General Focus for Each Prism

The Audit is great for tidying up your intuition and guidance, helping you to overcome interference, distrust in self and inability to make decisions.

Reality Bubble Buffer is great for softening outside overwhelm and bringing a sense of safety to self.

Evening Prayer is great for a good night's sleep and a general releasing of stress before sleep, as well as tidying up the dream space for a restful dreaming experience.

Shining Golden One is a great for bringing the self back to self in the remembrance of your true being. It helps you remember the glory of who you are and brings perspective to the human troubles you may be having.

Returning to Pristine is great for releasing stress and regaining calm, an excellent one for igniting peace, trust and presence.

Who Am I is great for remembering who you are and all that you are capable of as well as a return to strength and understanding of you.

Morning Prayer is great for releasing any lingering sense of fatigue or sluggishness from sleep as well as cleansing and clearing the self to return to presence.

The Audit

About The Audit

This prism is designed to clean up your unseen entourage and influences, you can think of them as guides and guardians, angels and masters, your higher self or in any other way that your life learning has led you to think of your unseen and intuitive guidance and protection. You can also think of them as the programs and belief systems that you hold within, that which unconsciously or subconsciously run you causing hidden biases, choices, actions and non-actions that lead you astray or may cause friction or unhappiness in your life.

Where The Audit refers to beings or harvesting, you can think of these as actual beings if that is your belief system, or you can think of it as anthropomorphising the inner landscape of belief systems that keep you in procrastination, avoidance, sadness or constantly believing your own sense of failure, or ineptitude.

How you think of these things does not really matter, the Audit is written as though there are actual beings and entities bothering you, so if that works for you, great, read it as is, otherwise consider it an exercise in compartmentalisation and anthropomorphising of your thoughts, your belief systems, your programs, your subconscious and unconscious aspects in order to pluck them out of the self as separate to the caring, encouraging and productive self of peace and love that is being smothered by these personal aspects and influences.

This is a powerful prayer; it is recommended that you do this daily for at least 30 days and revisit often.

The Audit is empowering and may cause great change in your life. Treat it with respect and see it as a spiritual practice of bringing the self back to self.

THE AUDIT PRISM

It is very helpful to monitor your mind set, your emotions and any occurrences and changes that occur in your life as you begin using this prism often. If you start to feel more negative, this may just be a sign that something within is resisting the change, shift or removal – keep at it! By taking ownership of self, whatever the resistance is, it cannot remain, but if you believe the negative emotions, then you may find that you stop the practice and remain where you are.

You can do the whole Audit to really get the flow and frequency of it, this will build and fortify your boundaries and shake up your entourage. Alternatively, you can simply take the last few paragraphs and use it as a prayer, frequency statement or mantra to maintain your level of flow and frequency.

Remember; there is nothing to fight! A simple denial of services, energy and attention will work. A simple removing of consent will work. There is only one choice, that is to choose sovereignty, which means that to a certain extent there is repetition in teachings because at the root of it all they say the same thing, be sovereign, claim sovereignty. This is what the Audit helps you do by realigning your unseen world to peace.

The Audit Prism

I in the ever-present moment of now call to all my friends, family, helpers, healers, guides, guardians and influencers in the unseen.

I call you all here for family and entourage meeting time.

Thank you for your presence.

I call you here now so that we may audit the entourage, audit the influencers and influences in my life as the apex being of the now incarnate here on earth in the graduating timeline.

I claim my place and space as the apex being of the now, and here we begin the audit of those who would influence me, those who would guide me, those who would partner with me, support me, help me, join me and accompany me on this journey.

I ask you all here now for your aid in this audit as we cleanse and clear all the influences and manipulations, the influencers and manipulators, that are leading, guiding or encouraging me astray. I refer to those that are whispering the deceits, the distractions and the manipulations that would detour me, that would hurt me or keep me bogged in the mire of mediocrity, in the mud of doubt and the suction of fear.

I include here those that get kickbacks, that take delight in deceiving or misleading me, providing enough benefit or positivity to me, providing enough promises of victory, help and aid to me, that I negate or become blind to the flow on draining, harvesting, limiting, distorting or ensnaring that comes from their aid.

I call forward now all the guides, guardians, friends, family, helpers, healers, supporters and influencers of light, those aligned with caring, sharing and Unity, aligned with do not harm.

I call forward those that have gathered and assembled for our greatest victory as an entourage in the light and a human aligning with emerging Earth, upshifting Earth, Eternal Source, the Heart of Creation and absolute love.

THE AUDIT PRISM

I ask you to please aid me with this audit as we search now for all of those in the seen and unseen, in the entourage and otherwise, that are feeding off me, non-beneficially influencing me, misguiding me, ensnaring, entangling and entangled with me and in any other way non-beneficially effecting me - including those that would alter, distract or encourage beings in 1, 2, or 3 degrees of separation from me, to disrupt me, to detour me, and to distract me. I ask that we search now for them and remove them from my energy fields, my body, my mind, my life, my light, energy, plasma and vapour bodies and my sphere of influence. I claim now my light, plasma and vapour bodies in pure pristine and perfect original immaculate grace.

I do not consent to the continued engagement nor presence of any of these non-beneficial beings, or those not aligned with do not harm, nor do I consent to any of their echoes, residue, mech or tech remaining or continuing to influence me in any way that is a deviation from do not harm or misaligned with my incarnational mission of healing evolution and growth into the light of the heart of creation and eternal source.

I only engage with, partner with and embrace those of unity consciousness, aligned with do not harm and equal exchange of ideas, energies and wisdom, those unified and accorded with community, affluence, prosperity, fulfilment, integrity, joy and love, that that have an alignment with Eternal Source and hold me in the respect, esteem and benevolence that I have for them..

I ask those beings in the entourage, those friends and family in the unseen, those of unity consciousness, to please escort away those that are aligned with harvesting, with unequal distribution of energy, with domination, victim victimiser games, those that reject equal exchange.

Please escort away all those that are misaligned with or do not encourage, validate or understand upliftment, expansion, and the budding, unfurling and growing of self into all that I am and could be, all that is possible for me in the lighted pathways of joy-filled delight, aligning with new earth, upshifting earth, loving earth of joy-filled, grace-filled, peace-filled, loving, prosperous and affluent delight.

I ask you, with grace and ease, to please escort these beings, influences and influencers to wherever is appropriate for them.

If those that are escorted away should object, if those that are not aligned with community, absolute love, integrity, respect and equal exchange of energy should object, if those that are aligned with draining, with procrastination, with distraction, domination and control should object then I ask for them to be escorted to the edges of our influence, to the edges of our being, to wherever is safe for them to plead their case. I ask for us to listen without judgement, for remedy and resolve.

If it should be the case that they become willing to align with peace, love, respect, unity consciousness and do not harm, we accept.

If it should be the case they become willing to give up their warring, dominant, controlling and harvesting ways, to become a part of the entourage again; we accept.

We ask for the appropriate reverence, humility, healing and respect to the family, to the entourage, guides, guardians, helpers and healers, to the soul matrix and other unity consciousness aspects of me, my entourage, my ancestors and the gestalt we are.

Upon showing of the appropriate healing and intentions, then the previously negative misaligned aspects may return, refreshed, renewed and restored, now working as the collective, as the entourage aligned with do not harm, releasing their parasitic hostile ways in favour of absolute love, aligning with upshifting, uplifting, emerging Mother Earth.

We are a being of absolute love.

We are a community of love, respect, integrity and peace.

We are the peacekeepers and peace makers of the now and we do not align with, nor do we allow, distorting, detouring or draining by, nor influence of, war makers, deceivers, half-truth tellers, leaches, parasites, exploiters, abuse game players nor those in service to such.

The shadow beings and the feeders, harvesters, instigators, triggerers and igniters, poking, prodding, deceiving, betraying and pushing from the unseen, you have no home here.

To those that affect me now and those that are in one, two, three and up to 10,000 degrees of separation from me, that are aligning, setting up dominoes of cascading events and occurrences, designed to disrupt my trajectory, to detour my journey, distract my focus and cause chaos, havoc, emergencies, distractions, confusion, equivocation, faltering, delaying and shilly-shallying in my day to day life, you have not haven here.

To those that are keeping me from my victory, my triumph, my destiny, my certainty, my confidence, my decisiveness and determination, my firmness and resolution, my gratitude and fulfilment, my grace-filled, graceful and harmonious ignition, emanation and living of prosperity, alacrity, affluence, and joy-filled abundance, of absolute love and endless resources to do all that I want and need to do, above and beyond any expenses and imposed limitations, you have no respite here.

I say unto you all now, you have no home here, you have no haven here, you have no respite here.

You are commanded to leave, you have no consent here, there is no consent given to your presence, nor to your disruption and stealing of vital force, of life energy, of emotional charge, of enthusiasm and of focused direction and self-healing.

Any consents or permissions you believe you have I hereby as the one present now and the chooser and decider for this body and this life stream, revoke, rescind and recant them now.

I as the present being of the now, the apex being of this incarnation, remove all agreements, permissions and bindings to any compact, contract or the like that allows your continued presence or return, revoking them now in any and all directions, dimensions, levels and layers of time, space, reality and me.

I step now into the present and empowered self as the I AM and say to all those that keep me tired, uninspired, flat, distracted, procrastinating, disconnected from my flow and inner genius, disconnected from my self-nurturing activities or fatigued and doubtful about my next move, about my next creation, about my future:

I release you now. You are no longer needed; I ban and banish you. I break all contracts and deals we have had in place and remove all permissions for you to harvest me and my energies, in any way, shape or form, including as a symbiotic or funnel system to, from or via others. All agreements we had were made in ignorance or incomplete knowing and stand now as not fit for purpose. I, as this ever present being of the now, hereby revoke and rescind these contracts, compacts, permissions and deals.

Thank you for your service, thank you for your help and protection in the past but I am no longer a frail nor ignorant being who needs this kind of limitation or oppression.

I do not need the bully to protect me whilst keeping me small and insignificant, operating from my own fear, doubts and illusions – I can and do self-nurture appropriately now such that you do not need to put the brakes on me, nor do I allow any further harvesting, you have been recompensed in full.

All programs feeding and igniting, instructing and controlling, all entities with what would limit me, tire me, block me, stop me, deviate me or distract me I say unto you now:

You are no longer needed, and I upgrade you now into supportive, nourishing, self-nurturing programs promoting vitality, vim and vigor, promoting self-nurture into peak-condition, peak-performance, regeneration, rejuvenation, replenishment and restoration to peak expression of perfect health through success, through prosperity, through grace, ease and thrival on all levels of me.

All is well.

THE AUDIT PRISM

To those who cannot or will not upgrade I say unto you:

You have no place here any longer. I do not need your inhibition. I do not need your curbing, regulating and smothering behaviour anymore.

It may have been helpful in the past, it may have been a rescue or a safety in the past, but I do not consent to it now. I do not need it, I do not consent to it and I do not allow it. I appreciate the input, the aid, the so-called friendship, the action in the past, but I am a person of the now.

I am here and I am the mighty I AM Being of the now, this ever-present moment of now.

All fatigue inducers, limiters, distractors, detourers, blockers, stoppers, procrastinators, avoiders and curtailers that are kicked off, ignited or initiated by any of my inspirations, any of my success, any of my self-nurture, any of my influxing or outgoing of money, any of my flow of triumph, victory, joy, glory, healing and/or prosperity for being me, through being creative and through being satisfied, appropriately and generously rewarded and awarded for any of these things, are cancelled, cleared, dissolved and resolved now in any and every direction, dimension, level or layer of time, space, reality and me.

All of those who have contracts, compacts, agreements or permissions associated with them, any of you that hold up the agreement, the decision, the pact or paper that shows you have the right to limit, curtail, overbear, scare, shock or interfere with me in any non-beneficial way, the definition of which is determined by my own eternal soul and unity consciousness entourage, I say unto you:

I, here now, as the apex being of this body and incarnation, as the voice that emanates from this incarnated being here now, cancel, clear, revoke, rescind and nullify all such agreements in any and every direction and dimensions of time, space, reality and me in all ways, shapes and forms.

I say unto all the entities and energies, parasites and otherwise, who drain me, harvest me, distract me or adversely impact me, especially those that do so as the payment for, or aftermath of, any summoning or manifesting I have done, including that which was messy, incomplete, desperate or ignorant I say unto you now:

You are not fit for purpose. The outcomes manifested from these clumsy and expensive alignments, agreements, arrangements or partnerships have been not fit for purpose or intended use.

I revoke all our contracts, and do not consent to any further syphoning or harvesting, on the grounds that I am a sovereign freewill standing light body of free-choice, and your outcomes and co-creation manifestations have been clearly, demonstrably and obviously not fit for my purpose or intended use, despite your promises and persuasions.

It is evidenced by my life that at best they have been a pale flimsy ephemeral imitation of what I wanted and at worst they have been a complete deception!

Anywhere and everywhere, I knew what I was doing, or was ignorant to what I was doing, I forgive myself for knowing no better and for believing the propaganda of humans and unseen alike trying to enforce their beliefs, techniques and/or processes as The Way or The Only Way.

I revoke all contracts and dissolve all connections, drainings and syphons with all manipulative non-beneficial beings who are getting kickbacks, onflows or residuals from any of the creations or manifestations I have made, partly made or attempted to make, knowingly or unknowingly, in partnership with these beings or alone.

I am a freewill human being.

I am a sovereign, freewill, free choice human being of the now.

You do not own me, and I do not owe you anything. Our partnership is done. Your free ride is finished. I am no longer your chattel, your cattle nor your food – I do not consent. I do not align with, nor agree to any contracts, compacts or the like that signify that you do own me in any way, including those which may have been made on my behalf or in my unknowingness, and I as the freewill conscious chooser for my own self and autonomy revoke, rescind, recant and nullify them all now.

I am aligned with, integrated with, upshifting with, emanating, outpouring and emitting with, effected by, blessed by, graced by, supplied by, Eternal Source and emerging, upshifting Earth, a constant stream of miracles and never-ending supply of solutions and opportunities, options, blessings and triumphs is mine now.

My life is miraculously blessed with clear and obvious help from the benevolence in the unseen. And I know it. And I see it. And I appreciate it. And I engage with it, easily, directly and joyfully every day.

I say thank you to my unity consciousness entourage.

I say thank you to the ancestors. To those that have been with me since the beginning of time, since my first individuation as a being and since my first incarnation on this Earth, I say thank you.

Thank you for being there.

Thank you for helping.

Thank you for your friendship, guidance, love, support and trust.

Thank you for your help on this day with this audit.

Thank you for your protection and your continued partnership with me. Together we step forward now in presence, in perfection and in readiness for the new, the magnificent, the beneficially surprising and loving outcomes of our guardianship, our friendship and our loving entourage and engagement with life.

Thank you, thank you, thank you

And so, it is!

Reality Bubble Buffer

About Reality Bubble Buffer

This prism is a calming, relaxing, cleansing exercise helping you to envisage the bubble of calm, of peace, of comfort that surrounds you and has the potential to work as a filter of sorts disallowing that which would attack or disrupt your calm, your sense of peace, your pristine and immaculate flows of self so preciously bought through all your personal attention and healing work.

This is good for when you are feeling harassed, harangued or chaotic in any way, it will bring you back to centre, to calm and peace and help you feel the protection, the space, to refresh, restore and replenish the self back to harmony.

This one, whilst short, should take you at least 15minutes to complete. It has breathing pauses scattered throughout, that should be taken as long slow in and out breaths as often as you need. These breath pauses are written as one breath in and one breath out, but take as many as you need - if you want to take 2 or 3 breaths between the statements do so!

Reality Bubble Buffer Prism

<Breathe in>

<Breathe out>

I allow the rainbow flows of my eternal soul to flow into my reality bubble soothing, calming and restoring me now.

<Breathe in>

<Breathe out>

I allow the shift and lift of all schisms and static, returning my eternal flow to me now.

<Breathe in>

<Breathe out>

I allow the healing of my mortal body, the soothing of my mortal mind and the calming of my mortal emotions.

<Breathe in>

<Breathe out>

I allow myself to return in calm sacred certainty that I am here and here is now and I am safe in the now.

<Breathe in>

<Breathe out>

I easily release all that which deters me from my calm and peaceful presence of now.

<Breathe in>

<Breathe out>

As I yawn and breathe, I release the static, the schisms, the overlay and imprints that buffer me from my calm and peaceful self.

REALITY BUBBLE BUFFER PRISM

<Breathe in>

<Breathe out>

I allow my reality bubble, my eternal flows, my rainbow flows of absolute love to buffer me from the buffeting of life.

<Breathe in>

<Breathe out>

As my reality bubble grows and flows more twinkling, sparkling and enlightened with every breath and imbuement of my rainbow flows, it becomes stronger in keeping me calm, in holding me safe and in providing the comfort of being held in a bubble of liquid peace surrounding me and dissipating all that which attempts to or threatens to disrupt my peace.

<Breathe in>

<Breathe out>

With each breath I am building my reality buffer, my bubble of protection and joy, my liquid peace bubble the dissipater of all that would stick to me as distraction or trauma, hold me away from or disrupt me from my peace, my joy, my health and calm.

<Breathe in>

<Breathe out>

I am here. In love and peace, I am here, and all is well.

<Breathe in>

<Breathe out>

Evening Prayer

About Evening Prayer

The Evening Consent prism is designed to help you wind down before sleeping and set various permissions and intentions for the sleep state. It helps put your mind at ease, dispelling doubts and worries about your safety and your state of sleep – whether you believe in dream spaces, the astral or in unseen beings interfering with your sleep doesn't matter, this is about addressing everything that your mind may throw at you that makes you feel fearful at night, or unsafe in your own bed.

If indeed you are living in an environment which is physically unsafe, that is something that you may need to alter for the self, but if you are living in an environment where your mind is creating the fears, where your dreams are disturbing your sleep with violence, terror and upset, then this prism will begin to help you feel calmer and safer in the sleep state and dream space

You may note some repetition during this prism, this is done to reiterate concepts to the mind. There are a few paragraphs in italics which are the paragraphs that address all that needs addressing so you can simply use them as your prayer each night. When you want to have a strong cleanse and boundary upshift, do the whole prayer.

This one is designed to be said slowly out loud to the self, whilst taking many pauses to breathe and relax. Done with presence this prism will help you create a space of calm, peace and relaxation helping you to drift into slumber more easily. It can also help you to enhance your dream space and begin to remember the scope and content of your dreams!

Nightmares

It is worth noting that if you suffer from nightmares or unpleasant dreams, or even if you tend to not remember your dreams, this prism can really help. It may not completely eradicate any nightmares or unpleasant dreams that you may be having but it will usually bring about a relieving change to them.

Nightmares and unpleasant dreams can occur for many reasons, so, if you continue to have them whilst using this Evening Consent prism, then it may be time to look into the other reasons they are plaguing you.

Quite often when we reclaim sovereignty and presence, the nightmares clear up, because often nightmares are associated with the mind dealing with some of the inner traumas and that which impedes you finding personal peace. If you find that nightmares are still a problem for you, there are solutions, so seek help! Your dream state should be pleasant and peaceful, if it is not – you don't have to suffer through it, you can heal it.

Nightmares, restless sleep or unpleasant dreams usually derive from an holistic space of unbalance, so they often need to be dealt with holistically – take care of your body, your peace and your spirit and you may find they 'clear up' on their own.

Evening Prayer Prism

I, in this eternal moment of now, as the apex being of this incarnation, as the owner of the voice that emanates from this body, call into presence my enclave of elders, my ancestors and lighted partners of unity.

I invite unto this enclave, called for recognition, remedy and resolve, all Unity consciousness family who would desire to witness and aid. I invite Eternal Source of All That Is to hold this space, keeping us free from harm and distortion as I make these declarations, revocations and invocations, as I state my prayers, needs, wants and desires for my experience in my life and the dream state.

I invite blessed, healing, upshifting, uplifting and supporting Mother Earth, who always has my back even when I forget that I am part of her and she is part of me, and I invite those beings of unity consciousness that have been my friends, confidants, supporters and encouragers, those who have witnessed my tears and my laughter, and those who have held me and inspired me when I could not find the way, those who would hold space in this enclave with me, those who glory in my triumphs and stand firm supporting in my moments of doubt, as I do unto them. I ask you all to be here as family, as brothers and sisters in light, as one, as I make my proclamations of consent, dissent, permission and denial.

I invite those beings of unity consciousness who would honour me with their support, their aid, their advice, their presence in my co-creating of the life of my desires, of the best of the best for me and of outcomes, experiences, timelines and moments aligned with the following statements of permission, consent, denial or dissent.

For the purposes of this document, the term 'the same' shall hereinafter refer to "Eternal Source of All That Is, Eternal beings of Unity, unity consciousness or the credo, belief system or alignment with do not harm".

EVENING PRAYER PRISM

I do not consent to, I remove all permissions for, and I revoke, rescind, recant and neutralise all contracts that allow, continue, reintroduce or reignite in any way shape or form any engagement or interaction with or from anyone or anything, that is not aligned with the same.

I do not consent to anyone or anything, in any way shape or form, by any means, entering my home if they are not aligned with the same. I remove, revoke, rescind and recant all permissions, contracts, compacts or that like that allow, continue, reintroduce or reignite in any way shape or form any consent that has previously been given in my knowingness or unknowingness for entry into my home or my spaces for anyone or anything that is not aligned with the same.

I include in the above statement all those beings that are tacitly, unknowingly, or in multiple degrees of separation not aligned with the same.

I do not consent to in any way shape, or form, nor by any means, entering any astral places, dream spaces, dimensional places or spaces, inter-dimensional, intra-dimensional or extra-dimensional spaces or places that are not aligned with the same.

Every place or space where I have previously knowingly or unknowingly given permission for me to enter or created some type of home or welcome that is not aligned with the same, I remove or reclaim, as appropriate, those permissions, contracts and agreements. I do not honour them. I disown them, I disavow them, I revoke them, and I dissent from them now. They were created in ignorance and have led me astray, as the present one of greater knowing now I revoke and rescind them in any and every direction and dimension of time, space, reality and me.

I choose to have healing dreams of peace and prosperity, allowing myself to integrate and upshift, to modulate and heal, returning to my immaculate, pristine, pure and perfect, peak condition, peak performance original uncorrupted template of health, flexibility, prosperity, profit, abundance, peace, love, fulfillment, lean, fit, healthy, slender, supple and strong, powerful, robust, and present in love for self in this lifetime.

I choose my eternal mission for this lifetime, my uncorrupted, unviolated, unpolluted, original, eternal mission for this lifetime. The original mission of my eternal soul for this incarnation. I choose to align with and fulfill my eternal mission in a win win and best of the best experience of life.

I choose alignment with my eternal soul. I am a rainbow shining one and I run the flows of my eternal soul. The rainbow flows of my eternal soul imbue me, flow through me and emanate from me as the modulators, minimizers, mitigators or vaporizers of all psychic splatter and matter, of all interference, imprints, overlays and assaults of distortion, deviation or domination, of darkness or diabolical oppression and control sent towards me, ignited within me or entangling me to corrupt me, to detour me, to distract me away from the immaculate, pristine and pure perfection of my original blueprint for this body and this life.

I do not consent to anyone or anything that is not aligned with Eternal Source, Unity Consciousness or 'do not harm' entering this home in any way shape or form including but not limited to physically, etherically, psychically, remotely or observationally. I do not consent to them violating the borders and boundaries of my home, my mind or my self, by any means, including, but not limited to, through mirrors, portals, worm holes, windows, doors, floors or ceilings.

This home is a protected haven for those of unity consciousness, peace filled, joy filled, absolute love and those choosing to heal and align with upshifting, uplifting Mother Earth.

I do not consent to the entrance or presence of any other being in this home in any way, shape or form.

All pets and children within this home are hereby placed under the same protection as I claim for myself, I hold them as aligned with these protections.

EVENING PRAYER PRISM

I ask Eternal Source to protect me during my dreaming adventures and homecoming into the astral, keeping my dreaming body and astral self safe and supported to return to my physical body unharmed, unmolested, untainted and without any distortions or time activated deviations of self from pure and perfect.

I am a being of peace and love, and I choose peaceful, calm and gentle learnings and interactions in the astral and dream-space.

I choose to remember my dreams.

I choose to understand my dreams and to experience them as the healing events they are. I choose to sleep, deep and restful sleep, regenerating and rejuvenating during my sleep and waking fully rested, regenerated, rejuvenated, replenished and restored with a full memory of my dreams and an understanding of their meaning and their purpose.

Tonight, whilst I sleep, I affirm to my body, through the power of eternal life, through the power of consent and attention, through the connection with Eternal Source and the flows of eternity that stream through you, you may heal. It is my intention to heal and I give permission for the healing process to begin, gently easily gracefully now.

I am a self-healing being, and I allow this healing to take place with ease, peace, grace and calm whilst I sleep, awakening tomorrow upshifted, uplifted and ready to continue my journey of baby steps into the enlightened, healed, pristine and perfected version of me.

I am grounded in this body with love and peace. I am joyfully replenished and made anew with each breath and I allow myself to experience life as the best of the best of outcomes in every way, staying in peace and calm, joy filled and ease fuelled each moment, releasing all attachment to my sorrows and all that perpetuates or encourages any steps further along the path of sorrow.

I claim my life of peace, happiness, contentment and fulfillment now, through ease, moment-to-moment, all is well.

Through this process I allow my connection with the eternal family of unity, and I remember who I am, who they are and who we are.

Thank you. Thank you.

My life is a blessing and a dream.

I am a rainbow shining one.

And all is well. All is well. All is well.

Shining Golden One

About Shining Golden One

This prism is written as a return to self into the glows and flows of your truly pristine and powerful self. It can be used as a form of abundance prayer and will help alleviate the fears and angst about the financial hardships you may be facing in your life. It may even initiate an inflow of your form of abundance!

This prism is so much more than just an abundance prayer though and can be used to ignite your glory in all ways, igniting the true abundance of self and the radiance of who you are beyond your human conditioning and sadnesses.

This one can help shift and lift the darkness when or if it descends upon you – but remember the darkness is tricky and will convince you not to do the prism! So, this may become a prism that you do by rote sometimes, in order to keep yourself reminded that there is more to you. The darkness does not want you to remember the glory of you.

Shining Golden One Prism

I am the shining golden one emanating the frequency match for prosperity of self beyond my mind's understanding, and all is well.

I am the shining golden one pulsing and emanating the light of prosperity of self beyond my mind's comprehension and all is well.

I am the golden shining one pulsing and flowing with light beyond description and understanding of the mortal mind and my true being shines with the vibration emanation of prosperity, wealth and abundance in all things, at rates and influxes beyond the containment of and limitation of my mortal mind.

I am a flourishing shining and radiant one, emanating the glorious light of attraction, leaving despair behind, my choice and alignment is the highest of the high and best of the best outcomes for me daily.

I allow absolute love to flow and override through all of my tributaries, all of my flows and lines, all of my potentials and trajectories, releasing and overriding all deviations from peace, joy, love, prosperity and affluence. Bubbling up, flowing out, and blossoming into peace, joy, love, ease, fulfilment, prosperity and affluence.

I release now all deviations, all distortions, all implants, techs and mechs, all parasites, entities, cords, syphons and attachments that impede my flow and glow, that diminish my blossoming and flourishing blooming into my prosperous now as a sovereign autonomous one.

I allow absolute love to override and flow, fueling me, blossoming up from within and flowing through all of my tributaries and out into all of my timelines and trajectories, moving and manoeuvring me gently, easily, gracefully into the trajectories and flows of my success, my peace, my love, my joy-filled ease-fueled timeline of original mission, success, peace, love and prosperity on all levels.

I allow the absolute love to bubble up and override all mech, all tech, all implants, invasions and deviations, all entities, beings, parasites, attachments, cords and syphons, all distortions deviating me away from true and perfect health, from peace, ease, love and prosperity, affluence and abundance of self on all levels including financial.

I command a cessation of all interference to, and deviation from, my beneficial healing progress that is affecting me via those that are 1, 2, 3 and beyond degrees of separation from me. I, as the eternal sovereign one, do not consent to the back door, tangential or parallel avenues of interference being open to use by you to affect me anymore – I close them and block them now with both my command and my love!

I choose, and align with, autonomy of self, autonomy of life and autonomy of choice.

I am free.

I allow the absolute love to flow through me, around me, embracing me and flowing through my body, physical, energy and light, flowing through my tributaries, my lines of light and flows of self, allowing all the distortions, deviations from true and absolute health on every level, to dissolve, disappear and diminish returning from whence they came.

Blossoming and blooming outwards from the core of self, I dissolve, diminish and disappear all internal and external influences leading me to stray from my own sacred eternal mission here on earth and my own sacred eternal flows as a precious one, a lighted one, a treasured one. I remove consent for their presence and disallow their reattachment.

Everywhere I do not believe of feel that I am a precious one, a lighted one, a treasured one, I allow my light of self to shine on that space and cleanse and clear my resistance to knowing this, feeling this and being this.

I allow the slow steady progress of myself into the knowing of who I truly am, into the owning of it and the integration of it in peace, joy, love and grace.

I allow, and align with, the diminishing, disappearing and removing of all markers, memes, schemes, blockages and damns, all inner and outer convolutions that prevent the flows of absolute love from being my present and perfect state. I align with and embrace my natural state of being in love, of living in love, of flowing with love and emanating love.

I allow the flows to blossom and bloom in my life as prosperity, as abundance, as precious perfect experiences and encounters, as peace and ease, with joy-filled and love-fueled moments in the now and always.

I allow absolute love to fuel, guide and direct me, to flow with me and through me, overriding all instructions, deviations, attachments and distortions to the contrary. I am absolute love. I am peace-filled joy-fueled delight and I am prosperous and abundant on every level of self, including financial.

I choose and align with my mission, the mission of my eternal family and the grace filled original contracts for me and my eternal self. All deviations to this are now disappeared and dissolved.

I am a shining golden one.

I am here and my time to shine is now.

And so it is, and so it has always been and shall continue to be. I am.

Thank you. Thank you. Thank you.

Returning to Pristine

About Returning to Pristine

This prism is mostly about truly igniting your flowing and peaceful health of self. It is really an exercise in physical self-healing and aligning back into calm and ease. It also helps you find a sense of realignment to Source and inner self.

It can result in truly life changing physical health changes and it is a beautiful relaxing calming peaceful and reconnecting prism with a visualization of healing built into it.

Returning to Pristine Prism

<Breathe in>

<Breathe out>

<Breathe in to the centre of your being>

<Breathe out>

<Breathe in>

<Breathe out - Hold the focus on your core and imagine the pulsing out from your very centre through the entirety of you as you breathe out>

I am here.

I am a lighted shining one breathing the flows of eternal love, eternal creation, eternal bliss.

I am a loved and loving one.

I am a shining rainbow one of peace and presence.

<Breathe in>

<Breathe out>

I connect through my breath with the eternal flows of me, the rainbow flows of my eternal soul.

I allow those flows to stream through me and from me. Flowing and pulsing the eternal flows of absolute love and healing.

I stream the rainbow flows and allow myself to be filled with their love, to be imbued with their healing rays of peace and calm.

I do not doubt their power, nor do I doubt my ability to ignite them and flow them.

I know, by simply saying this, by simply intending this, that my lighted and plasma bodies know what to do and begin the ignition and streaming of the rainbow flows of my eternal soul, my uncorrupted, unpolluted, inviolable eternal soul and its rainbow flows.

<Breathe in>

<Breathe out>

I allow the rainbow flows to lift me, shift me, elevate me, in the bliss and heavenly peace as I rise to meet the lofty realms of my eternal soul. Flowing with the streams of eternal source and the pure and perfect Christic core of the heart of creation.

<Breathe in>

<Breathe out>

I am a divine one of grace and peace. Stepping down from eternal source as a creation of love and an emanation of purity, peace, love and divine grace, I am. Everywhere that I believe that I am not, I allow the rainbow flows to streams there, and work their blessing of peace, their emanation and vibration of purity and their grace of healing to quell, quash and quieten that which would object to my purity, to my belovedness, to my grace and divinity, to my peaceful birthright of being a divine present one of rainbow flows and true power, of angelic human embodiment aligned with do not harm and fed by, backed by and supported by the absolute, uncorrupted, pure and perfect love flows of eternal source. I am.

<Breathe in>

<Breathe out>

Peace is my nature. Peace is who I am. In that peace, I flow. I feel the love of the heart of creation. I feel the bliss and divinity of the creation that is me. I now align with the original intention of my eternal soul for this lifetime, in this body, at this time.

I am here.

I breathe in and I breathe out. With my breath I know that I am here, I feel that I am here. I allow myself to return to me and now in this moment.

<Breathe in>

<Breathe out>

Whilst flowing the streams of my eternal soul, the rainbow flows of benevolence, perfection and original imprint of me and the perfection of who I am; I call in the white flame.

I call in the christic core of the heart of creation, white flame, to bathe me in its light and power.

I allow the flame to settle within me, wherever I feel discomfort.

I ask it, humbly, gratefully and respectfully, knowing that it is my right and my expectation to partner with this white flame of pure and perfect creation; I ask for the release, removal, upshifting, uplifting, lifting off, burning off, dissolving, resolving, correction, or simply the neutralising, of all deviations from pure and perfect, immaculate and pristine, true and present health and being now.

<Breathe in>

<Breathe out>

Every overlay and deviation, distortion or desecration, that is leading me away from, detouring, denigrating, disallowing or stopping my ability to access, hold, replicate or return to true and perfect health is targeted by the white flame and my intention.

I command now the cessation of all distraction, all deviation, all overlays and imprints that encourage anything other than pure and perfect, immaculate and pristine, true and present health now.

<Breathe in>

<Breathe out>

I am lean, fit, healthy, slender, strong, powerful, flexible and I emanate and embody a stamina and robust vitality that plays out as the experience of vim and vigour. All that I am encoded with or emanating that is to the contrary of this, I ask to be brought easily to the surface and sloughed away as redundant or brought to my attention gracefully, easily and practically for healing and release now.

I ask the white flame and the rainbow flows to immerse my whole body and allow this sloughing off, this correcting, uplifting and upshifting to continue. I take this moment now to be with me and allow the healing, encourage the healing.

<Breathe in>

<Breathe out>

I go within. I focus within. I place my attention within. I breathe. I breathe in. I breathe out. I am centred within. I breathe and feel the stillness, the peace of who I truly am. I am here. I am now. I allow.

<Breathe in>

<Breathe out>

I commission the white flame with the instructions to burn off, lift off, dissolve, resolve, disappear, correct, remove or neutralise all deviations from my original template of true and perfect health. Dissolving, resolving, lifting and shifting all that keeps me from being a true and present, pure and perfect, expression of pristine and immaculate original imprint of health and vitality for this incarnation now, as dictated by the original template of true health by my eternal soul, eternal source and the divine human.

I breathe. I am here. I am peace. I am love.

I am graced by the healing moment that I am in now. Thank you.

I allow the white flame to return from whence it came having finished its role as partner in my healing. Thank you, thank you, thank you.

<Breathe in>

<Breathe out>

On my next outbreath I expel all the debris from the healing, from the alteration, from the upshifting that has been delivered with grace and peace, with dignity and kindness, from this engagement with the white flame.

<Breathe in>

<Breathe out>

I remember now who I am.

I remember that I am a rainbow shining one, streaming the flows of my eternal soul.

I return now to my original template, to the intentions and designs of my eternal soul before any bargains, before any polluting, before any caveats, overlays or deviations. I return humbly and gratefully to who I really am. I am here.

<Breathe in>

<Breathe out>

Blessings and gratitude to Eternal Source, Eternal Family, Eternal Soul. Thank you for allowing me to know all that is at my behest, at my fingertips and available to me to heal, to upshift and to return to who I am.

In peace and gratitude, in love and respect, in kindness and knowing, thank you thank you thank you.

I know now that all is well and getting better.

Thank you.

Who Am I? : Mini

About Who Am I : Mini

This one is created as a type of personal mantra, to very quickly and simply remind you of who you are and help you to realign with the emotions, actions and feelings of peace, truth, love, integrity and stillness.

Note: the expression in the last statement is 'on purpose' not 'of purpose' – we are far too focused on what our purpose is, how can we have purpose or be of purpose. The reality is, you incarnated for a reason, you are here on purpose. You cannot fail to fulfill your purpose because incarnation has already fulfilled it! Now all that you need focus upon is how to feel better, be better and live a fulfilling and replete life of satisfaction for the self and soul. That is your purpose!

Who Am I : Mini Prism

I am the rainbow lighted one

I am the peace in the midst of the storm

I am the truth in the midst of the lies

I am the love in the midst of the hate

I am the integrity in the midst of the deception

I am the stillness in the midst of the chaos

I am the stone that outlasts the barrage of the angry seas

I am eternal

I am here

And I have come to Be on purpose

Who Am I?

About Who Am I

This prism is a reminder of the gloriousness of you – it is also a reminder that within you there is a connection to the mighty I Am, the true self and the inner guidance. This one is fairly self-explanatory – just go on the journey. Read it out loud and remember who you are!

Who Am I Prism

I am the observer of the consciousness housed in the cellular structure of the human in this lifetime called <insert your name>.

I am the awareness of the thoughts of <insert your name>.

I am the observer, guider, supporter of the thoughts, emotions, programs of <insert your name>.

I am the one who is of the body *and* beyond the body.

I am the one from beyond, the Beyonder, aware of the thoughts and understandings, of the programs and belief systems, sharing the thoughts and emotions in the mind and body of <insert your name>.

I am the separate one who is part of the whole.

I am the immersed one, dreaming I am the human in this life.

I am the Observer, the Knower, the Supporter, the Guider.

I am the one aware of the thoughts, actions and emotions.

I am the one who has always been here and always will be.

I am the Ever Was, Ever Is and Evermore!

I am now and I have always been.

I am not limited by the tiny life.

I am the one who chose to immerse in, be constrained by and housed in this body, this life.

I am part of the body – I am held by the body, aware of the thoughts and emotions.

I am the one that knows that I am more, that there *is* more.

I am the one that remembers.

I remember the memories, both remembered and lost, both now and ancient.

WHO AM I PRISM

I am Ever More.

I am now and always have been.

I am the blink, the sparkle and the materialisation of all that I am, have been and will be.

I am the one who knows.

I am the Observer of me.

I am the eternal one having a human experience.

I am the one who is aware of the human experience.

I am the one aware of the thoughts, choices and actions of the one in the body.

I too am in the body, of the body, but not wholly constrained by the body.

I am here – and I am everywhere.

I am immersed in the body, and I am the streams and flows of so much more than the body.

I am the Observer of the thoughts and emotions and the one aware of the programs and belief systems beneath, that have been forgotten, rejected or neglected allowing the consciousness and body to operate in absentia, manipulated by the programs and belief systems.

I am the might of Me returning to me.

I am the past, present and future of me.

I have always been and will always be.

I am the Evermore.

I am the was, is and will be.

I am the now and always.

I am.

I am the one who chose the life.

I am the one housed in this body by choice and I am the flows and streams of more, of all of me that cannot be contained by this body.

I am the Dreamer of the dream of me – I hold to the hope of more.

I am the peace, the love, the joy of all that I am.

I am!

I am the one who sees through the eyes, hears through the ears, tastes through the mouth and touches through the skin.

I am the one that knows through the heart.

I am the one that is here aware of it all, agreeing and disagreeing with it all.

I am the one whom the consciousness may try to quiet and overwhelm.

For I am the one who whispers "again, try again, there is more. You. Are. More".

I am the breath of wind, sometimes hidden in the storm, that will hold you tight and carry you through.

Listen for me. Sometimes I am no more than a tiny stillness. Listen for me – I am ready to roar!

I am here.

I have always been here.

I am more than you are, more than you allow and more than you think.

Yet, I am you!

I am beyond the you you think you are.

I am the minds, the streams and flows of creation, condensed to be associated with, partly housed in the body of, and flowing, streaming, glowing through the life of, the mind of, the cells of, the memories of, the nature of, the being in this life called <insert your name>.

I am all that was, is and will be.

I am the unlimited, the eternal and the Everwas choosing to align with the limited, finite and Now Is of this human life whilst retaining, in some way greater or smaller, all the knowing, memory and understanding, that I am so much more!

And I am here to return the conscious memory that I AM so much more!

I am the love, peace, calm of creation stored within, expressed as the pain, trauma and kicking out of the crushed, oppressed and disappointed.

I am here.

I am here.

I am here!

Remember me – you are more!

I am more.

Sprouting up and flowing in, I am here to show you, remind you, deliver to you the streams and glows, the sparkles and flows of all that you are with me. All that we are! The eternal one of absolute love, the Everwas of peace and joy, the smiling one of blissful comfort, the one before time, before life, before having been entangled and ensnared in that which is painful in the here now, that which causes you to writhe and cry out in despair and destruction for that which is missing.

I am not missing.

I am here, I am here, I am here!

Listen for me

I am you and in each present breath I am more powerful with you again.

This is who you are!

This is who I am!

Morning Prayer and/or Cleansing Prism

About the Morning Prayer

This prism is an activating mediation followed by a prism. It is called the Morning Prayer prism because it was written specifically to deal with the residue of a bad night's sleep, but truthfully it will cleanse and centre you at any time.

The meditation at the beginning is done simply by reading the words and imagining the process. It takes you through the breathing that aids the meditation so all you need to do is read it, envision it and breathe through the process.

You can do the prism without the meditation action, but the two together word synergistically to give you a deeper experience of cleansing and bringing the self to presence.

Morning Prayer and/or Cleansing Prism

<Start with your breathing, breathe into your core and see the pinks, blues, yellows, whites, golds and silvers sparkling and twinkling there, igniting and lighting up, beginning to shimmer with your attention and your breath.

Breathe down into the Core of Mother Earth and feel your connection with her, the beloved one connecting with the Beloved one, knowing that you are hosted and supported by her in your life on her form, as a child of earth and a chosen one for incarnation with and on her form.

Bring the connection with her up to just below your feet and feel the chakra there (the 12th Chakra, usually envisaged as white, but it can be any colour that feels right to you!) being fueled and filled by the stream of energy running between you and the Earth you live upon. Feel that energy filling and flowing into the chakra below your feet until it pops out as a sphere of vibrating pulsing and radiating light and frequency below your feet.

With your breath and attention feel into that space below your feet and watch it as it flows and glows, drawing and sharing energy from and with Mother Earth, until it feels so full and so vibrant and alive, that it pops up into a column of light around and through you. See this column of light filling you with the energy and frequency of white, bright light tinged with the flows and swirls of pink, blue, yellow, gold, silver and platinum all twinkling and sparkling as bright metallic flickering of crystalline beauty.

This pillar of light imbues you, surrounds you, fuels you, cleanses and clears you, igniting you on every level down to the cells and beyond.

It ignites you right down to the smallest of the small, the micro aspects of the very building blocks of the universe that you are created from.

Flowing and glowing, right down to the very essence of the creation that you came from and pulsing with you there. Fueling you and healing you, filling you with the white glimmers, the pink and blue shimmers, the *gold, silver, yellow and platinum glowing, pulsing and vibrant lights of love and peace.*

Breathe that up into the space above you and follow it with your attention up to its connection with the Eternal Source of all-that-is. Bring your attention back now, drawing the flows of Self, Mother Earth and Eternal Source back to you and into your core. Observe this, the core of self, the connection to your Eternal Self, fueled by and fed by Eternal Source, as it pulses and glows now, within you the flows of Mother Earth, Eternal Source and Eternal You bubbling and glowing within you, in your own core.>

Blessed Mother Earth thank you for holding me, supporting me, hosting me here on your body. I choose to see now the beauteous actions of your upshifting. I choose to notice the glimmers of joyful life that are unfurling all around me. I choose to align with, engage with, upshift with, I choose to heal with, walk with, move with, your upshifting, uplifting, healing and awakening joy-filled trajectory. The return of Self to self, aligned with your journey back to peace and love, with reverence, respect and trust for life, and in life, once more.

I am a child of Earth, and I align now with the peace covenants, the healing choices, of Earth and her bioforms. As a freewill conscious choice of the now moment, I do this.

I choose peace, I choose fulfilment, I choose 'do not-harm'. I choose respect, kindness and ease. I choose healing sovereignty and prosperity, on all levels thriving as me.

I choose my Eternal Soul and original mission, releasing now all overlays and deviations agreed to, accepted, taken on or implanted for any reason including those accepted or implanted to keep the peace or because I knew no better.

I align now with the needs and wants of my incarnate self, blended in alignment with my eternal soul's, mission to co-create my life here now as one of peace-filled, ease-fueled, joy-full delight, fulfillment and personal and financial prosperity.

MORNING PRAYER AND/OR CLEANSING PRISM

I allow the absolute love that flows through the universe, the immaculate, pristine and absolute pure love that started it all, created it all and was never polluted with human ideas of true love, unconditional love or romantic love, I allow this love to flow through me, to imbue me, bubble up and blossom out from me. I allow the absolute love to fill and fuel me, unfurling and unfolding from my uncorrupted, pristine and sacred core to cascade through me, emanate from me, fuel and saturate my reality bubble and every level and layer of me in every direction. Glittering, glowing, twinkling and sparkling, emanating from me, ignited through me, from my sacred inner core and eternal self. Flowing and streaming through every level and layer of me, physical, spiritual, emotional, mental, known and unknown.

This powerful, pulsing, gentle, unstoppable, inexorable, resilient flow of incorruptible, inviolable, sacred, secure and sacrosanct absolute love is me, from me, for me. I am this love, and it is me. I allow this flow, this pulsing glow, of absolute incorruptible love, to flow through me, on every level.

I allow this absolute love to flow with each outbreath, pulsing through me and around me, to dissolve, resolve and neutralise all the remainders and remnants from the dream spaces, astral places and beings still engaging with me in any non-beneficial way. I allow it to dissolve, resolve or neutralise all of the thought forms, dream forms, implants and ideas, the wispy ephemeral cobwebs and attachments from the dream spaces and astral places, experiences and engagements, that do anything other than align me with, imbue me with and support my remembrance, embrace and pursuit of my joy-filled, ease fueled life, my eternal mission and the uncorrupted pure desires and choices of the original incarnate me in this life.

I allow the powerful, indomitable, absolute love to gently, insistently and completely, with grace and ease, burn away, dissolve and resolve all the cords, syphons, attachments, muck, mud and mire, the thought forms, dream forms, additions and subtractions, wispy cobwebby pulls and triggers, the emotional yearnings, hollowness, sadness and emptiness remaining and the bubbles of distraction left over from any dream space or astral place engagement or experiences.

I designate it now to dissolve, release, resolve and relieve all entanglements and attachments, formed, maintained or agreed to in any time, space or place, that are deviating me from, delaying, stopping, perverting or distorting the uncorrupted, desires of my choice pre and at incarnation, of my eternal soul, eternal family and of my now choice for ease, joy , fulfillment, happiness, satisfaction, comfort and autonomy, prosperity and sovereignty of self on every level.

And with his final out breath, I am clear, glittering and glowing, radiating and pulsing as a pure sacred present one aligned with, emanating and imbued with, crystalline purity of who I really am and why I am really here.

I am a shining one, a radiant one, clear and here, here now and living each day in happiness, peace, love and fulfilment, from my core of absolute love, respect and reverence for life.

I disallow all trespass against this, my kindness, my love, my peace.

I forgive and move on, choosing my peace, my presence and joy filled mind.

I am love. I love life. I am a lover of love. I am a lover of life. I am a liver of love.

And all is well.

Thank you.

Thank you.

Thank you.

Chapter 18

Closing Thoughts and Ideas

You many have noticed throughout this treatise on the use of words, that there really are no specific don't 'say this and do this' moments. There is no calling out for particular phrasing nor suggestions for particular phrasing. There are no specific conflict resolution words or phrases such as say 'this' to him/her to resolve the argument or make the self understood. This is done for a reason; there are concepts and ideas that help, but there are no 'one rule fits all' phrases that can be used by anyone that will magically resolve their issue. You are a complex and dynamic being, your speech and your spoken resolutions and creations will differ from those of others.

The assumption of this book is that you are a freewill independent human being who is old enough, wise enough and clever enough to analyse your own language and your own thoughts and identify that which is self-castigatory, self-demeaning, self-defeating and/or life deteriorating.

The focus is always on self-healing, self-analysis and self-responsibility, so your words and your thoughts are yours. They are also yours to upshift and heal if you feel it would aid you in your experience of life. When you observe your thoughts, when you observe your speech and habitual conversational patterns, you can notice where you are stuck in a loop of nonproductive thoughts, words or emotions.

This book is about looking at the types of patterns we get into, the types of attitudes we hold that we can become blinded and ignorant to or dismissive of. Yet, to change your life, to manifest better outcomes for the self and to experience the life of your dreams, you cannot go on as you are – change must occur.

Changing yourself is the only reliable thing you can do – you are in charge of your inner landscape. Change you, change your thoughts, change your words and engagements with life to something more aligned with who you truly are and what you truly wish to experience, and your life changes.

Change or manifestation has become such a big business the last few years that you might be forgiven for thinking that it is hard. It is not! It is a very easy process, but we live in a convoluted inner and outer environment that accidentally, incidentally and sometimes deliberately thwarts us in our efforts.

When we open our hearts, minds and eyes and recognise that the impediments, resistance and blockages exist, and we become brave enough to determine our role in all of this, wise enough to determine where we have entangled ourselves in situations that have minimised our own impact, our own power and our own sovereignty then strong enough to do something about it, at such a time we open up to reclaiming ourselves once more as the sovereign one and as the creator of our own lives.

We live in communities on a planet that is supporting us and hosting us through her upshift and return to awakenment, the return of glorious crystalline flows of loving light once more. Whether you believe this or not doesn't matter, if it is true, it is occurring whether you believe it or not, if it is not true, the belief does no harm. Your belief or disbelief is not required for the process to occur, if it is indeed occurring.

Any of those who are aware of this upshift and align with it, may be seeing it, sensing it and understanding it from many different perspectives. As has been said many times throughout this offering, it doesn't matter whether you believe or not. It doesn't matter if your belief is something different to someone else's, or if your understanding is different – none of the specifics matter, none of the 'accuracy' of understanding matters.

It may be nice to have. It may help you feel connected, happy, wise, secure. It may. And that's ok! But the actual understanding of the specifics, the minutiae and the physics of it all is a little irrelevant – it's just a nice way to help the doubting brain to understand it and perhaps to remember that there is something more, something bigger, going on.

What is important, what is in fact vital, to creating your life the way you wish it to be, is to know thyself! This knowing of self is crucial. This comes from the ability to be utterly truthful with the self – not castigatory, not brutal and abusive with self, not telling the self off and finding fault in all that you do, but aligning with self and loving the self through the changes, through the upshifts and though the stumbles and falls that you will have as you attempt to heal the self into the igniting, imbuing and immersing of self into the life that you desire.

The life that you desire, the life of fulfilment, joy and ease, the life of prosperity on every level of self, only comes from self-healing. You may not believe it, you may not want it to be true, and that's ok, you can do and be whatever and whomever you want to do and be. It's ok. No one in the unseen is judging you about your choices, no one is diminishing you for those choices. You and those other humans whom you listen to are the only ones judging you.

You have freewill and can choose whatever you desire. It is you and your choices that are causing the detouring of your life from the dream life.

Healing the self of the dramas, traumas, wounds, belief systems, programs and limitations that keep you reacting in certain ways, triggered by certain things, believing certain things, involved in certain things and limiting the self is what directs you into and drives you toward the living of your desired life.

You actually are your own sage and mage, and yet you are immersed in a society that is constantly attempting to make you believe that you

CLOSING THOUGHTS AND IDEAS

are not. A society that is constantly attempting to force beliefs upon you, and encouraging you to pass your attention, your money or your emotions onto something else.

Bring yourself back to self and truly, kindly and lovingly help the self move through the sorrows, the longings, the hurts that you hold – all of this is what is keeping you lurching from one thing to another, attempting to assuage the inner emptiness, the inner yearning for the love you seek, for the fulfilment you seek, for the satisfaction your seek.

There are multiple ways to reframe your view, and bring your self back to self, some of which have been explored in this book.

You can compartmentalise the aspects of self, allowing you to address that aspect of self as though it is not you. This is not about shirking responsibility for the action, this is about recognition that you are more than that one aspect of self, that one habit, action or pattern of self. The compartmentalising of self is a quick and simple way to remember that you are more than the surface, diminishing, often abusive thoughts, words and actions that you have about self, others and situations.

You are more.

You are not irrevocably cemented into the negative, abusive or sorrow filled thoughts, behaviours and actions – you are also the one that yearns to be better, kinder, happier.

You can also view your life as guided from beyond, maybe by God, Eternal Source, Guides and Guardians, Angelic Beings, Higher Self, Ancestors, Starry Beings – there are so many ways that humans consider themselves accompanied in the unseen. All of it is helpful when considered from the point of view of sovereignty.

You are an equal partner, you have just forgotten far more than those in the unseen have. When you bow down and prostrate the self to any intuition, inner voice or unseen guidance you are giving away sovereignty. Consider it a supportive equal partnership which deserves

CLOSING THOUGHTS AND IDEAS

respect and humility but not self-flagellation and prostration. Be discerning as to who and what you are listening to.

Remember, not every feather is a sign, not every triple number is a sign and not every butterfly is a sign, be discerning with your experience of life and recognise the patterns that repeat. Signs, calling cards and support abounds in life, but being discerning as to what is valid and what is distraction and handing over autonomy is very important.

Noticing patterns helps you to become more adept at aligning with the unseen guidance, if you experience 'uncanny' coincidence a few times, that *may* be a sign. That may be the unseen connecting with you but don't give your power away simply because something is a mystery. Some mysteries are not healthy or uplifting for you to engage in at all!

Viewing your life as guided from beyond, from the unseen, can be a really comforting and powerful way to create your life experience, but giving all of your choices to the unseen is simply releasing responsibility for your own human life. It is tantamount to being a slave to someone else's choices, whims and decisions for your life. You are no longer a child; you have autonomy to make your own choices. You came here to be human, live a human life and take responsibility for self.

The art of a fulfilling human life often involves the return of self to a connection with divinity in some form – but it is the mutual living of life hand-in-hand with the unseen, in communion, not in prostration of self and giving all power over to the unseen to make every choice for you. There is no self-responsibility and healing in that, that is simply an abdication of any autonomy and sovereignty that you have as your birthright. Consider it a joyful, respectful and helpful friendship, mentor or loving advisor type relationship and get busy living your life.

So, why are these the closing thoughts? Because what is helpful for you to see is that you are a powerful creator. You are a manifester of extraordinary potential. You are a spiritual being in a human body operated by DNA technology that is creating your life as you go, day-to-day, moment-to-moment.

CLOSING THOUGHTS AND IDEAS

You have been doing this in unawareness this whole time.

Perhaps it is time to try to do it in awareness? With conscious deliberation?

Perhaps it is time to try to remember who you are and what you are capable of?

Maybe you could try to be a conscious word weaver speaking and spelling your reality into creation?

As a closing offering you will find on the next page a Prayer Framework ceremonial action that you can use as the opening to any inner work or spiritual work that you do throughout your life.

This prayer framework invites in the love of the benevolence and any unseen players of unity that may be present in your life. If you don't believe in any of that, you can consider the unseen players simply the other aspects of self, the loving one, the kind one, the gentle one etc.

Use this prayer framework any time you settle down to meditate, do breathwork, contemplate, create or wonder.

And take the time every day to remember who you are Word Weaver!

Prayer Framework

Breathe into the heart and send the energy down to the centre of the earth.

Breathe down to the centre of the earth and back up to the Self. Watch as the pink, blue, gold, silver, white and platinum colours bloom and blossom throughout you, in you and around you.

"Thank you, Mother Earth, I invite you to be present with me and hold me in your energies and safety bringing your energy of remedy, resolve and healing. Thank you"

Breathe up the cord of light from Mother Earth's centre to about 15cm below your feet. Allow the energies to unfurl into a shield shaped sphere beneath your feet. Filling this shield shaped sphere with the energies and light from Mother Earth.

Breathe in and up drawing the shield of lighted energies up and through you, a cord in the centre and a pillar of light up, around and through you to about an arm's width above your head. Here let the energies settle out into a capping of light to the pillar and watch as the cord of light goes beyond to connect with the Great Benevolence, Eternal Source, the centre of the universe, the Great Spirit who lives within Great Mystery, whatever that looks like for you.

Draw the light in the cord and your attention back down to your heart.

"I invite in the Great Benevolence, the Great Spirit who lives within Great Mystery to bring the energies that hold this space in unity consciousness for swift healing and resolution.

I invite in those who know me, those who know the bigger picture of my life and love me, those who would guide me from a place of absolute love and unity, those who support me, those who host me, upshift me, uplift me and help me, having my back at all times. Thank you, thank you, thank you.

I invite in the guides and guardian, the helpers and healers of unity, to be present here with me now in this space of sanctuary held in unity consciousness for caring and sharing.

I invite in the star brothers and sisters, friends and family, of peace, love and unity, aligned with Eternal Source, those who are willing and available to care and share here with me now and aid in this (ceremony, session, meditation) to be here in unity consciousness.

Welcome and thank you."

(and now go into a conversation, a meditation, automatic writing, breathing session or other spiritual practice as desired)

A Final Reminder

You are a glorious radiant golden shining one poured into this tiny human body to live a life of remembering who you are.

Your life is your creation.

Create it wisely.

Create it beautifully.

Create it tenderly and lovingly.

Create it as a reflection of the utopia you dream of.

Your life is yours to create.

About the Author

Jodi Maree lives in Western Australia and has worked as an Energy Medicine Practitioner and Spiritual Counsellor for the past 20+ years. During this time, she has worked with many clients helping them to move through very painful and debilitating emotional and physical situations to return to hope, happiness and understanding of the deeper meaning in their lives.

Working hand in hand with the Universe and the human energy systems she helps people to find balance, healing and guidance for themselves. Jodi's work is focused upon self-sovereignty, self-healing, self-empowerment and self-responsibility and it is this focus that is the foundation of all the work she does in both her products and her sessions.

www.ingramcontent.com/pod-product-compliance
Lightning Source LLC
Chambersburg PA
CBHW071529160426
43196CB00010B/1718